VANTAGE POINT

VANTAGE POINT

50 YEARS OF THE BEST CLIMBING STORIES EVER TOLD

COMPILED BY THE EDITORS OF
CLIMBING MAGAZINE

GUILFORD,
CONNECTICUT

Vantage Point is dedicated to all the courageous, passionate climbers and story-tellers whose words appear on these pages. Your adventures and exploratory spirit in the mountains and at the rocks continue to inspire us all, as do your honesty and craft in making these adventures relatable to the rest of us in the form of the written word. It is your spirit and passion that make *Climbing* magazine and this anthology so timeless, special, and unique.

FALCON®

An imprint of The Rowman & Littlefield Publishing Group, Inc.
4501 Forbes Blvd., Ste. 200
Lanham, MD 20706
www.rowman.com
Falcon and FalconGuides are registered trademarks and Make Adventure Your Story is a
trademark of The Rowman & Littlefield Publishing Group, Inc.

Distributed by NATIONAL BOOK NETWORK

Essay introductions written by and essays compiled with the help of Chris Van Leuven.

British Library Cataloguing in Publication Information available

Library of Congress Cataloging-in-Publication Data available

ISBN 978-1-4930-4848-9 (paperback)
ISBN 978-1-4930-3478-9 (e-book)

♾™ The paper used in this publication meets the minimum requirements
of American National Standard for Information Sciences—Permanence
of Paper for Printed Library Materials, ANSI/NISO Z39.48-1992.

CONTENTS

PART FIVE: THE 2010s

INTRODUCTION

50 YEARS OF AWESOME

BY MATT SAMET, EDITOR OF *CLIMBING*

In recent years, a new term has entered the climbing lexicon: "overstoker"—when you're so psyched to climb that you ignore obvious obstacles and fling yourself at the rock, ice, or mountain regardless of consequences, including snapping tendons or imperiling you and your partner. Examples include bouldering on a 10-degree-Fahrenheit snowy day, jumping on a 5.14 with no warmup, or leading that melting ice pillar on a balmy spring afternoon even though it's clearly about to topple.

I was 15 when I began climbing, in the mid-1980s in Albuquerque, New Mexico. And, as is common with boys of that age, I was a perpetual overstoker. There was no rock gym in town yet, so I'd beg my parents for rides to the boulders in the foothills of the Sandia Mountains and join every possible New Mexico Mountain Club outing. But it still wasn't enough. Like a tireless golden retriever, I was always ready to climb, even when my muscles burned with lactic acid and my hands were bloodied from jamming. I had to put that energy somewhere, and so at night—after I'd finished my homework or come back from the rocks—I'd immerse in climbing magazines. Hell, I loved them so much I'd tuck them between the pages of my textbooks and peruse them avidly during class at Highland High School, pretending to be focused on the academic subject matter.

In addition to the current editions that I'd rush out to pick up at the local mountain shop, the Wilderness Center, I also had a giant stash of old *Climbing* and *Mountain* mags dating back to the 1970s that my friend Jessica had gifted me. Nights in my bedroom were spent reading and rereading them. To my young, overstoker mind the lore in those pages was priceless. And it helped form the perspective of our sport that I still carry to this day: that climbing is a historically and culturally rich *lifestyle*—and not some mere athletic pastime.

My collection started with the oldest issues, staple-bound and in black-and-white, and from there I gradually worked my way forward. The 1970s and 1980s were times of rapid transition, when the gear improved by light-years, bringing with it the birth and then begrudging acceptance of hangdogging. Then sport climbing pushed free-climbing standards into the stratosphere: from 5.12 to 5.14. From grainy 1970s photos of climbers wearing clunky Kletterschuhes and placing slung hexes on 5.10 cracks up to images of honed athletes in brightly patterned Lycra tights clinging to blank 5.14 bolted walls—the magazines had it all.

In particular I was drawn to the first-person writing in *Climbing,* which from its very first issue, in 1970, has always featured essays and trip reports from that perspective. Climbing is an immersive, sensory, visceral sport, one with high stakes at every turn (*gravity doesn't sleep*); it is, like the best things in life (sex, fine dining, sleep), best experienced for oneself. But since no one will ever have the time or ability to do every climb everywhere, the next best thing is reading and seeing photos of others doing it. And the best writing is that which puts you there on the rock, ice, Himalayan big wall, or desert tower with the author, feeling his or her fear as your own. Because *we've all been there. We've all been gripped out of our gourds.*

Climbing magazine, like this author, is soon to turn 50—a half-century of existence—making it the world's oldest continuously published vertical publication. It has the name—*Climbing!*—and the weight of those decades rooting it firmly in the canon. During this time, the top climbers and climber-writers have been at its helm, from its founder, the desert-rock pioneer Harvey T. Carter, to the Himalayan super-alpinist Michael Kennedy, to the Southwestern badass free climber Jeff Achey, to the veteran climber and current *American Alpine Journal* editor Dougald MacDonald, to the seasoned photojournalist Julie Ellison. All, myself included, have worked our hardest to preserve the magazine's mission, as laid out in the editorial on page two of issue No. 1, May 1970: "We are a magazine directing itself to the interests of rock climbers and mountaineers. . . . The editors of *Climbing* claim no authority for assuming this task other than the fact that we believe that the magazine is needed and we have the desire and the capacity to supply it."

And finally: "Being climbers ourselves, we relish the task and will do our best to serve satisfactorily."

Over five decades the sport has continued to expand and evolve: It is simultaneously old, with its roots in the Alps in the late 1700s, and young, with the modern era of bolts, gyms, training knowledge, and reliable, lightweight gear dating back only to the 1980s. Each decade has its own advances and its own flavor, and each one has built on the last to bring us up to the present moment, when 5.15d is a reality, 5.15a sport and 5.14a trad have both been flashed, WI7 has been onsight free soloed, and the 8,000-foot South Face of Annapurna has been soloed in a 28-hour round-trip push.

With this *Vantage Point* anthology, we offer the best first-person or essay-style writing from each decade, to give the broadest but also deepest possible snapshot of the last 50 years of *Climbing*. I'm proud of the stories we've selected, and many are the favorites I read and reread during my youth.

As examples, take these few highlights from the 1970s up through the 2010s, among the 33 stories selected: There's Michael Kennedy's spare but poetic two-page account of perhaps the most epic alpine climb ever undertaken—his, George Lowe, Jim Donini, and Jeff Lowe's to-within-a-whisper-of-the-summit attempt on the North Ridge of Latok I ("Latok I: A Climb Without a Summit," No. 53, March-April 1979). And the late Tobin Sorenson's "Witlessly Bold, Heroically Dull," detailing his and Jack Roberts's white-knuckle ascent of the *Central Couloir* of Mount Kitchener in the Canadian Rockies (No. 58, January-February 1980). Then there's John Sherman's mud-epic "Tales from the Gripped" (No. 140, October-November 1993), about unearthing forgotten desert treasures with Rob Slater in Utah's Mystery Towers. There's also Tommy Caldwell's dramatic first-person account of freeing El Capitan's VI 5.14a *Dihedral Wall* ("The Dihedral Wall," No. 234, October 2004). And, finally, the late Micah Dash's classic story of alpine brinksmanship with his partner, the late Jonny Copp, on the unclimbed Shafat Fortress in Kashmir ("The Line of Control," No. 263, January 2008).

To add context and glue the chapters together in a continuous narrative, we tasked climbers active from each decade to write an introductory essay for each chapter. For the 1970s, Jim Erickson gives his perspective on the big leaps in gear and how free climbing came to supplant aid. For the 1980s, Paul Piana talks about the Lycra era, the scruffy Brits who came to American shores to dirtbag, and of course his and Todd Skinner's paradigm-busting first free ascent of the *Salathé Wall* (VI 5.13b) of El Capitan. For the 1990s, Randy Leavitt talks about the explosive growth of sport climbing and his role in its dissemination. Beth Rodden, at the cutting edge of big-wall free climbing and first ascents in the 2000s, details how that decade built upon its predecessors to explode world standards. And for the 2010s, Chris Sharma, one of the best free climbers the world has ever seen (and may ever see), talks about the current state of the art with rock climbing and where he hopes to take the sport next.

These days, instead of filling my garage with boxes of back issues of *Climbing*, I have a 5-foot filing cabinet in my office housing every issue of *Climbing* ever printed—many in protective cellophane—from May 1970 up to the most recent issue, February-March 2018. Not only is this archive a useful reference tool, these three shelves' worth of magazines also represent the living, breathing history of our dynamic sport, an archive of accomplishment and courage and perseverance and tragedy.

This book, I believe, fills a similar role. May it keep you in overstoker mode—always!

PART ONE:
THE 1970s

THE 1970s: CLIMBING BECOMES CLEAN, FREE, AND A LITTLE BOLDER

BY JIM ERICKSON

As the 1960s gave way to the 1970s, American rock climbing entered a period of rapid change. Stretchy nylon kernmantle ropes imported from Europe replaced hemp and Goldline. Free climbing on nuts and hexes eclipsed the use, as protection and direct aid, of rock-damaging soft-iron, and chrome-moly pitons. And footwear evolved into tight-fitting, smooth-soled rock shoes like the RD, PA, and EBs from the Austrian Kletterschuhe (essentially hiking boots) we'd been wearing. Though the sole rubber on these new rock shoes was a far cry from today's sticky compounds, that didn't stop the advance of free standards up to 5.11 and beyond.

Then there was the changing garb, fashion-forward fare like sun-reflecting white painter's pants and durable rugby shirts that replaced the corduroy knickers and wool sweaters. We saw the rise of comprehensive guidebooks, instead of relying on around-the-fire-climbing beta to share route info. And we began to see more women on the sharp end—gone were the ubiquitous all-male teams. Rock climbing was coming into its own, no longer one facet of training for the complete mountaineer, but an independent sport.

Meanwhile, 1970 marked the first year of *Climbing* magazine, which celebrated bouldering, offwidths, slabs, high-altitude objectives, free soloing (including onsight), and grade V free climbs. It even included projecting, which had been largely unheard of in the previous decade. These styles were now legitimate pursuits in and of themselves. As the tools evolved, along with the emerging new media to report on the scene, climbing became more popular and better understood.

MY TEENAGE YEARS IN WISCONSIN

Caving was my introduction to the vertical world. I was 13 in 1962, when my family and I entered the previously explored caves near our hometown of Racine, Wisconsin. Once inside these gloomy limestone grottos, it became obvious that in order to explore further, we needed to climb and rappel. So I visited the local library to find out which skills and tools cavers used. The first book I opened had a drawing of two men fastened together by a rope. The leader, with a thick, burly cord tied around his waist, was hangdogging while his belayer held his weight from a piton fastened to a carabiner. The leader was smiling.

Before then, I had never seen a piton, carabiner, or a lug-soled mountaineering boot.

I showed my parents the illustration, and together we visited the University of Wisconsin Outing Club in Madison, where we purchased two soft-iron pitons and three steel carabiners at the closet-size store. With our new rack, the family headed for the quartzite bluffs of Devil's Lake State Park.

There, in the box canyon near Balanced Rock, I started up a 30-foot wall pierced by a thin crack, while my brother, Dave, belayed. The first 10 feet were a breeze, but after that the wall steepened. *No problem,* I thought. I got out my pitons and clubbed one in with my hammer, just like in the book. Then I clipped my US Army steel carabiner into it and leaned back on the rope. I was as happy as sliced bread.

Three feet higher, I placed the second piton and asked Dave for slack to clip it. To my surprise, I dropped 3 feet. This was clearly not progress; I was not smiling. After ten minutes yo-yoing around and clutching the upper piton and carabiner, I'd grown so exhausted that I had to be lowered. Summarily defeated, we retreated to the parking lot.

Six months passed. Then one day my mother, who was an avid ornithologist, was out looking for birds when she ran into a group of real-life mountaineers from the Sierra Club. She told them about our defeat and our eagerness to learn the sport. They responded by inviting us on a weekend climbing trip, during which we learned proper climbing skills under their tutelage.

For the next few years, we'd take family weekend trips to areas like Devil's Lake, or longer trips to the Tetons and the Gunks, where Dave and I acted as ropeguns. Then Dave and I started putting up new routes: First were leads of climbs that had only been toproped, then came first free ascents of aid climbs. We slowly progressed to the (still-sandbagged) Devil's Lake and Gunks 5.9s and an occasional 5.10. All were led ground-up, sometimes onsight. To Dave and me, these lines were training for big objectives like the Eiger Nordwand and the

Walker Spur. To reiterate, back in the 1960s, rock climbing was seen as practice for the big ranges and not a pursuit unto itself.

BOULDER AND BEYOND

As my high school years came to a close, I began to look at colleges based on their proximity to climbing. Boulder, then as now, was a major climbing center, so I opted for the University of Colorado Boulder. I arrived in 1967, eager to start climbing in Eldorado Canyon, the Flatirons, and at Castle Rock in Boulder Canyon. Yet I had a hard time finding partners, until I met Jim Walsh in the far wing of the dorm. That spring, we also met "Magic" Ed Wright in our dorm and taught him to climb. Soon the three of us were onsighting 5.9s on Eldo's slick Fountain sandstone and on the water-polished granite of Castle Rock.

By 1968, I had led most of the 5.9s in the Boulder area, so I began trying to free obscure aid lines with the hopes that the legends—Layton Kor, Pat Ament, Royal Robbins, Larry Dalke, Bob Culp—had overlooked their free potential. Fortunately for me, these 1960s-era greats had been mostly interested in speed and length. Only occasionally had they slowed down enough to push free climbing. When they did, however, the results were spectacular, like the 5.11 (and harder) routes by Robbins, Ament, and Gill at Castle Rock, and the free ascent of *Crack of Fear* in Lumpy Ridge by Chris Fredericks and Jamie (Jim) Logan.

Because free ascents were there for the picking, by 1973 I had established many new lines and first free ascents. Perhaps the most famous was the first free ascent of Eldo's *Naked Edge*, which I completed with my longtime climbing partner, Duncan Ferguson, in 1971. The 460-foot 5.11b was widely considered the hardest multipitch free climb in the United States at the time. Suitors had to be proficient in all the disciplines, including slabs, finger and hand cracks, overhangs, and chimneys.

Other notable routes first free ascents I completed from Colorado to California, ground-up and onsight, were *Rincon* (5.11a; 1969), the first pitch of *Wide Country* (5.11a; 1972), *Insomnia Crack* (5.11; 1972), *Scotch and Soda* (5.11c; 1973), and *Dead on Arrival* (5.11c; 1973).

CLEAN CLIMBING

I still remember that pivotal evening in December 1971. I had been climbing for almost 10 years on my prized chrome-moly pins, which had saved my life on many falls. But I'd also seen firsthand the damage caused in Yosemite (namely *Swan Slab* and *Serenity Crack*) and elsewhere by their pounding-in and pounding-out retrieval.

I was in my apartment in Boulder reading the May 1967 issue of *Summit* magazine and happened upon an article about using nuts for protection by the late Royal Robbins. The piece, "Nuts to You!", was America's introduction to a practice Robbins had picked up in the United Kingdom. I unequivocally decided to no longer be part of the problem—now I would be part of the solution.

I told Duncan that from then on I would only use nuts. I was aware that this change in style would likely result in a drop in my climbing numbers, moving down from 5.11 back to 5.10, but it was worth it. I needed to walk the walk to protect the rock—in the direction we were headed, there wouldn't be any clean cracks left for future generations, just blown-out scars and ugly holes. Duncan agreed. Together we unloaded our pitons and replaced our rack with a small selection of new Chouinard Stoppers. Six months later, Steve Wunsch joined us. Nine months later, the leading Gunks climber John Stannard did the same, and in one fell swoop he (almost) singlehandedly converted the East Coast to nuts. In spring 1972 Chouinard Equipment released its now-famous catalog featuring Doug Robinson's essay "The Whole Natural Art of Protection," which revolutionized clean climbing from coast to coast.

In May 1972, using only Stoppers for protection (and no chalk), Duncan and I had freed the first pitch of *Wide Country* (5.11a), just right of the famous *Bastille Crack* in Eldo. I went away that summer, and in autumn when I returned, I asked Duncan what new climbs he'd done. In his typical self-deprecating manner, he answered, "Oh, not much. I finished *Wide Country* with Don Peterson. The first pitch, as you know, was the crux, about 5.10-, and the last three pitches were 5.9." (At that time, 5.11 was not an accepted grade, and it was never applied to any first ascent that went onsight. The Gunks climb *Foops*, surely the hardest short route in America, free climbed only after many days of falls, was still graded 5.10!) Shortly thereafter, Roger Briggs led the second ascent of the *Wide Country* integral route and thought it was much more difficult than 5.10- and also quite dangerous. Today one of Duncan's "5.9" pitches is the technical crux at 5.11b R, and much of the 5.8 and 5.9 climbing is poorly protected.

5.11 ON NUTS ONLY

In March 1972, I made my fourth visit to Tahquitz Rock in California, home of the first 5.9 and 5.10 climbs in America, and also Bob Kamps and Tom Higgins's record-breaking face climbs. My partner was Devil's Lake legend Scott Stewart, perhaps the best dead-vertical-face climber at the time. Scott handily led many of Tahquitz's hardest face climbs, including *Jonah*, *Chingadera* (5.11a) with one fall, and the first pitch of *Valhalla* (5.11a), while I struggled to follow. We had our eyes set on freeing *Insomnia Crack*, the overhanging aid climb on the southwest side of Suicide Rock. My rack was six or seven small Stoppers, two Hexes, and a Dolt Super Chock (a 1.5" piece). Footwear was RDs, great for edging but poor for smearing.

I cruised the first 25 feet of *Insomnia* to reach a rest in the chimney, steeling myself for the overhanging, thin-hands section that loomed above—the crux. Here I reached left and placed the Super Chock. My hands were too big to jam the next 10 feet, so I laybacked in those stiff RDs until I finally reached sinker 2-inch jams that led 30 feet to a small belay. I could have continued, but I wanted to allow Scott the option to lead the final part. The backs of our hands were roughed up from the jamming, and Scott, gassed upon reaching the belay, decided he wanted no part of it, so I onsighted the final section as well.

Insomnia became a classic free climb. Our 1972 first free ascent was not only a cutting-edge onsight, but also possibly the hardest first free ascent in the United States using only nuts for protection. I was very lucky to be a small part of this important eco-change in American climbing.

THE RISE OF WOMEN, AND ADVANCING STANDARDS

One morning in June 1973, I was walking up the main road in Eldo past the Bastille and noticed Diana Hunter belaying a climber above. "Henry is going to take me up the third ascent of *Wide Country*," she said. Diana was perhaps Colorado's first outstanding female free climber. She was Steve Wunsch's college girlfriend, and, after graduation in 1969, she and Steve traveled across the United States repeating hard classics and putting up new routes.

I looked up and saw "Hot" Henry Barber hanging from the bolt at the crux of the first pitch. Only a few months earlier, Henry had arrived on the free-climbing scene and was quickly repeating (or establishing) virtually every hard and dangerous climb from Yosemite to Eldorado Canyon to the Adirondacks. I had just climbed with him in Yosemite, where a week earlier he'd put up *Butterballs*, then the hardest single-pitch climb in the Valley, rated 5.11c.

"I can't figure this out," he called down, perplexed by the thin edges. I yelled up a greeting and walked on to do my route farther up canyon.

Apparently, after I left, Henry lowered, and Diana shyly asked if she might give *Wide Country* a try. Henry nodded, and Diana tightened her EBs and proceeded to onsight the 5.11a pitch. Although the (late) great Beverly Johnson had redpointed a 5.11a in Yosemite the previous year, Diana's lead was, I believe, the first onsight of the grade by a woman in the United States.

Henry quickly redeemed himself. The next day he partnered up with Art Higbee for the third free ascent of the *Naked Edge*. In June 1975 Diana died during a descent in Rocky Mountain National Park.

In autumn 1972 I did the first ascents of the Eldo climbs *Blind Faith* (5.10b) and *Sooberb* (5.10c/d), and the Ralston Butte climb *Cassandra Direct* (5.11a), free solo, chalkless, ground-up, and onsight. These may have been the first multipitch free solos at the grades, although I didn't tell anyone about the ascents for many years. In 1976 Art Higbee and I freed nearly all the pitches on the *Regular Northwest Face* of Half Dome in Yosemite, at VI 5.12, the longest and hardest multipitch climb in the United States.

THE DRAGON ROUTE

JULY-AUGUST 1973, NO. 20

BY KARL KARLSTROM

Deep, dark, ominous, steep, severe. Those words sum up the quarter-mile wide, half-mile-deep Black Canyon of the Gunnison. Climbing long routes there these days is no joke, but back in 1972 and armed with the era's primitive hardware, it was downright terrifying. Add in poison ivy, loose and sharp rock, and crack systems that all-too-abruptly end, and you've got the makings of an epic. Armed with six ropes and supplies for twelve days, Rusty Baillie, David Lovejoy, Scott Baxter, and Karl Karlstrom reanimated an abandoned Layton Kor project from the 1960s, via "a myriad of ghostlike crack systems and a thousand phantom ledges," to reach the top of the canyon's largest formation, the Painted Wall.

The Painted Wall is the highest wall in the Black Canyon of the Gunnison, Colorado. It is about 2,700 feet high and is composed of dark metamorphic rocks cut by bands of pegmatite. The first time I saw the Painted Wall was in July 1971. I sat for a whole day on the south rim, peering at the wall with binoculars, trying to piece together a route. It's a strange wall: shadowy black rock streaked and spattered by whitish veins. Its appearance is sinister, nearly demonic, and its features are elusive.

During that first day a myriad of ghostlike crack systems and a thousand phantom ledges appeared and then vanished before my eyes. The wall was in a state of flux, constantly changing its appearance with changing light conditions and never revealing its true aspect. The route I was looking for was one that Layton Kor had tried several times in the middle sixties.

Kor was fairly active in the Black Canyon in those years, putting up numerous grade IVs and Vs at a time when few other people were interested in the Black Canyon as a potential climbing area. He had established the style of climbing the Canyon walls very quickly, not hauling much gear. It is my guess that Kor approached the Painted Wall with this style and found it unsuitable for a rapid, two-man first ascent.

The magnitude of the wall and the intricate route-finding problems apparently demanded more time and gear than Kor estimated. At any rate the highest Kor got on any of his attempts was about 1,300 feet up. On his last attempt he came back with Rusty Baillie to finish the route. That time they never even got to the base of the climb due to flooding river conditions, but from then on it was Baillie who provided the momentum for attempts on the Painted Wall, Kor having apparently lost interest. Baillie tried the wall later with Wayne Goss, but they couldn't find the route and were suffering effects of poison ivy that fills the descent gully (appropriately named S.O.B. Gully).

Kor and Baillie were trying to push a route up the central portion of the wall, up through the "two dragons" (huge pegmatite bands that resemble oriental dragons). In this area of the wall there is a long crack system that extends diagonally down about 800 feet from the top. This crack became known as the "Summit Crack" and all the early attempts were aimed at gaining access to this feature, although there was no apparent line leading into it.

The best possibility seemed to be a series of discontinuous dihedrals and flake-formed cracks in the lower section of the wall; however, this line of cracks ended a good 200 feet to the right of the base of the Summit Crack. The traverse, across vertical and shattered rock, to the Summit Crack was the major uncertainty of the route. We dubbed this traverse the Stygian Traverse because, like the River Styx, once one has embarked upon the journey across it, there is little hope of returning. It was this traverse that apparently stopped Kor on his best attempt.

The Painted Wall presented problems other than those of route-finding and climbing. The wall has an aura of strangeness about it that created another sort of obstacle. I experienced a feeling of anxiety; an empty sensation in my stomach, as if I were out of place and in a forbidden world. I think we all experienced this sort of feeling on our first attempt, and, perhaps as on any new type of rock, this initial strangeness needed to be worked out before a successful ascent could be made. It's hard to define just what causes the weird aspect about the Painted Wall, but it undoubtedly results from a combination of things.

In the first place, the wall is vertical or overhanging for its entire height such that the top of the wall is visible from the very bottom. This verticality was accentuated by the bases of ledges on the climb, so that nearly all of our belays and bivouacs were hanging. The rock itself is shattered and brittle and although not unusually reliable, it fractures into large blocks and flakes that occasionally gave us cause for uneasy speculation.

Another factor was the situation of the wall. The Black Canyon is an extremely narrow gorge and the Gunnison River at its bottom is a rumbling and raging torrent. We were climbing in a dark slot that was sunlit only part of the day. Below us the river roared incessantly, echoed and seemingly amplified by the closeness of the other wall.

The roar of the river was actually loud enough to make communication nearly impossible when we were separated by more than half a rope length. This was especially the case with Baillie, whose Rhodesian-British accent made it sound like his mouth was full of marbles. We learned afterward that there were times when the people on the South Rim could hear and understand us while we had to struggle to communicate with each other.

In July 1971 Rusty Baillie, Scott Baxter, and I made our first attempt on the Painted Wall. Baxter and I had met Baillie in Arizona, and after numerous climbs around the Southwest together, the Painted Wall seemed like a worthy project. Baillie was a master of persuasion in getting us interested in the wall. He was like a snake doctor persuading the folks to try his elixir, or a spider spinning a web for unsuspecting flies. We were quickly caught up in Baillie's passion to climb the Painted Wall.

The actual attempt started off relatively smoothly. After a few false starts and difficulties finding the route we finally reached Kor's high point in four days. That lower section is a tribute to Kor's knack if not his prudence. Kor reached his high point in two and a half days, and then on the retreat had to reverse a large roof over which he could not rappel. Kor's high point marked the level at which we figured it would be necessary to strike out across the long traverse toward the Summit Crack. That was my lead.

I climbed up, then pendulumed, then did some skyhook moves, and then stopped. The rest of the traverse looked hopeless to me at the time. We had all been getting increasingly uneasy about committing ourselves on the wall. The strange aura had been working on us slowly as we climbed and it finally took control of me on that last lead.

I called back to Scott and he called down to Baillie. We were each at separate hanging stances on the wall, each thinking his own thoughts. Our hoarse discussion lasted only a short while. We decided not to push on across the traverse. In a way it was my decision since I was the only one who could see across the traverse. I can't help wondering that if it had been Baxter's lead or Baillie what would have happened (useless speculation, I realize).

Our retreat was an epic. We were approaching the extreme condition in which it is nearly impossible to think logically. Just trying to figure out how to reverse the pendulum and clean that short pitch, and set up a rappel taxed us to the limits. Two rappels and we were at Kor's Cave, the route's only ledge. We proceeded to demolish the rest of our food while Baillie explained to us the logistics of our retreat.

Beneath us was the overhang that Kor had had to reverse on his attempt. Baillie planned to rappel off into space and then start swinging, hoping to reach our belay bolts below the overhang. It proved to be too overhung and he was unable to reach the bolts. At a lower level, at the very end of his ropes, he was just able to reach a handhold that allowed him to place two rappel pitons.

When we finally reached the river I was firmly convinced that I would never return to climb that route. Yet I think that even as we were retreating, Baillie was planning to return although we didn't discuss it for some time. Baillie was undoubtedly reserving the discussion for just the right moment. He must have found that moment because before I knew how it happened we were all planning to go back the next summer.

Three is a good number for a big wall but we decided four would be better for our all-out effort. That way two guys could climb while the other two did the hauling. Then, on the next day, the two teams would switch; the two climbers would have been burned out from the strain of climbing and the haulers would be desperate from the boredom of hauling and sitting in belay seats. With this variety we figured we could sustain ourselves for a long period of time.

Our threesome had been fairly well balanced as far as assets. Baillie provided the spirit and the passion for the climb, Baxter was amazingly good at finding his way past blank-looking, desperate aid sections, and I was well suited for hauling the heavy sacks. What we lacked on that first attempt was a sense of joviality. David Lovejoy, as our fourth climber, provided the laughter that helped ease the strangeness of the wall.

A short time before we were to leave for our 1972 effort we heard a rumor that the Painted Wall had been climbed. A Frenchman, Chris Jones, Bill Forrest, and Royal Robbins; these were the appellations that reached my ears over a period of about a week. Rumor eventually gave way to fact and we found out that Bill Forrest and Kris Walker had done the first ascent of the Painted Wall. They had chosen a line of dihedrals to the left of our route.

They reported loose, dangerous rock and difficult climbing. The news was naturally disheartening. We were now faced with the question whether we still wanted to go ahead with our plans even though ours would no longer be the first ascent of the Painted Wall. The four of us got together in Flagstaff to discuss the question. It was an interesting meeting. We were basically talking about climbing motives and our own rationales regarding climbing.

Once again it was Baillie's cunning and his passion to make the climb that determined the decision. He was as interested in going as ever. His arguments were along two lines. First, the magnitude of our achievement wouldn't be hurt by the fact that Forrest and Walker had made a major achievement. Second, Baillie felt that our proposed route would be superior to the Forrest-Walker line both in terms of safety and interesting climbing.

Our route was up the central portion of the wall and nearly all the climbing along diagonals so that rockfall danger was minimized. In addition there were nearly always roofs and overhangs to belay under. The nonsuicidal character, and the unique climbing on our route, Baillie maintained, might even make it a classic in its own right. We decided to call our route the Dragon Route and to go ahead as planned.

Our actual ascent of the Dragon Route on the Painted Wall took place in June 1972. We started out with enough food and water for twelve days and six brand-new ropes. We reached our old high point without much difficulty, and this time it was Baxter who set out across the Stygian Traverse.

He led out past my high point and reached a belay stance. He spent the next four hours trying to drive a bolt into that brittle rock. Drill bits kept binding and breaking and finally, in near desperation, he had me jumar across on a tied-off bolt and about ten assorted pitons and nuts. Then I tried to drive a bolt, with the same difficulties. We weren't willing to bring Baillie and Lovejoy across until we were sure we could get in good anchors, and we were too far around the corner to be able to communicate (the river was still loud at the 1,300-foot level).

Baillie lowered Lovejoy out on a haul line so we could talk, and there occurred a conversation similar to the one we had had the year before. The decision this time was to persevere. Perhaps the memory of the previous year's retreat influenced our decision, and also the fact that there were two of us in each spot to give each other support. Also we had more food and water the second time, and the weird effect that the wall exerted on us was diminished by the facts of having been on the wall before and having a stronger team.

We finally discovered that moisture entering the bolt hole through our blower tube was turning the fine powdered rock to cement and binding the bit in the hole. After that we used the blower only to scrape out the hole, and we finally managed to place two good bolts. We named the stance the Three Bolt Belay, including the bolt that sticks out about 3 / 4 of an inch.

The next lead should have been mine but it looked hopeless, and, in a single instant, I gave the lead to Baxter. He has always said that he would just as soon lead as belay me (I weigh about 50 pounds more than he). So off he went on what was perhaps the hardest and most intricate pitch on the climb.

Lovejoy led another A-4 pitch above that, and we finally reached the base of the Summit Crack. From there it was one day to the Lovely Bivouac Ledge (Baillie's description of a two-foot, steeply sloping ledge), another day to the Buzzard's Roost, and then one more day to the top. In total we spent nine days on the wall. Six of the nights were spent in hammocks and untold number of hours were spent in belay seats.

It is surprising how accustomed one gets to a vertical environment and the things it entails: exposure, always being anchored, and always using your arms to brace yourself. This became evident when we reached the sloping summit. Lovejoy led the last pitch of the climb. He was so used to a vertical frame of reference that the gradual change of slope apparently confused him and he bumped into a tree at a crawl before he realized that he could stand up.

All of us experienced some difficulty in making the shift back to a horizontal environment—those first steps after nine days were surprisingly unsteady. Aside from this and the normal state of exhaustion, we were all in remarkably good shape. We finished with enough food and water for a few more days, and we all agreed that it wouldn't have been too difficult nor even disagreeable if we had had to climb for those extra days. Our ascent proved to be everything our attempt wasn't. It was a smooth, flowing effort in which the difficulties seemed to iron themselves out as we climbed.

It is a shame about the recent ban on climbing the Painted Wall. It was unlikely enough that anyone would repeat the route even without the ban. We all decided long ago that if ever there was a second ascent of our route we would all get some lounge chairs and a couple of cases of beer and sit on the South Rim and watch.

ROUTE DESCRIPTION

THE DRAGON ROUTE: VI, 5.9, A4, 20 PITCHES

The Dragon Route begins from a huge scree slope about 200 feet above the river. To reach this scree slope walk up and left (west) from the beach through talus and poison ivy until one is able to climb (3rd class) to a ledge system leading left. Follow this ledge system (still 3rd class) to a point directly beneath the right-hand margin of the scree slope. Climb 100 feet to the scree (5.3). Follow the scree to its top, then down the other side to its extreme west margin. Two or three pitches wander up and left for about 250 feet to a rubbly ledge. aid pitches lead up to the level of the prominent roof above. A short to Kor's Cave, the last ledge on the climb. Exit Kor's Cave at the right side up and slightly right to a small belay stance. The next aid pitch goes up and to another small stance at a rock horn. Climb left then up (A-4) to a very exposed hanging belay (the Bugger Belay). Traverse 10 feet left, then climb a crack 50 feet to a pendulum point. After being lowered to just above the level of the belayer, pendulum or tension traverse around the comer and continue free climbing to the Zuider Zee. Then traverse left and up on hooks and knife blades (A4) to the Three Bolt Belay. Climb slightly right, then up a decomposed section (A4) to a small roof. Nail left under the roof and belay. Climb up and left (A4) to the base of the Nose (a prominent overhang at the base of the Summit Crack). Follow the Summit Crack, free and aid, through the first dragon, to a tiny sloping ledge (the Lovely Bivouac Ledge). A long pitch, free and aid, leads up to a hanging belay beneath a small roof. Climb left then up to a chockstone in a chimney (the Buzzard's Roost). From here three free pitches lead to the top.

HOT HENRY: AN INTERVIEW WITH HENRY BARBER

MAY-JUNE 1974, NO. 25

BY DEMETRI KOLOCOTRONIS

These days, climbing-news outlets teem with blurbs about the rock stars and their latest formation-to-formation linkups—like the El Cap–Half Dome speed days we hear about routinely. But forty years ago, such linkups were far less common. Perhaps the heaviest hitter of the time—and a climber who sought challenges in this vein—was "Hot" Henry Barber, a nickname coined by the late Mountain *magazine editor Ken Wilson. For example, after Hot Henry in 1973 onsight-soloed the 1,600-foot* Steck-Salathé *(V 5.9) on Sentinel Rock in Yosemite—one of the Fifty Classic Climbs of North America—in a brief two and a half hours, he was back on the Valley floor that morning hunting down partners for the rest of the day.*

Barber is an original dirtbag who traveled and climbed full-time during the 1970s, and everything he climbed was done ground-up. This meant no rehearsal, no hangdogging, and climbing up to 5.12b R barefoot. He didn't take rest days. During one trip to Australia, he put up sixty-seven new routes at more than twenty different crags during a forty-two-day trip, raising the country's standards by two to three grades. Today Barber still climbs every chance he gets, and true to style, he visits the crags with his ultralight rack of ancient Hexes and Stoppers—no cams.

You've come a long way since you last climbed with me. At what time and place did you break through to your present level of accomplishment?
The spring of 1972 was the turning point for me. I started doing harder routes and I made my first trip to Yosemite. I had done many routes in the East which I thought were difficult, and I became very aggressive. Bob Anderson and I were regular partners and we did some hard second ascents in Yosemite such as *Sacherer Fredericks* and the *Left Side of La Esquela*.

On our way West I was chuffed when I did *Supremacy Crack*, a 5.11 in Boulder, with a toprope first try. I fell off *Supremacy Crack* trying to downclimb while leading it later.

How old are you, and at what age did you start climbing?
I'm 20. I started climbing with the Appalachian Mountain Club when I was about 15. The AMC provided me with wisdom and encouragement, but I learned techniques primarily by myself. I climbed 5.6 first day, but it took almost a year before I did 5.7. Now I get people up 5.7 first day.

What climb do you consider your best so far?
That would be hard to pick. I've had several good days. The day I did *Naked Edge* in Boulder was fantastic. The route is superb. I had an excellent day in the Valley doing *Nabisco Wall* and *New Dimensions*, and free soloing *Midterm*.

One of my most exuberant moments was the second free ascent of *Foops* (5.10+) in the Shawangunks. Other unforgettable moments occurred on the first free ascent of *Recidivist* near Boston and first ascents of *Whaleback Crack* on Cannon Mountain in New Hampshire and *Butterballs* in Yosemite.

The best climbs I've done were four free solo first ascents in Utah one evening while on a river trip down the Green and Yampa rivers. They have been the ultimate for me.

Do you consider yourself America's best rock climber?
When I'm in a difficult situation, I put myself in a frame of mind that I'm the best climber to approach the problem. I don't actually think I'm the best rock climber. There are many good young climbers coming along. I know many climbers technically better than myself. Everyone has their specialty.

Would you like to compete with Europe's best rock climbers?
I don't want to compete with anyone. I think top climbers have a competitive urge within themselves to surmount difficulties. I would give up climbing if it became directly competitive with others.

I recently had a successful trip to England where I climbed in most of the areas except Cornwall and visited many of the pubs. I will return this spring.

Considering the interest in the ascent, do you regret using another party's fixed ropes to ascend the first four pitches of the Nose *of El Capitan?*
No. I don't particularly like big walls. I climbed the *Nose* for my personal satisfaction and to climb with Keith Bell, who's a good bloke. We climbed in the best style we could. This meant to us climbing fast, using mostly nuts, and free climbing as much as possible. Donini and Mink's ascent was similar. You can't go for everything and succeed, as recent attempts of the *Nose* have shown.

People can criticize the ascent if they want. Criticizing is very popular. Anyone near the top of the totem pole can expect knocks.

Will you back off a climb?
Yes. I'll back off if I don't feel right about the climb. If I feel the only reason to stay is because of what others might think, I'll come down. I'll back off if I'm uninterested. An indifferent attitude can be dangerous on a cliff.

Do you consider your free soloing dangerous?
This is a tough question. Of course climbing without a rope is risky. If you make a mistake there is no one or nothing to help you. I don't think my free soloing has been dangerous because I have always free soloed within my limits.

Two climbs, a 5.6 and a 5.9 in the West, were the only climbs I've free soloed without using proper judgment. On the 5.6 my attitude was too carefree. On the other I pushed to my limit on a delicate move of a type I had not done before. I feel free soloing is most dangerous for climbers who haven't sufficient experience to know their limits.

What led you to free solo hard routes?
Climbing free of a rope in misty weather, early in the morning, or late in the day is very pleasing to me. I find the challenge of free soloing difficult routes very rewarding. When I'm free soloing easier climbs, I feel joyous moving rhythmically, unencumbered.

Were any of your free-solo ascents, such as the Steck-Salathé *on Sentinel in Yosemite, repeat climbs for you?*
All the routes I have free soloed in the West, including the *Steck-Salathé*, I did onsight. I had previously done the last pitch of *Hair City* in Boulder. All my free soloing in England was onsight.

Do you consider that future breakthroughs in climbing will be free solo?
I hope that free soloing will not be the line dividing good climbers in this country. This isn't the attitude in England where much more free soloing is done. I think that if this happened it would limit freedom of expression on the rock, and lead to tragic competition.

The expert who strives to compete and the less competent climber will both be in trouble. I advise anyone who is thinking about free soloing to look within and consider others' sober thoughts on the subject before committing himself.

What are your climbing goals in the future?
Besides visiting England, I will go to Australia this season, and will probably turn to bigger mountains between the ages of 22 and 25. I have several Alpine seasons in mind. I also wish to do something in South America and the Himalayas. I would like to have been invited to join the American Alpine Club's U.S.S.R. Pamirs expedition this summer. I love the mountains and would rather be in them than anywhere else. I am impatient sitting in a tent waiting for a storm to pass.

How is your snow- and ice-climbing technique compared to your ability on rock?
I don't have the ability to lead on snow and ice as I do on rock. My cramponing is fair. Ice climbs in the East are too short for me to really judge. I don't have the head to monotonously hack with an axe and to trust all the hardware necessary for ice climbing.

CLIMBING AND THE ALPINE ENVIRONMENT: ETHICS OF PRESERVATION

NOVEMBER-DECEMBER 1975, NO. 33

BY MICHAEL KENNEDY

~~~~~~

Climbers' impacts on the environment have always been a hot topic. With the Internet, the modern climber is only a click away from videos on proper crag etiquette—brush off your tick marks, remove your trash, stay on existing trails, and so on—thus educating new members and showing by example what is acceptable and what is not. But back when rock climbing—and climbing media—was in its infancy, preserving the crags was a new topic.

In the 1970s, former Climbing *editor in chief Michael Kennedy wrote: "Climbing is about two things: ascending direct, natural lines with a minimum of technical aid and protection and preserving the climbs through the use of the least destructive methods possible." In the same article, he also drew attention to the "extreme" use of chalk in Eldorado Canyon—an area today whose holds are so white that there's an annual chalk cleanup on the Roof Wall. This essay is a looking glass back into our sport's roots—what has changed and what has stayed the same. One thing rings true throughout: It is our responsibility to minimize our impacts on the vertical environment.*

~~~~~~

I have become increasingly disturbed over the last few years at some of the changing directions climbing has taken. These fall into two very broad categories: that of physical damage to the climbing environment, and that of damage to the sport itself.

The physical damage is easy to see, and has been well documented, but the damage to the spirit and essence of the sport is much more subtle, much more subject to variations of opinion and rhetoric. It seemed that this was an appropriate time to put some of these concerns into perspective, and perhaps offer some solutions. By no means do I intend these as the "final answers"; they are based on my personal experience and observations. The climbing community as a whole will determine what the "final answers" will be, if indeed they exist.

It would perhaps help if we looked at what might be called the traditions of climbing. These traditions were best defined in the early part of the century by Rudolph Fehrmann and other climbers active in Saxon Switzerland as:

". . . (the) undertaking (of) climbs by 'Great Lines' (routes laid out in the most direct way, tackling great difficulties; hence, the ideal, most beautiful line), which represent the uppermost total performance in route-finding, agility, technique, strength, endurance, and, particularly daring . . . with poor or limited possibility of belaying."

And further, referring to protection, which consisted of drilled-in rings, as the rock was too soft and crackless for ordinary pitons:

"Considering the great difficulty and exposure, very few safety rings are used. Only the leader of new climb has the right to place a ring, and it stays as a permanent fixture, no one being allowed to remove it. It is considered bad form to employ many rings, so as few as possible are used. . . . The rings are meant only for belays and are not used for hand or footholds." (From "Oliver Perry-Smith: Portrait of a Mountaineer," by J. Monroe Thorington, *American Alpine Journal*, 1964.)

To summarize, then, climbing is about two things: ascending direct, natural lines with a minimum of technical aid and protection and preserving the climbs through the use of the least destructive methods possible. Saxon Switzerland was one of the first pure rock climbing areas, and the first to have climbs of the Sixth degree. The cliffs are small and easily accessible, and therefore subject to damage. The leading climbers, through writing and lectures, established traditions to preserve not only the physical aspects, but also the challenge of the climbs themselves. These traditions were made to last not five or ten years, but much longer. This has resulted in a high standard of climbing, and permanence of the routes.

Technical climbing in this country developed in a different way. The American traditions of freedom and independence and the greater range of activity led to a less defined "do as you please" ethic. When the crags and peaks were many, and the climbers few, this was a reasonable way of doing things. But times have changed, and perhaps we need to look at the traditional rules and adapt them to the American situation.

Most of our problems stem from sheer numbers of climbers, and a resulting competition for both climbing space and recognition. Add the vast range of technical advances that have made climbing both easier and safer and you end up with a general deterioration of the climbing environment.

Pitons have wrought permanent damage: broken flakes, ugly scars, cracks widened beyond use, all are familiar and lamentable remnants of the Iron Age. The introduction and popularization of nuts and other forms of natural protection by Chouinard, Robbins, Stannard, and others have halted the destruction to a great extent. The trend toward free climbing has also helped, but damage continues to occur. Nuts are tapped into place, resulting in certain damage, although it does take longer. In most rock climbing areas, wads of slings, excessive numbers of fixed pins and bolts, and stuck nuts all contribute to the aesthetic deterioration of the natural rock surface. The practice of leaving permanent slings on pins (so they are easier to clip in to) is not only destructive to the appearance of the rock, but leaves unsafe anchors for future parties when the nylon rots away, and reduces the challenge of the climbing.

By all means we need fixed pins and occasionally bolts. Many routes, if not impossible, would be significantly harder without fixed protection. But moving up one move, clipping in, moving up one move, clipping in, and so on is not what climbing is about.

Fixed protection should be logically placed to allow a reasonable margin of safety, yet not destroy the challenge of the climb. Minimal protection should be the rule, rather than the exception. I see no point and, in fact, view it as bad style to replace a single fixed point of protection with several poor nuts or whatever.

In many cases nuts have made routes easier; large nuts have made formerly unprotectable cracks routine problems, and there has been a general trend toward overprotection due to the ease and speed with which they can be placed. In most instances, a greater number of nuts must be carried for safety and security; this has led to an increased consciousness, indeed an obsession, with technical gadgetry. This is not to say that bold leads are not done, or that nuts are always easier, but in the main, they have made most leading both easier and safer.

One of the biggest problems is chalk. Telltale white marks mark everything from boulders to big walls, 5.0 to 5.11. In Eldorado, the problem is so extreme that chalk is visible enough on some climbs to glow in the dark.

In Aspen, routes that have been climbed as little as once or twice show the stains already. I, for one, would prefer to find the holds myself, and not follow the paint by number syndrome.

The question is not whether the stuff will wash off with the rain, or even if someone will come up with a colored chalk that won't show up. In an ethic of clean climbing, the use of chalk is hypocritical to an extreme. More important, it is completely outside the traditions of climbing; it is another gadget, another barrier to overcome and discard. Climbing is above all a sport of boldness and control. If we are to preserve its character, we must consciously limit the use of technical aids. Perhaps we can look forward to the day when chalk is regarded with much the same disdain as using aid on free climbs, or adding bolts to existing routes.

Trash along the trails and at the base of the climbs, as well as on the climbs themselves, has become a problem of epidemic proportions. A few examples will serve to illustrate. On a recent trip to the Diamond, we collected a full duffel bag of cans, webbing, paper, food, water bottles, and tarps from Broadway. The summit, by comparison, was clean. On the Grand Teton we found dozens of cans on the East Ridge just below the summit. These had obviously been thrown off the top, with the attitude "Out of sight, out of mind." Also on the Grand: While the trails up to Surprise Lake and Garnet Canyon were well constructed, well maintained, and clean, the track (I would hesitate to call it a trail) to the Lower Saddle was an abomination. In the absence of an "official" trail, many side paths and shortcuts have been worn, and the land has suffered as a result.

It is an outrage that a place such as Broadway, visited by a handful of climbers a year, is infinitely dirtier than the summit of Longs Peak, which sees thousands of tourists each year. And what is ultimately more destructive to the wilderness experience: a single, well-made trail, or a maze of muddy ruts, broken bushes, and trampled meadows?

It has become all too common recently for climbers to rappel down, cleaning holds, pre-placing protection, practicing moves, or even top roping a route before leading it. An ascent is then made and called "free." I disagree; it is both illogical and a use of aid to employ such tactics. How much better to try the climb in classic style, from the ground up and perhaps back off, or use a few points of aid to establish protection. At least this leaves a bit of uncertainty, a bit of the challenge of discovery.

An equally bad habit is the practice of down rating. Routes are dismissed as easy, when in fact they may have involved several attempts by the leading climbers of an area before completion. There is no point in saying that a 5.10 here is harder than a 5.11 there; this indicates a breakdown in communication and an infantile desire for ego gratification.

One often has a tendency to down-rate familiar climbs as well; this is destructive to the climbs themselves, as it encourages people to get in over their heads. Routes need to be graded realistically on the basis of an onsight lead using standard protection. When several people do a particular climb, a consensus will emerge as to the difficulty, protection, and worth of the climb. This should be consistent with other areas and the standards of the grading system. Naturally, there will be some disagreement over details, but in my experience, this system works.

Competition has always played an important role in climbing, by providing incentive and push to do better and harder routes. But it seems that at times the competitive urge has gone too far, resulting in bitterness and distrust and some truly ridiculous actions. In at least one case, a fixed pin was removed from a route en rappel by someone who hadn't even done the route, and is probably not even capable of doing it!!! This was a pin that every party that had done the route had used (and often fallen on). In other cases, pins have been removed (and replaced with bad nuts) because some felt that the original ascent party, if they had nuts, would not have used the pins. Surely many pins are now unnecessary, but this is a case of rather blind, and I think, shortsighted reasoning.

But perhaps I dwell too long on these subtle and difficult matters. After all, I am hardly a member of the elite who set the style of the day. I must also admit that I have violated virtually all of my own rules. Again, I must stress that these are my own opinions, based on what I have seen and read and experienced. I would hope that anyone who disagrees (or agrees) will put their experience on paper for others to see. It is only through a free exchange of such ideas that climbing will mature.

OGRE DESCENT

NOVEMBER-DECEMBER 1977, NO. 45

BY DOUG SCOTT

When it comes to adventure lore, only a handful of stories make the rounds again and again. By now (almost) everyone has heard of Sir Ernest Shackleton and his 1915 epic aboard the Endurance *in Antarctica. However, Doug Scott's essay about his nightmare on the Ogre (Baintha Brakk) in Gilgit-Baltistan, Pakistan, is no less remarkable. After he and Sir Chris Bonington completed the first ascent of the 7,258-meter (23,901-foot) peak, Scott broke both legs in a pendulum rappel fall. What resulted—an endless crawl down the vertiginous formation—is one of the greatest rescues of climbing history. To make matters worse, Bonington was hurt in a separate rappel accident that broke two of his ribs and damaged his hand. All the while, storms circled the wall. Yet just like Shackleton and his crew aboard the* Endurance, *everyone survived—barely.*

The peak wasn't climbed again until 2001, when Thomas Huber, Urs Stöcker, and Iwan Wolf ascended the South Pillar. The late climbers Kyle Dempster and Hayden Kennedy climbed the Ogre again in 2012. Scott's 2007 book The Ogre: Biography of a Mountain and the Dramatic Story of the First Ascent *is available from Vertebrate Publishing.*

A fine day's climbing was brought to an end on the Ogre's rocky summit; snow faces and steep, iced-up rocks, sinuous cracks cleaving brown granite wall, crazy pendulums, and delicate traverses, combined tactics up into a bottomless gully and the final weary grind up a sloppy summit snow couloir were all behind us. For

Chris Bonington and me the summit simply marked the end of the route, for there was little to see now that the light had gone out over Hunza, bringing darkness to the valleys and a cold gray light to the featureless snow peaks all around.

Mo Anthoine and Clive Rowlands had already traversed back to the snow cave from their high point 500 feet below us, for they were satisfied that the climb had been completed and felt no urge to reach the summit and risk an unplanned bivouac. I thought of Tut Braithwaite, who but for a twenty-pound boulder smashing into his thigh muscles would have been up there with us, perhaps instead by the South Buttress. Now Tut, having evacuated most of Base Camp, was fifty miles away in Askole. Ten thousand feet below and five miles distant, Nick Estcourt sat out the last few frustrating days awaiting our return. Nick had made an abortive attempt on the summit ten days earlier with Chris, reaching the Southwest Summit, but had found that a combination of altitude, very little sleep, and poor food had left him with insufficient energy to try it all again.

Now it was time to go down and fill our emaciated bodies with *paratas* and honey, to walk along quietly through Baltistan free of fear and high altitude exertions, and to go home to that initial elation that comes after being away two and a half months. A miserable cold wind saw us shuffling down a crumbling snow arête until we could fix a sling around a flake of rock for the first abseil. The imminent darkness threatened to terminate our downward efforts, so I pushed my aching body down the frozen double ropes in a series of jerks and hops, all the time moving left—left to a crack I had pegged up some three hours before. Right at the end of the ropes and at full stretch I reached the crack and prepared to clip in to a couple of pegs still sprouting from it. I couldn't quite reach them so I stepped my feet up to hold my body in better balance. Without looking I stepped onto a veneer of water ice. In that careless moment I lost control.

My feet glided across the ice off into the air and away I went, galloping for all I was worth across the rocks, striding faster and faster, then spinning, rolling, wildly round and round and away into space, clutching the ends of the ropes, into the gloom to who knows where. Exhilaration turned to fear and I gave an appropriate scream. All in a split second I had twisted and turned in an effort to face the unknown squarely and saw great cracked walls of rock blocking the way ahead. On inexorably, on and on, zooming in, no stopping it now. Splat went my flesh amongst a clatter of gear, down went my specs and I came to a halt with every bone shaken. The surge of blood around my head slowed to a trickle and all was quiet after that period of total involvement. A quick examination revealed no head injury, back O.K., femurs O.K., knees O.K. . . . Oh! Oh! What's wrong with my ankles? They seemed to crackle as I moved them.

I had come to rest hanging free but could just reach the rock with a toe stretched out, so I pushed with my right foot trying to start myself swinging. There was not much pain at first, only a weird sensation of grating bone and unnatural movement. I tried the left foot for I needed to swing myself onto a ledge. This time there was more pain but less bone movement, but now I could lean over and push the rock with my hands. I eventually reached the ledge, sat on it, and hammered a peg into a crack, slotted in two wired chocks, and tied myself off.

Having taken my weight off the ropes, I yelled up to Chris to come on down. As the rope ends dangled and danced about in front of me, I slowly realized that this game had new rules, for winning would require that the descent would have to be made without using my lower legs. "That'll be interesting," I mused. "I wonder how it's done? I suppose it can be done? Still there's a long way to go with the South West Summit to get over. Oh, it will work itself out!" I concluded optimistically.

I suppose my initial reaction was bound to be fairly rational, as there was so much with which to occupy my mind. But now having tied off, fearful thoughts battled for a place in my head until Chris arrived from out of the night. "What oh!" he said airily. I told him as casually as I could that I had broken my legs down at the ankles. There must have been a note of concern in my voice for he told me not to worry, adding, "You're a long way from death." "Why did he think nasty things like that?" I wondered, for so far the thought had never crossed my mind. Now it did. So I had quick flashes of lying out there strung up on some granite ledge my body all stiff and cold. That vision went as quickly as it had come. It had not been wasted for it had the admirable effect of stiffening my resolve and all fanciful fears evaporated as we abseiled down another rope length to a snow patch clinging to the granite. Chris went first, down the gully and out of sight, although I could hear him hacking out a step in the snow and ice. I went down the ropes with my legs stuck out—out of the way of jutting rocks, and let my left thigh make contact with the rock as I slid intermittently down. I joined Chris, who by now had made a long narrow ledge into the ice. Without thinking I put my legs down, took a step along the ledge, and collapsed onto my knees. After the pain subsided, I shuffled along the ledge on my knees and with no trouble at all. "So that's how it's done." I thought. And that's how it was done over the next seven days with a little help from my friends—Chris, Clive, and Mo.

We remained tied on to the abseil ropes while both of us increased the width of the ice step, oblivious to the void below. After an hour we had a space suitable for sitting up, facing each other. In that position we took our boots and socks off and pushed our toes into the warmth of each other's crotch from where it was convenient to massage warmth into each other's feet. The cold would have been a problem anyway at 23,500 feet, for we had nothing to warm us except the clothes we wore, but I was especially worried in case the swelling of both my ankles should shut off the blood supply to my toes. So every time this thought entered my head, I would grab Chris's toes and rub them furiously in the hope he would do the same for mine. This he did with a great deal of care, which helped to pass the night away to a fading memory of a miserable, cold, shaking body painfully wriggling about trying to find a comfortable position on that hard freezing ledge.

With the dawn coming up, we put our boots back on and Chris prepared the next abseil. We were now on unknown ground and so Chris could only hope that there would be abseil stations suitable for a fastidious cripple. Luckily each time it was possible to find a place to kneel down while I clipped on and off the ropes. The last abseil brought us on the snow basin of the Southeast Face. It was still a desperately cold morning and we had hardly warmed up from the bivouac, so as Chris kicked steps up to the ridge between the Main Summit and the South West Summit I followed in an effort to stave off frostbite. Chris took short steps and I was able to follow by jabbing my knees into the snow, although sometimes it was necessary to cut the steps bigger where the snow was hard. Chris disappeared along the ridge to the Snow Cave and then Mo came down followed by Clive. They rigged up our four ropes as a safety line and I was soon in the cave eating up a freeze-dried meal and catching up on lost sleep. That night we finished off the last of the food, never really thinking there might be delays in our descent. In fact we looked forward to moving without all the hardware we had so laboriously carried to the very top of the mountain and without all the food that was now largely eaten.

So far the Karakoram Mountains had enjoyed a very favorable summer, but on the morning of July 15th we looked out from the quiet insulated world of our snow cave to a holocaust of swirling snow that went on and on at the same furious rate throughout the day. Clive and Mo went out to find a way over the South West Summit 300 feet above us, but soon returned, clothing plastered in snow and Clive's large beard encrusted in ice. Spindrift had worked its way behind their snow goggles so they had been unable to see, nor could they make much progress anyway on account of thigh-deep powder snow and the wind that made standing up a problem—never mind climbing the 55-degree slope. During the night the storm increased in violence, blocking the snow cave entrance so that we had to dig our way out the next morning. Mo, muttering something about "Karakoram storms don't last long," burrowed his way out only to find the same howling blizzard was still raging.

This was serious. Apart from having no food we would only deteriorate by staying up here at 23,000 feet. Already Chris was feeling extremely lethargic having been at this altitude two weeks before. Clive set off to try for the South West Summit again while Mo belayed in the cave entrance until Clive yelled him up to the first stance. I followed next trying to keep up with Mo so that I could knee up into his steps before the snow blew into them. Chris brought up the rear pulling the ropes up with him. As we climbed up and over the South West Summit we caught the full blast of the wind viciously blowing spindrift into our frozen faces. In this condition Mo went on down fixing the abseils. It took us until dark to drop down 750 feet and traverse across to a snow cave we had used five days before. I had been quick enough down the abseils but I had slowed everyone up on the long traverse. Feeling guilty at this I pounded along on my knees, never stopping to warm my wet and frozen hands. At the snow cave I dived inside to help dig it out, for it had filled up with drifting snow. Before it was properly finished the sky was pitch black and the temperature made it impossible for anyone to remain outside any longer. With the cave only really large enough for two men, the four of us made the best of our cramped quarters. Powder snow seeped in through the entrance and covered our sleeping bags.

Mo and Clive already had damp bags, and these became quite wet during the night. It was the worst night of all; no food, wet, still above 23,000 feet, and me slowing them all down with the 1,000-foot pillar still to come. Next morning, Mo emerged from the cave and announced in his Birmingham accent that the storm was, if anything, worse. He went off followed by Clive, then me, then Chris—all of us bent on reaching the tents, for there we had left a pound of sugar, which was something we had not had for two days. Food seemed to be a number one priority. But also there was no real resting place between the snow cave and the tents, so we had to make it.

It was a nightmare descent. Whenever there was a ridge of level ground, I found crawling painful, seeming always to be catching my legs on protruding rocks. Only on steep snowed-up rocks did I feel comfortable, for then Mo would have fixed up the abseil ropes and I could slide down with my body making contact with the mountain side, while my feet stuck out of the way of obstacles. In this fashion I started to descend the 1,000-foot West Pillar.

Unfortunately, on the way down, Chris abseiled off the end of one of the double ropes. Luckily, Clive had tied the other off to a rock, so Chris fell only about 20 feet or so, but he still broke two ribs and painfully damaged his right hand. Cold and getting colder, he had no alternative but to continue the descent. Mercifully, he did not at once start to experience the pain in his thorax that was to dog him later. It was a sorry little band that made the tents. Mo was the first and he had to re-erect them, as they were both flattened under 3 feet of snow.

The rest of us were happy to crawl straight in out of the tearing wind and into our sleeping bags. For me, it was a long and painful process removing gaiters, boots, inner boots, and socks. But it had to be done so that I could rub my frozen toes back to life—for circulation was somewhat restricted by having my legs permanently bent at the knee. More serious, though, were my frozen finger ends, but all I could do was hope that things would improve now that we were losing height, and we all kept thinking that the storm could not go on for many more days.

Mo came into the same tent as Clive and me, to warm up, as his sleeping bag was now reduced to a useless clump of wet, soggy feathers. We played cards, and Dr. Hook on the tape recorder, hoping the storm would blow itself out during the morning, so that we could move the tents down to the Southwest Col later in the day. Chris was now in a bad way—coughing, his throat hoarse, his voice down to a whisper, and every cough increasing the pain under his ribs. He burst into our tent during the morning, announcing that he really must go down as he thought that he had pulmonary edema. We discussed this with him, but he did not seem to have any of the gurgling noises one hears about. It was probable that he had mild pneumonia, which wouldn't have been helped by spending the day out in the swirling spindrift. Neither did the three of us fancy the subzero temperature and harsh wind, for Mo announced that he had not felt his toes for nearly a week and Clive's digits were also numb. Despite it being our fourth day without food, we decided to give it one more. At least now we had enough sugar for the next dozen brews of tea. We had been taking tea without milk or sugar for breakfasts, and half a curried meat stock cube for dinners, and we were lacking energy but now noticed a slight change for the better with the sugar.

It was still blowing hard the next morning as we roped down to the Southwest Col. By now I had become quite expert at knee-climbing. I found that being on my hands and knees was actually an advantage in particularly deep snow, and I did a bit of trail breaking. Mo unearthed some old Japanese ropes from 1976, and we slid down the first 500 feet to the Southwest Col. We went to our former campsite and dug around until we uncovered a waste bag, in the bottom of which was some boiled rice mixed with cigarette ash, which we ate. Mo rummaged around some more and found an ounce of milk powder and, in another bag, three packets of fruit sweets and two packets of cough sweets. We shared them out when Clive and Chris arrived. We moved off to the top of the fixed ropes that would take us to Advance Base the following day. I carried Clive's pack as he had to go and recover a tent that had fallen off it higher up. There was now about a mile to go across the snow, but at last the clouds were rolling back to reveal the mountains all around, sparkling with fresh snow down to the glaciers. My arms kept sinking deep into the snow with the weight of Clive's pack pressing down over my neck. Despite following Mo's footsteps, I took many rests, flopping down flat out in the snow.

Expeditions are usually good times to sort out a few things in the head—times to drop down a level or two—but it occurred to me then that since my accident

I had brought such iron will to bear on every moment of the day that I had not given such matters a thought. But there had been compensations, for whenever I shut my eyes I went off into a hallucinatory world of lilac and purple coloring, incredible shapes and forms, caricature people and stylized views of distant times and places. It did not make a lot of sense, but it was one way to while away a few minutes and recover enough to take a further twenty or so crawling paces.

Mo and I dug out tent platforms, put up one of the tents and then the other when Clive arrived with it. Chris came in very slowly, coughing up a rich yellow fluid from his lungs. Chris and Mo set off at first light for Advance Base. Clive and I followed four hours later, for then the sun would be up to warm our frostbitten hands and feet. Also, Chris and Mo would have had time to cut big steps at various key places for my convenience.

Abseiling down fixed ropes was no real problem for me, so I was able to descend 2,500 feet in four hours. Crawling over soft snow down to 17,000 feet was also relatively easy, but after that the snow became thin, and I had to crawl over hard, sharp glacier ice.

We arrived at last to find that Advance Base was no more—either blown away or taken away by Nick and Tut—so there was nothing for it but to follow Mo and Chris down to Base Camp. The next section was the most painful of the whole retreat. The distance was about four and a half miles from the end of the fixed ropes. About one mile was on soft snow, two and a half on ice, and one on moraine. At 10:30 that night (July 20) I crawled over the last of the moraine rocks. My legs were very swollen from knocking them countless times. I stopped to examine them and was horrified to find that I had worn right through four layers of thick clothing and that my numb knees were bloody and swollen.

One last bank and I was on the triangle of moraine that surrounded the thick green grass of Base Camp—a little oasis amongst the chaos of shifting rock and ice. I crawled to the old kitchen site to find that Mo had gone off in hot pursuit of Nick, who had that same morning given us up for dead. "If you get as far as reading this, then it presumably means that at least one of you is alive," he wrote in his note, adding that he was going down to fetch Tut from Askole and form a search party.

They obviously did think us dead from the meager supplies that were left. However, it was good to eat Purdy Cake with a cup of milky tea and then fall asleep on that little meadow.

The next morning the sun shone onto our wet sleeping bags—you could feel the warmth come right through into the murky interior. Pulling open the draw-cord from inside, poking my head out to see the grass, the flowers, and the stream running across, then getting out, brewing a mug of tea, eating a powdered-egg omelet, and feeling the sun burning my skin: beautiful memories those.

For four days Clive looked after Chris and me, and still there was no sign of the porters that Mo should have sent. On the fifth day, however, when we were down to soup and "Tom and Jerry" nougat bars, Nick arrived with twelve porters to carry me down, together with the remnants of our gear. Mo, in the meantime, had gone off with Tut and our liaison officer, Captain Aleem, to Skardu, in order to dispatch a helicopter for arrival outside Askole on July 28th. When Mo arrived in Askole, Tut had already been there a week and had made good friends with the headman and many of the villagers. As each day passed it had seemed to Tut and to the Baltis that our chances of being alive were growing increasingly slim, especially when Nick arrived alone. Thus, when Mo walked in, they were all overjoyed to discover that we were safe, if not exactly 100 percent sound. The headman sent off to other villages to ensure that we had twelve strong and able porters. And that was exactly what we got.

In three days they carried me down the Biafo Glacier to its snout and then to a flat field near Askole, where a helicopter could land. It was a remarkable journey on a homemade stretcher constructed of juniper wood poles, a climbing rope, and sleeping mats. Never once did they look like dropping me, and I seldom felt a jolt. It was good to lie out, listening and waiting as they made decisions as to route-finding, choice of camping place, who should fetch wood and water, who should take the heavier part of the stretcher, and so on. They inevitably made the decision after a gentle murmur had gone round the motley band—no one ever shouted or became excited. Their voices blended into a sing-song melody that seemed completely in tune with the rhythm of their village lives. They knew just what to do. And I for one have nothing but admiration for these hardy people, who are all very individualistic and full of character, yet are easily capable of working to a common aim in complete accord. This is how good expeditions can work.

It was sad to be suddenly plucked away from them by the noisy helicopter. There was just time to make arrangements to see them again next year on K2 and to shout a few words to some of the American Trango Tower Expedition, Dennis Hennek, and Kim Schmidt, and then away, to civilization. Coming into Skardu the engine cut out, and we suddenly plummeted twenty feet to the ground some hundred yards short of the helipad, but escaped with only a severe jolt. (As a result Chris had to wait a week in Askile while the helicopter was repaired, but eventually he also was flown out to Skardu.) Three days later, after fine hospitality at the British Embassy and a first-class flight home, courtesy of Pakistani International Airlines, I was being plastered and pinned in Nottingham General Hospital.

PUMPING SANDSTONE

JANUARY-FEBRUARY 1978, NO. 46

BY JOHN LONG

*John Gill—who began climbing in 1953—is credited as the father of modern boul-
dering. He introduced gymnastic chalk to climbing, embraced dynamic movement,
and even went ropeless on giant, pre-crashpad-era highballs, including the iconic
Thimble in the Needles of South Dakota. Back when Gill did it, there was a guard-
rail at the base that he would smack into if he blew the moves on the 30-foot spire.
Bouldering historian John Sherman has called the Thimble "the most famous boulder problem in America before Midnight Lightning seized that crown." It clocks
in at 5.11+/5.12-.*

*Stonemaster/writer John Long idolized Gill and decided he had to climb with
him. He looked him up in the phonebook in Pueblo, Colorado, and when Gill picked
up the phone, the men arranged a meetup. The next thing Long knew, Gill was sharing his bouldering circuits on southern Colorado's steep, physical Dakota-sandstone
boulders. "Soon enough we were venturing through colorful sage, scrub oak, and
assorted cacti en route to the [boulders]," writes Long. During the sessions at the
blocks with Gill, Long learned fluidity of movement, precision, and the subtleties of
cutting-edge bouldering.*

Some years ago John Gill published several explanatory-philosophical articles on
specialized bouldering. During this time the aces of the climbing community were
pursuing the last of the natural big walls, with the extreme-type movements of
Gill's fancy being predominantly overlooked. Shortly thereafter the paradigm

shifted to free climbing, with the rising standards usually demanding some bouldering from those in pursuit. Today (with the assistance of considerable hearsay, fable, and actual documentation) the accomplishments of Gill are gaining notice, and in turn his feats provide much in the way of inspiration for those who have tasted them.

Sixteen years ago Gill demolished the current free standards by soloing the *Thimble* in the Needles of South Dakota. Few even knew of it then and only a handful now. Through the years I had caught a glimpse of the odd scope of Gill's exploits, though no firsthand knowledge existed. My first exposure to any Gill propaganda occurred some half-dozen years ago. Someone, somewhere along in my climbing career, had produced a picture of himself posed on the "crux" of a supposed Gill problem. His motive seemed twofold: to astonish us with his performance and to verify his good taste. He failed at both. The photo was cropped at boot level—a feeble attempt to conceal his feet firmly anchored to the turf. Eye-level graffiti told of his true location. To be sure, the stone above this trickster's fingers appeared quite smooth, only to become smoother as memory became colored by imagination.

Reliable friends had forewarned me of the absurdity of Fort Collins bouldering, this being but one of Gill's many playgrounds in the '60s. Driven from Yosemite by summer heat and from Tuolumne by a funky social scene, we headed east for Colorado and our first peek at the boulders. Under the guidance of John Bachar we visited the notorious *Eliminators*, Mental Block, Torture Chamber, Sunshine Boulder, and more, the likes of which had haunted us for some time. John, one of America's foremost free climbers, had frequented Fort Collins for three summers, systematically bagging most every problem there. Knowing this in advance I banked on a personal advantage, assuming that John could reveal the keys to sequence solving, enabling us to simply work on the moves.

The difference between these boulders and others is the rock—Dakota sandstone—which holds no secrets in sequences, these usually being solved via long moves between unreliable holds. Dynamic techniques play no small part in their execution. Hence, Bachar's presence served us little pragmatic value, save the reefers he continuously scrolled.

Anyway, these outrageous problems were proof positive that Gill had indeed mastered the intricacies of dynamic movements. The Mental Block has six standard classics, four of which involve considerable gunnery to succeed. *The Eliminators, Left, Center,* and *Right,* are all dynamic problems. This is unique considering that most bouldering is intentionally static movement, with dynamics being avoided and sometimes even scorned as a false technique. For those with an aversion toward lunging, Fort Collins is to be avoided, as static efforts will generally insure certain failure regardless of strength.

A tad after experiencing Fort Collins a second time I concluded that exposure to Gill was obligatory—but how? Dave Breshears, my only contact, was in Canada, which vetoed any possibilities for a proper introduction. I briefly pondered requesting Pat Ament to introduce us but surmised he would charge me. A childish attitude, but stuck I was, so I simply looked up Gill's Pueblo number, and as a relative stranger, called him up. Acknowledging my wonderment, he immediately arranged for a guided tour of the "more outstanding areas." When we talked later to verify the plan, he mentioned an itinerary he had drafted, the details of which, I imagined, would surely prove my undoing. As we finally approached the door of Gill's two-story Pueblo abode my mind was void of expectations, as the endless tapestry of fable coupled with my own experiences had left me somewhat numb. As time passed we learned that Gill was exempt from all the preconceived notions that climbers and books had transposed upon him. Soon enough we were venturing through colorful sage, scrub oak, and assorted cacti en route to the Fatted Calf boulder. Just then, I believe, John began to display that unmistakable smirk that reminded me of an old film I'd seen of Mohammed Ali watching amateurs box.

I spent half my energy attempting the numerous problems on the Fatted Calf. Gill's smirk only grew as he knew all too well to what I aspired—re: to bag all the problems in the shortest time possible. At this I failed. One problem (described on pages 145–46 of Ament's book, *Master of Rock*) proved responsible for a host of holes in my fingers. No description could justly portray the absurdity of this leap.

Soon after we were swinging from the razor edges of the *Ripper Traverse*, a paramount of finger strength. This problem seemed so severe that to reverse it would certainly usher in some type of injury. If one could harness the torque involved in crossing the *Ripper*, he or she could conceivably turn coal into shining gems. Shortly thereafter, John rigged a toprope on the sensational *Little Overhang*, perhaps the most enjoyable problem I climbed that day. A series of swinging aerobatics led twenty feet to the crux move to the top. Once there I wobbled over to unclip the cord from the anchor a fixed blade behind a loose block. Shocked, I reflected on how marginal my climbing had been, in addition to the barrel cactus at the base. Laughing over my cowardice we were off to lunch and then to a third area.

This final tour involved more looking than climbing, as by this conjuncture my hands felt as if they had been stroked with a bastard file. This area, referred to as the Badlands in *Master of Rock*, had the most unlimited possibilities conceivable. Following a warm-up on the Penny Ante boulder we crossed a quick-sanded creek bed to the final problem of the day—the phenomenal *Juggernaut*. Not having enough energy to even come close, I became stupefied by the bizarre and unique sequence involved in ascending it. Completely spent, we left the lost canyon talking of a future visit.

A month later I returned with John Bachar, both of us having tuned up considerably during that time. On this second tour the problems became more realistic, though still the hardest both John and I had seen. Heavily psyched, we warmed up on Saturday for our appointment with Gill on Sunday. The training had paid off as we both managed problems that had thwarted us previously, most pleasurable being the *Ripper Traverse* Gill's way (from right to left). Exuberant we retired in lieu of the following day.

On Sunday we drove straight to the lost canyon for a swing at the *Juggernaut*. Warming up again on the Penny Ante I mostly loafed while Bachar familiarized himself with the problems. Gill slipped on his boots for the first time and powered over several B-1's. With this as inspiration we headed for the *Juggernaut*.

In the weeks previously I had devised a way to train for this climb (30 feet) by swinging from the support beams of a basketball backboard. The aim was to limit the lower body swing by levering off one or the other arm. With the toprope set I tried it and, deliberating past mistakes, managed to succeed. I stood, then sat on the small summit, astonished. I yearned to write home, but realized I had none— my folks left no forwarding address after moving in 1975. Shortly after Bachar succeeded and we spent the remainder of the day exploring for new problems and attempting several. I think we only did one of the many we saw. We left the lost canyon talking of yet another visit.

THE FOOLISH AND THE WISE: THE FIRST FREE ASCENT OF THE *WISDOM*

JULY-AUGUST 1978, NO. 49

BY GLENN RANDALL

~~~~~~

Like Yosemite National Park, Eldorado Canyon is a hotbed of American climbing. Both areas have cutting-edge routes—lines that have stood the test of time—like Yosemite's Bachar-Yerian (5.11c X) on Medlicott Dome and Eldorado's The Wisdom (5.11d R) on Redgarden Wall. Perhaps not coincidentally, both routes were also authored by the late John Bachar (1957–2009), perhaps America's best and boldest free climber in the 1970s and 1980s.

The Wisdom was originally an aid route established by Layton Kor and Pat Ament in the 1960s. "When the cracks ran out, Kor would hook and nail the most fragile sandstone flakes, and if those ran out he would start free climbing again," Climbing.com stated in a tribute to Kor in 2013. While the first two pitches were freed in 1975, it wasn't until 1977 when Bachar came along that the integral route— with its crux third pitch in all its intimidating, overhanging glory—was freed. "His ascent added the last piece to a long-standing puzzle," writes Glenn Randall.

~~~~~~

"*The Wisdom* isn't really very significant in terms of the history of climbing," Dave Breshears (the *Kloeberdanz* Kid) said to me recently. "After all, there is only about 15 feet of hard climbing in it." I looked at him for a second.

"Well, that's true, if you consider everything under 5.11 easy," I said.

Last October John Bachar struggled up the only "hard" climbing on *The Wisdom,* an overhanging route in Eldorado Springs. His ascent added the last piece to a long-standing puzzle. Bachar is a California rock-jock who has made climbing hard free routes a career. With Jeff Lowe belaying, Bachar led out from the cave at the top of the first pitch and across the 10-foot Wisdom Roof. Art Higbee had succeeded on the roof in 1975 after failures by many people.

Bachar clipped into the bolt above the lip and took one more look at the old aid line that had defeated him and all others. Bachar had personally tried that route twice before. Once again the moves eluded him. He later said the aid line "looked horrendous, B3."

There was another way, however, one Bachar had examined before and shunned because "it looked so flaky and loose." "I'm basically chickenshit," he told me.

This alternative was to undercling 10 feet right from the aid line and climb a long overhanging bulge with a small arch. Bachar traversed out, placed a nut behind a slightly expanding flake just below the bulge, and started up.

"I got into the arch and really freaked out," Bachar said, "I kept grabbing the wrong nut off the rack. Finally I got a three Stopper in halfway." Bachar grabbed the Stopper as his strength fled. "I could barely hold on to the nut to clip into it. Then I fell, got back on the rock, and underclung back to the bolt."

Bachar knew the nut was shaky. He also disliked placing protection in that style, so he clipped into the bolt with a runner, untied, and pulled the rope through the Stopper. He hung off the bolt for a minute to retie and got back on the rock.

"It really scared me the first time," he said. "Second time, though, I didn't even get pumped." Bachar said, but after talking with Lowe he decided to rate it *hard* 5.11.

More than one party has gotten gripped on *The Wisdom.* The first attempt on the route, in 1973, avoided the first pitch by a 50-foot traverse down a rotten dike from a neighboring route, *Le Toit.* Steve Wunsch led it and Bob Hritz, noted for a girdle traverse of the Rotwand Wall, had to follow.

"That traverse really scared Hritz," Wunsch said. Hritz had to rig a back rope to protect himself.

On that first attempt they tried the roof high and failed. Wunsch returned with Chris Reveley in January 1974 and tried again, this time lower. Wunsch peeked around the corner but failed to pull over the lip.

The Wisdom had for many years intrigued Jim Erickson, a Boulder resident well-known for his first free ascents in Eldorado. In the spring of 1975 Erickson teamed up with Hughes and started exploring the first pitch. They reached a fixed pin after 30 feet of steep, poorly protected climbing, but were stopped there and climbed down. Erickson arranged to meet Higbee at noon a few weeks later to try again. While waiting, Erickson ran into Ed Webster and Roger Briggs. Higbee was late, so the three hiked up to the first pitch. Erickson led up to the pin, then climbed down.

When Higbee hadn't shown up by 12:30 Webster gave it a try and made it. Erickson and Briggs followed, as did Higbee when he arrived.

They didn't get far on the roof that day. Erickson and Higbee returned to the roof a week later. On Higbee's first attempt he got his hands above the lip and grabbed a big loose flake. The flake came off—and so did Higbee. Several years later he solved the main roof problem but failed on the next roof above it.

It was established now that the main roof would go. In an effort to simplify work on the smaller roof, Erickson aided the main roof and placed a fixed pin and a bolt. His plan was to belay at the bolt if it could be done without hanging from the gear.

"I would have tried to belay legally; if I couldn't then I wouldn't have belayed at all," Erickson commented. "I still think people have the right to decide on permanent protection when doing a first ascent. They can leave it as a horror or rappel and place bolts."

Unfortunately, Erickson' decision to place the bolt generated controversy. Higbee told me recently he thought the bolt had "degraded the climb psychologically," Breashears said flatly. "The bolt ruined the climb. If I do the route, I'll chop it."

Partly because of the controversy, Erickson lost interest and never returned to the route.

In the summer of 1975 Wunsch returned, this time with John Bragg. Wunsch led the main roof with one fall and belayed in slings at the bolt. To protect himself while following, Bragg aided out to the last fixed pin in the roof and tied into the pin with an old red sling that Wunsch had found. Then he aided back and followed free with the sling as protection. (The sling is still there, slowly rotting away.) Except for a pin just off the belay, the sling was Bachar's only protection on the roof.

Both Wunsch and Bragg tried the second roof several times. Wunsch recalls it as very scary, as the protection consisted of an upside-down pin with a broken eye and a "shitty sideways two hex."

Eventually Bragg tried to go right down low. Already tired, he took a look at the way Bachar eventually went and rappelled off. A two-year lull preceded Bachar's ascent. Two weeks after his success, Dan Stone, Wunsch, and I gave the route a try. Our encounter with the route proved nearly as exciting as Bachar's.

We agreed that I would lead the first pitch, Wunsch the second (to a sling belay above the big roof), and Stone, undoubtedly the strongest member of the team, was to lead the section Bachar had freed. Rumor had it that Bachar was fighting rope drag on the crux. Since we didn't really need that sort of thing, a sling belay seemed logical. It did draw criticism later from Higbee, Erickson, and others.

The first pitch provoked some thought, but finally went smoothly with some fancy footwork. Wunsch's feet were scraping a little as he followed. Stone, the gymnast of the group, ignored the fancy footwork and just pulled up on the hold. Steve led out on the giant roof in his beautiful, controlled style, then fouled up the foot sequence and had to let his feet fly for an instant. When he reached the lip he hooked his heel between his hands and threw us a huge grin. Stone and I covered our fear with nervous laughter.

While Wunsch set up the anchor, Stone and I puzzled out how to protect Stone as he followed the roof. The ultimate arrangement of our three ropes made it possible for Stone to get back on the rock if he fell, but made it unlikely that I would be able to do so when I came third. Stone reached the belay after chalking up three times in the middle of the roof, took one look at the third pitch, and refused to try it.

Wunsch traversed out to look at the crux. I waited below the roof, unable to see what was happening. Finally Stone called down, chuckling, "Hey, Glenn, want to give it a go?" I felt I was being sandbagged, but I agreed to look at it. After scurrying across the main roof as fast as my arms would carry me, I crawled through Stone's and Wunsch's legs to reach the undercling, and climbed out to have a look at the crux.

It looked BAD. I had no protection at the end of the undercling, and didn't trust the flake. It looked as if I might get a wired Stopper in the arch, but to find out I had to commit myself to some ferocious climbing. Without protection at the start it was a terrifying prospect. I had not talked to Bachar at that time and so did not know his story.

After several trips back and forth along the undercling I worked out the first moves. I knew I could reach the nut placement—if it existed. It was the uncertainty about both the protection and my ability to do the moves that gave the pitch its terrible fascination. The price of knowledge about either one was total commitment; the price of failure was not the embarrassment of grabbing a bombproof nut, but a long and very serious fall. I felt like a trout pondering a baited hook—take a big bite and swallow? I had already nibbled on the bait as much as I could.

It was quiet and warm at the belay; the sun was getting low and the shadows were creeping up the wall below us. The crowd that had watched us do the roof had left. I went back out the undercling and committed myself. Steve later said he was really impressed at the way I moved into the arch. Then he saw me starting to shake and had to turn away.

The rock was flaky and the footholds were crackling under my feet. My forearms were numb. I got in a marginal nut and tried to get back down. There was no way. The mental glue screamed with the strain. I grabbed for a hold and pulled up, praying the fragile footholds would maintain. I reached blindly over a bulge—it was an act of desperate faith— a bucket! The rock still overhung but any thought of choice was laughable and I kept going. More buckets appeared, giant ones, some of them loose, and I was waltzing when I reached the belay. My throat was too dry to whoop; I croaked my jubilation.

Wunsch followed with a struggle and Stone, as usual, wasn't even out of breath. Shortly after our ascent Bob Candelaria and Pat Adams tried the route. Candelaria led the main roof, then traversed to the crux. To avoid rope drag he skipped placing protection behind the flake and just went for it. Halfway over the bulge he reached down to place a nut. As he jerked the nut to set it, his foothold crumbled. Instantly he was tumbling through space, the nut still in his hand. "It was like doing a double backflip with a full twist and deciding halfway through you're not going to do it. You just start looking for something to grab," he told me later. He fell about 70 feet. The arc of his swing was so great he could easily have reached back up to the lip.

Jim Logan saw the fall from the other side of the canyon and came running up the scree slope. Candelaria says Logan was giggling when he saw Candelaria was all right. "Are you trying out for a trapeze act?" Logan asked him. Adams later said of the fall, "It amazed me. He came over the roof sideways. He was kicking like he was on a swing, trying to get back up to the lip of the roof." Adams lowered Candelaria to the ground, followed the main roof, and rappelled off. At this writing no one has been up there since, to my knowledge.

Others will follow, though, and I think they will agree that while *The Wisdom* may not be a significant climb, it certainly is an exciting one!

FRIENDS: A LOOK AT NEW TECHNOLOGY IN CLIMBING

NOVEMBER-DECEMBER 1978, NO. 51

COMMENTARY BY STEVEN LEVIN

From 1973 to 1977, the aerospace engineer and dirtbag climber Ray Jardine perfected his design for the Friend, the spring-loaded camming device (SLCD) that would forever change rock climbing. It's hard to believe it now, given SLCDs' universal use by climbers, but at first the invention wasn't accepted worldwide—and in some cases was even seen, like chalk and sticky rubber, as cheating. Forty-plus years have passed since Jardine sold the cams out of the back of his rig in Yosemite's Camp 4, disseminating an invention that would, by making parallel-sided cracks easily protectable, allow huge advances in the sport. Below, current AMGA guide and author of the 2009 Eldorado Canyon: A Climbing Guide *Steve Levin plays devil's advocate with the then-newfangled invention, asking a series of questions about what direction the tool was poised to take rock climbing.*

With each new mechanical or technological advancement in climbing equipment there also comes the related questions of ethics in its use. This applies to the latest breakthrough in clean-climbing protection, Ray Jardine's Friends. It is not my intent in this essay to draw any conclusions, nor do I want to advertise or disdain Friends; rather I would like to mention several pertinent arguments against Friends, each of which the ethic-conscious climber should consider before carrying

Friends on his or her next climb. I must stress here that each of us climbs for different reasons and that there are no right or wrong sides in this debate.

The most obvious argument against the use of Friends is whether they are an aid in difficult free climbing, particularly on strenuous and continuous crack climbs. Because of their ingenious design and principle, the placement of a Friend takes much less time and effort than does the placement of a traditional chock. If you will agree with me that a major factor in doing a difficult crack climb is endurance, and that climbing fast is of utmost importance, would not the use of Friends then significantly aid in the climber's chances of success? Put into other words, would the climber be able to climb a certain pitch without the use of Friends? Is the climber relying on Friends to complete the pitch? Does the use of Friends on established climbs that were originally done with traditional chocks lower the technical difficulty of the climb? Would a climber doing the second ascent of a climb without Friends be doing it in better style if the original party used them? And likewise, would it be in poor style to repeat a climb using Friends when they were not used on the initial ascent?

Another argument against Friends is that they take the challenge out of placing nuts. On a poorly protected route originally done without Friends, isn't the question of doubt in one's ability threatened if Friends are taken? Again, is the climber relying on Friends? Placing a Friend is reminiscent of placing a pin in that the regularities and contours of the rock are overlooked and the protection blindly thrown in. It's true that by placing chocks we become more aware of the rock surface, but aren't we enlightening ourselves to the textures of the rock in conjunction with a manmade device? In effect we are only contriving our awareness to the rock and its surface. So why waste our time playing with technology when we place a nut and just concentrate on the climbing? One might also consider the personal rewards of climbing without technology backing you up. Perhaps instead of looking in the direction of harder and harder routes we should be looking deeper into the quality of the climbing experience. Doing a 5.10 lead with a minimal amount of equipment could be equally as impressive as attacking a 5.12 route with an armory of Friends, tape, benzoin, and quickdraws.

I think we should also consider the impact Friends will have on the climbing scene and competition (that is if you care at all about it). In advertisements for Friends it reads, "Climb The Big Ones With Friends," or as I interpreted it, "Now You Too Can Be a Hotshot." We should decide whether our reasons for climbing agree with this statement. Friends should open new doors for everyone who decides to use them, but should this progress be gauged in terms of other people? In our efforts to improve at climbing are we trying to get better than we were, or are we attempting to get better than the next guy? I agree that competition, in reasonable quantities, can only enhance the standards of the climbing game. With open eyes competition is an inspirational device for us to progress by. But the progress should perhaps be personal and should not be reflected back into the maelstrom of competition.

There are several situations where Friends are a bonus. Desert cracks tend to be very parallel and standard nuts very often are useless. Friends will undoubtedly open up vast numbers of desert lines. Also aid pitches could be climbed much faster and cleaner, thus ascents of major aid lines will do little to harm or alter the rock surface. Lastly, major undertakings such as free climbing an alpine wall could go a lot smoother if you didn't have to waste time fiddling with chocks and you could simply place a Friend.

It will be interesting to see if Friends catch on, and if they do, what considerations, if any, people give them. A major prohibiting factor is the price—at close to $25 apiece not all climbers will be able to afford complete racks.

At times I feel the climbing game should not be taken so seriously and many of you will disregard the points I have made. But to those climbers seeking higher levels of climbing prowess, the style that these climbs are being done at is as important as the ability to get to the top of a certain pitch. If you decide that Friends are against your ethic you will save yourself a lot of trouble and money. But if you feel they will make some unattainable climbs come within your grasp, then use them. Whatever choice you make is your own.

LATOK I: A CLIMB WITHOUT A SUMMIT

MARCH–APRIL 1979, NO. 53

BY MICHAEL KENNEDY

A whisper from the summit. That's how close the dream team of Michael Kennedy, Jim Donini, George Lowe, and Jeff Lowe came to completing the first ascent of the North Ridge of the 7,145-meter (23,440-foot) Latok I in Pakistan's Karakoram range. For twenty (or maybe twenty-one—Kennedy doesn't recall) days, they worked up the wall. With them they carried 450 pounds of gear, including eight ropes and seventeen days' worth of food. Along the way, they endured three storms, one low on the route, one high on the route, and a bad one during the descent, but "The climbing was magnificent . . . the finest and most direct line to the summit," Kennedy wrote. The quartet was thwarted a mere 400–500 feet from the summit when Jeff Lowe became terribly sick and the team had to descend. They were back on the ground twenty-six days after starting. In the forty years since, at least twenty teams have attempted the line, though none have succeeded.

After this historic climb, Kennedy didn't come home and write a long-form essay; instead, he collected his favorite shots from the climb and laid them out in a photo essay accompanied by a mere 339 words and let the images speak for themselves. (It's worth seeking out this original for the photos alone.) This for what is regarded as "The Most Remarkable Failure in Climbing History!"

In July 1978, a small American group—Jim Donini, George Lowe, Jeff Lowe, and myself—made an attempt on Latok I (23,440 feet) in the Karakoram Himalaya of Pakistan. The mountain had been attempted three times previously, all from the south, we chose the *North Ridge* as the finest and most direct line to the summit. It also appeared to be the safest route, perhaps the only one on the peak.

After some delays and a long walk to Basecamp, we spent three days reconnoitering the route, packing loads, and resting. We planned to climb alpine-style, with none of the tedious buildup of fixed ropes, camps and supplies common to most Himalayan ventures. Nevertheless, we did stack the odds a little in our favor with seventeen days of food, eight ropes (to allow some flexibility in campsite selection), full winter bivouac gear, and a large selection of hardware, 450 pounds in all.

We stayed on the climb for a total of twenty-six days, failing to reach the summit by 400 or 500 feet. Half of this time was spent in storms, one low on the route and the other near the top. The climbing was magnificent, ranging from 5.9 rock with the odd bit of aid to 85-degree ice, never desperate but always sustained. We spent four nights above 21,000 feet on tiny ledges hacked out of the ice, including one in a storm on the descent, the most horrible night I have ever spent in the mountains. Jeff became very ill at our highest camp, a snow cave at 22,800 feet, but managed to get down under his own power.

But it wasn't all grim; there were days of pure enjoyment when the sun, rock, ice, and sky all blended into a blissful state of movement and exhilaration. But how does one write about a twenty-six-day climb? To describe each pitch, each day would be tedious, and the experience was so overwhelming and so ultimately disappointing that I'm not sure that I could, even six months later.

PART TWO: THE 1980s

THE 1980s: A DECADE OF RADICAL CHANGE AND TRANSITION

BY PAUL PIANA

My life as a rock climber began in 1966 at age 11 with 120 feet of Goldline, a few pitons, and a few carabiners. The crags near my hometown of Newcastle, Wyoming, were fun, but I learned early on that attaining any summit in the nearby Black Hills/Needles in South Dakota was real climbing—committing and often run out.

In those days, rumors circulated of the couple Herb and Jan Conn, who had "climbed all the Needles," so for twenty-five cents I purchased their ten-page *Rock Climbs in the Needles*. I learned from the Conns and others, including Renn Fenton and Bob Kamps, that first ascents are where it's at.

In my early 20s, in 1978, after having climbed from coast-to-coast while serving in the US Marine Corps, I enrolled at the "University of Vedauwoo," near Laramie, Wyoming, and began searching out new routes. One spring day in 1979, I started up what would become *Spider God* (5.11b) on the *Fall Wall*, placing the first three bolts from granite cobbles and thin edges. At the time, I felt hooking was cheating and hadn't considered rappelling in to bolt. Finally, I placed the fourth bolt up and left, thinking I would return when my feet weren't on fire. So, I stepped onto nearby *Fall Wall*, a 5.10a, and followed that to the top.

As I crested the wall, a troupe of climbers arrived. Their fearless leader, shod in Robbins boots so large he wore four pairs of wool socks to make them fit, wore a newfangled Whillans Sit Harness bedangled with 1950s-era Bedayn and Marwa carabiners slung with Moac chockstones. He also carried a collection of army surplus pitons and several figure-8 rappelling devices. The owner of the vintage gear, the up-and-comer Todd Skinner, asked if he could give the climb a try via toprope.

After falling many times, Todd made his way up *Spider God*, and it was this climb that convinced him to purchase a tight-fitting pair of EB rock boots. Soon after, he began a career of authoring free climbs at the highest level on walls both small and huge, routes on which I would often join him.

The early 1980s were exciting—first ascents were everywhere, and gear was rapidly getting lighter and safer. Take the time at Devils Tower, Wyoming, when Ron Kauk showed me Ray Jardine's game-changing No. 1, 2, and 3 Friends . . . wow! The first Friend I purchased was a No. 2, and I was sick with the guilt of spending $18.50 for a single piece, but the potential for protecting Vedauwoo flares was irresistible. Then I discovered the revolutionary RPs from visiting Aussie Chris Peisker, who had a fistful. These micronuts, which so handily protected seams and tiny tapers, were just as revolutionary as Friends.

NEON LYCRA AND EVOLVING ETHICS

In the 1980s, the climbing magazines flaunted photos of honed athletes clad in flashy Lycra tights sending super-steep, bolt-protected routes. It was these articles and word-of-mouth reports of sport climbing in Europe, plus Alan Watts's ground-breaking sport climbs at Smith Rock, that began a revolution. The controversy over rehearsing moves and rappel-placed bolts, plus the subsequent outrage of chopping said bolts, kept the discussions heated—and often in the press.

In 1986, the American Alpine Club hosted the "Great Debate" in Denver, where whoever wished could speak his or her mind. Climbers interested in preserving an ethic of bold, poorly/sparsely protected climbs spoke alongside climbers who were establishing cutting-edge sport climbs on rappel. Many passionate opinions and viewpoints were presented. In the end, no solution was agreed upon, but I think a lot of steam was vented, and climbers went back to climbing however they wished. As we all now know, sport climbing came to be accepted.

Today, climbing news can be learned almost immediately via the Internet. But I recall the excitement in the 1980s when a new edition of *Climbing* or *Rock & Ice* appeared. During that decade, I moved to Boulder and worked at Neptune Mountaineering. Famous climbers would often stop in to visit Gary Neptune—and, of course, Gary would often throw a party. One of the most memorable was the 80th birthday party for Anderl Heckmair, the leader of the Eiger North Face FA in 1938. When the birthday cake was presented, he didn't know what it was. We were all surprised, as we assumed that birthday cakes were a tradition in German-speaking countries.

The Brits were especially entertaining. One of their rest-day sports was to "nick" merchandise. Of course as employees our job was to curtail this. One hot July day, a Brit climber strolled in wearing a Mount Everest–size down coat. As he strolled through the store, we noticed that his coat appeared to get even larger and hang lower, until he sidled over to the entrance and stepped out the door. Fellow employees Clyde Soles and Larry Coates and I walked outside and asked the lad to open his coat. He promptly sped off, the three of us in hot pursuit. As he raced away, carabiners flew into the air . . . a bivouac stove bounced on the ground. Socks and gloves were next, followed by one climbing shoe and then another. As he booked it down Broadway, an unbelievable quantity of equipment flew into the air. Laughing so hard we couldn't breathe, we gave up the chase, slowly reclaiming the long trail of merchandise that led back to the store.

It was a different era, a scruffy epoch of transition and change when our little sport took its toddling first steps to modernization. Todd Skinner was a driving force in this shift, wholeheartedly embracing the new tools like hangdogging and rap-bolting. He spent a fair bit of time at Smith Rock and quickly adapted to the new ethic, taking it onto the international stage.

Todd, Lynn Hill, and Alan Watts were the first Americans to be invited to Bardonecchia, Italy, in the mid-1980s to compete in one of the first international rock-climbing competitions, Sportroccia. Unlike today, the comps were hosted on outdoor cliffs, and they didn't achieve the general public's interest. However, what little press that came out of them resulted in Todd's first sponsorship.

The sponsors liked Todd not only for his climbing skill but also for his buoyant personality and peripatetic lifestyle. They also liked the slideshows he put on at climbing stores, college outdoor clubs, and universities. His performances made Todd a valuable spokesperson. All of these things fueled his full-time traveling lifestyle, one we take for granted with professional climbers today, but that back then was still in its infancy.

SALATHÉ WALL

When Todd and I were students at the University of Wyoming, we often studied Tom Frost's wonderful black-and-white photographs from the first ascent of the *Salathé Wall* on El Capitan. We wondered what it would be like to climb those long, beautiful cracks—so far above the ground. Many years later, Todd called me to come out to the Valley to try the *Salathé* with him—on a recon mission to see if it would go free. He planned to leave the very next day, so I missed out, but two years later he asked again, and this time I said yes.

Todd and I were very tight-lipped about our *Salathé* plans because we were worried that a talented team would swoop in. Our good friends Mark Hudon and Max Jones had already come close when they unlocked all but 350 feet on a single-push ascent in 1979. Eventually, in 1988, we succeeded, eliminating all the aid. [See *"Salathé Wall*: 1988," page 85.]

After the *Salathé*, we were supposed to climb Mount Everest from the Chinese side. It would be the first time that Westerners were allowed there since before WWII. However, both Todd and I had broken bones, sustained in an accident atop El Cap after our free ascent when a giant block we were anchored to cut loose. Todd had broken ribs, and the tip of his pelvis was snapped off. My lower left leg was deeply gouged and crushed in five places, with badly squished tendons and muscles. Todd recovered quickly, but it took me several years to heal reasonably, and though I could climb, I couldn't hike very far. We missed out on an epic journey.

One morning after the *Salathé*, I returned to Boulder and went to a wonderful French bakery. There I sat, bruised, scabby, and hurting with a casted leg, when Ed Webster came in. His hands were heavily bandaged and his face severely scalded. He told me he'd just made the first ascent of Everest's Kangshung Face and had been badly frostbitten when he took his gloves off to take photographs. Then he asked what happened to me. When I told him, we both laughed and ordered another round of coffee and pastries!

Five years after Todd and I freed the *Salathé*, Alex Huber, an extremely talented German climber, made the second free ascent. While working the route alone, Alex often rapped in to try pitches. He also endured a number of cold, wet bivouacs. However, in the mornings, he was still tough enough to stay up there and continue working the route. On his successful ascent, Alex chose to follow the *Bermuda Dunes* (pitch 19) offwidth just below the Alcove and El Cap Spire. By doing so, he missed out on the most difficult, and one of the coolest, pitches on the climb. However, he made up for it by linking the first two pitches of the Headwall. I think he did a terrific job on the second free ascent. I was disappointed to read an account of Alex's climb in *Climbing* magazine, which, I felt, sought to discredit Todd and me.

A few years later, Todd, Dave Doll, and I were in Yosemite working on freeing the *Dihedral Wall* (later, Tommy Caldwell, with our encouragement, brilliantly made its first free ascent). Our efforts on the *Dihedral* mixed lots of hard work and lots of fun. Randy Leavitt, Glenn "Machine" Svenson, and other friends came by and worked some of the pitches. We would holler beta up and down. They laughed at our names for individual pitches such as "The Mouse Cookie" and "The Wind-Up Badger Toy." One day after climbing, we returned to Todd's place outside the park and listened to a message from Huber. He asked to meet us the next evening in El Cap Meadow. I figured he wanted to join our team.

The next evening, Todd, Dave, and I, along with Randy and Kevin Worrall, met Alex, Heinz and Angelica Zak, and another climber whose name I've lost. I was surprised to learn that Alex and Heinz were writing a book and wanted us to admit that we had not freed the *Salathé*! Alex had a litany of reasons for why he (and not us) had made the first free ascent and why we should renounce our climb. My story in *Climbing* in 1988 and my book *Big Walls: Breakthroughs on the Free-Climbing Frontier* recount our climb. Alex has written several books, and Jeff Achey, among others, has written of our *Salathé* climb. These accounts, articles, and opinion pieces are easily found on the Internet.

I could write that every generation makes improvements in style, which is true. But at what point does the argument "I did it a bit better, so I get all the credit" lose its steam? Since Alex's ascent, there have been many refinements to the *Free Salathé*. For instance, the entire Headwall has been climbed in one pitch. When Todd and I were working the *Salathé*, we talked about climbing from stance to stance with no hanging belays. We thought the "saddle spike" halfway through the big roof—and not the belay at the lip—below the headwall was the most logical spot for a belay, when future climbers would be climbing from hands-down stance to hands-down stance. A stance-to-stance lead without the "saddle spike" would be a run of 440 feet from Sous Le Toit Ledge to Long Ledge atop the Headwall! Someone, someday, will climb this super-pitch. It will be the next evolution of the *Salathé*.

So many wild stories and wild climbs emanated from the 1980s. I was lucky to have met and learned from those who established world-standard climbs. And I'm happy to have gotten to know and share the rope with some of our sport's most entertaining and colorful personalities.

WITLESSLY BOLD, HEROICALLY DULL

JANUARY-FEBRUARY 1980, NO. 58

BY TOBIN SORENSON

~~~~~~

In this story, the exceptionally bold alpinist and famed Southern California Stonemaster Tobin Sorenson (1955–1980) describes ascending the Central Couloir of *Canada's Mt. Kitchener with partner Jack Roberts (1952–2012). The same year this piece came out, Sorenson died during a solo climb on the north face of Mount Alberta. He was only 25 at the time of his passing.*

~~~~~~

The January cold had been devastating, more often crippling. School was to begin in a week and I could not wait to get there; anything but this cold. Having completed a winter ascent of the North Face of Mt. Robson, we were heading home out of Jasper, Alberta. Jack had both the throttle and the heater wide open and I think he was planning on keeping them that way until we crossed the California border. "Pachelbel" was playing on the tape and I was thinking about the surf in Baja.

Around the next corner, Mt. Kitchner's north face pulled us to the side. The *Central Couloir* that splits the face was running silver and gray with ice. I had never seen it in better shape for climbing. The following day we were back by noon with sharpened tools. The remainder of the day we spent skiing to the mountain's base.

The *Central Couloir* on Mt. Kitchener is 4,000 feet long. Somewhat like a giant *Point Five Gulley*, it is broad and mild for the first half and then steepens and narrows for the remaining 2,000 feet. From looking at the couloir one gets the feeling he will be climbing in a tube. From history we knew it sucked down both cornice and rock. Like a mass converter, it would throw out that which it has collected at well over terminal speeds. Of Canadian ice, the *Central Couloir* of Mt. Kitchner is the most feared and least done.

Many had come to take a look but the only ones who had managed to climb the couloir were Jeff Lowe and Mike Weiss in the summer of 1974. By climbing the lower section at night they were able to avoid the rock fall and be at the crux section at dawn. It has proved to be a tremendous ascent with loose rock and soft rotten ice.

The winter after that first ascent, Adrian and Phil Burgess and Charlie Porter attempted the couloir. Because of the severity of the cold, they adapted a moving fixed line. This was done by progressively moving a 600-foot rope slowly up the face. The temperature was 45 degrees Fahrenheit below zero, the problems were mounting, the ice slabs were ever tightening, and finally Charlie broke his axe. From about the halfway point they started back down. Adrian was making a diagonal rappel out of the couloir when he heard a small "whoof" from above. Seconds later, and only a few feet to Adrian's left, the entire couloir was in holocaust. The summit cornices had broken from the tension of the cold.

Our own plan was to move as quickly as possible. We would take no sleeping bags or bivouac gear. The stove would be enough. In the winter there is no stone fall and all we would have to worry about was the summit cornices. We could climb all day and all night. If need be we could climb through the next day until we reached the summit. Of course, this is cutting thin our margin of error, but I could not harbor the thought of carrying another heavy winter pack.

The tent was up and a brew on when the sky cracked. Jack jumped into the tent and I started taking pictures. An untold number of tons of snow and ice were dropping 3,000 feet off the northwest side of the mountain. I had never really seen a full-scale avalanche. "This is quite something," I was thinking to myself, until I realized that the whole thing was going to stop nothing short of our tent. I jumped into the tent with Jack. Fortunately, by the time the avalanche had traveled the horizontal mile across the glacier, all it did was meander about us like a small snowstorm, leaving only a few inches of snow over everything. I had been wondering why we had gotten in the tent.

The chore of cooking and getting ready for the next day went as planned. At 11 p.m. we were quiet, each thinking to himself. Occasionally the thunder of a small avalanche would come down and roll to a stop against the colorless cold on the glacier.

The nights before a climb are always the same for me. I lay there with my eyes vainly shut and think about all the potential problems and their possible solutions.

I think I shall always be praying for courage. Even still, it seems long after my prayers that I finally fall to sleep.

The watch is hanging down on its strap from the top of the tent. Five o'clock on its face, it stares at me like an animal in the night. We are supposed to be up at four; Jack is still asleep and I lay there until six before doing anything. It will not be light for two more hours. Jack starts the stove and our day has hesitatingly begun.

Crawling out of the sack on mornings like this is for me the hardest time of climbing. The air outside is brittle and seems to crack from my presence. Once again I am left wondering where I am going. My initial commitment is all I have to go on in these times when my cowardice is at its peak. I should have cursed them both but chose the latter.

We were off by seven. Having to leave the skis behind, the progress was slow until we reached the ice, which began a few hundred feet up the face. Initially we were forced to climb under a small hanging serac system. Its cracks and groans kept us wincing. Soon we were out from under and moving rapidly. The ice was not as hard and brittle as we had expected, thus we were able to climb together fairly quickly and safely.

The hours went by, and by 2 p.m. we were nearing the crux halfway up the couloir. The ice was getting harder and as a result Jack shattered the tip off one of his ice axes.

"Hey, there's not supposed to be rock here," Jack yelled. The couloir had closed off to a steep corner with loose rock and intermittent ice on both its sides. I could only stop and stare motionless for a while. It all looked very disgusting for at least 300 feet. Both of us knew by the looks of things that it was going to take far more time than we could afford. Jack fixed a secure belay and I wandered up to take a look.

The climbing, it must be said, was confusing. My left side followed a thin runnel of ice in the back corner. On my right I utilized loose rocks that moved around in their housings of verglass. It was only by being most uncautious that I was able to make any progress at all. At one point I looked down and saw my ice hammer bouncing wildly into the mist below. For the remainder of the climb we shared our only two tools.

By the time it was Jack's turn to come up, our day had grown thin. The next difficult pitch was finished in the dark. Here we stopped briefly to take a rest and prepare ourselves for the night climbing.

We were both very weary now; the cold at minus 30 was draining us. We knew we had one more difficult section, but that wasn't for a thousand feet. For now the angle of the ice was a moderate 60 degrees. We pushed on into the night using headlamps for light.

As we continued, Jack's headlamp began to fail. My headlamp rapidly grew dull because of the cold. At 8:00 p.m., at the point of stumbling, we came to a stop. We had reached the final crux.

I had wondered about this section before but had continued to remain optimistic regardless of how hard it had looked from the bottom. However, having arrived, there was hardly any room for optimism. I could feel the difficulty much more than I could see it. We both knew without question that the remaining 400 feet was going to be hard, very hard. With no more light and very little strength, we decided to wait until dawn.

Soberingly we began to cut a ledge in the ice that we might stand on. Sitting down was out of the question; to stay alive we would have to keep moving. Running in place seemed to be the best method we could think of. After two hours of dull hacking at the stone-hard ice, we had a ledge 2 feet deep and 4 feet long. The temperature was dropping rapidly.

The cold had already taken our light. It had taken our strength, and was now trying for our lives.

Frustration was the theme as the snow blew off the top and down onto our ledge, constantly dousing the stove. In the blue of the flame, we would look at each other with haunting eyes while each took his turn to bend and cry at the pain in his fingers.

Somewhere in the night we stood alone. Each in his own world, sometimes running, always silent; as if holding our breath, we waited for dawn.

After twelve hours on the ledge, light finally began to sift into the morning. As quickly as possible we were off. The ice was thin and inconsistent, often just smattered over loose rock. I began to push with all my force into the wall. Jack was hurt below from my efforts. Running up against a short overhanging section I was stopped. Twenty desperate feet and the summit could not be far beyond. This section was breached solely by a thin slash of ice. After exploring all other alternatives, the slash was the only possibility left. It hung there like a tattered piece of tapestry. Reaching past an iceless gap with my axe, with no place to put my feet, I pulled up on my arms as high as possible and recklessly smeared my crampons against the decaying wall. A few more muscle ups and I had my feet on the ice as well. The angle was kicking back to vertical.

I had the only tools we had left and Jack jumared the line. Two more moderate pitches led up to and over an easy cornice to the summit.

The summit of Kitchner is broad and flat and thus gives a person an astounding feeling of safety. The sun was barely peeking out through while clouds swirled about. We could not see much, just waves of gray and white. It all looked very similar to a movie version of Heaven. For the first time in thirty hours we could sit down. We were both very happy and could not help but just sit and smile at each other. But soon the smiles wore out and the fatigue set in. It would be hours before we could truly relax. The descent, but for the avalanche danger, would be easy, down the northwest flank.

"Jack, do you think you will ever come back in winter again?"

"I'm not sure, Tobin."

"Yes, I know how you feel. For now let's go home."

THE DANCE OF THE WOO-LI MASTERS

THE FIRST ASCENT OF THE EAST FACE OF THE MOOSE'S TOOTH

NOVEMBER-DECEMBER 1981, NO. 69

BY JIM BRIDWELL

From March 17 to 21, 1981, two of America's heaviest hitters, Jim "The Bird" Bridwell (1944–2018) and Mugs Stump (1949–1992), made the first ascent of the East Face of Moose's Tooth in the Ruth Gorge, Alaska. Playing on the name of Gary Zukav's award-winning physics book Dancing Wu Li Masters, *they named the 4,900-foot route, rated VI 5.9 WI4+ A4, The Dance of the Woo Li Masters. Stump died in a crevasse fall on the South Buttress of Denali in 1992 at age 41, while Bridwell died at age 73 in early 2018.*

A jet . . . yes, I was sure it was a jet. The sound was uniquely different from the roar of avalanches thundering down everywhere around us. It was probably headed for Oslo or some such place, and would arrive in the morning (or evening?). I couldn't figure it out, but that's the way jets are; you're never sure what time it is. My thoughts started to race on into the relationships of time and its necessity for place, but I was harshly interrupted by the sudden realization that I was looking down 3,000 feet to our tent. The spacious North Face dome looked like heaven, and we were in hell. What was I doing in this inhuman zone? Was it choice, happenstance, or fate, or possibly some combination of these that brought me to meet my climbing partner Mugs Stump?

Only four months ago we had been strangers, meeting in an outdoor cafe in Grindelwald. We drank strong coffee and shot the bull about the Eiger and similar experiences on the North Face. One cup of coffee equals about one hour of bullshit, and before three cups were gone we were both jawing each other about the East Face of the Moose's Tooth. We had both failed on the "5,000-foot" face, along with a large contingency of other climbers. At least we were in good company; we figured that the face had been attempted over ten times by different parties, all very competent. We made plans, not for the Moose's Tooth, but maybe that's where fate came into play.

In early March, Doug Geeting flew us toward the Great Gorge, but when we looked for our objective it wasn't there. Conditions were bad indeed. All the faces were in the worst possible condition; no good ice where we'd hoped, just a thin veneer of aerated ice with a light dusting of spindrift, overhangs bulging with snow clinging incredibly to their undersides. It wasn't just bad, it was inhuman. What could we possibly do in these conditions? We had to think of something quick — Doug's a good guy, but he wouldn't fly us around forever. The Moose's Tooth was close, so we decided to have a look. The East Face looked equally horrendous, but we couldn't impose on Doug's patience any more. It would have to do; these were our cards, we'd have to play them.

The landing was fine, but getting Geeting aloft took some digging and pushing. As the plane sped away we gazed at the hoary specter before us. Just thinking about it made my bones brittle and my spirit fragile. My imagination balked at more inquest and I set about erecting the tent. At least home on the glacier would be luxurious and the ogre above could wait for inspection when my courage was well braced.

The next day was clear and oh so cold; in March Alaska still doesn't really feel the sun, it passes but doesn't touch. I remembered my hand freezing white like a burn when I touched the metal on the Cessna the day before, and it felt the same as I adjusted the ring on the spotting scope. The face looked impregnable, and the invaders were armed with slingshots.

We thought that just maybe we could pull off the ol' David and Goliath sketch, and decided on a route to the right of our previous attempts. These technical aid routes were hideously plastered with ice and out of the question. Our new choice was a more perilous passage, but the only reasonable possibility. A lightweight alpine-style approach would be the key.

We were bluffing with only a pair; it would be like grabbing a tiger by the tail, you couldn't let go or you'd be eaten. The lower half of the climb consisted of avalanche chutes and faces fed by the whole upper wall, and if a storm came in while we were on the climb, retreat would be suicide. The only way down was to go to the top; conquest or death, so to speak. It sounded ridiculous, but it was true. Retreat in good weather would be very difficult, but you probably wouldn't be retreating in that case anyway. Unless, of course, there was something up there we couldn't climb.

The barometer rose but the storms came without caring. We didn't mind; it gave us time to psych up and sort out the gear. The minimum would be the rule: Four days of food and fuel could be stretched to six or seven. Food was an austere allotment of gorp, coffee and sugar, and two packets of soup. The hardware rack was skeletal; we had trimmed away the fleshy bolt kit and second set of Friends, leaving the bones; ten ice screws, fifteen rock pitons, six wired nuts, a set of Friends, and the essential hook. We planned to rappel mainly off slings around horns for the descent. We opted for a technical and swift descent, hopefully not too swiftly down a 1,500-foot rock face into the East Couloir. This of course would also be suicidal in a storm, as two huge faces on either side fed the couloir lethal doses of snow. But it did lead directly to the tent, while the Bataan Death March down the North Ridge lead only to the homeless Ruth Amphitheater. We chose what fate decreed.

Clear skies came, but the first day was spent watching the face and timing avalanches, trying to feel for some intuitive glimpse at the secret of its pulsating rhythms. The night was spent deliberating on whether to wait another day while consuming large quantities of whiskey. Something inside told me to go in the morning, perhaps the whiskey. It wields a strong opinion indeed.

We agreed, and in the morning found ourselves trudging to the base, laboring under our packs and hangovers. I didn't want to give myself a chance to know what I was doing until it was too late. Needless to say, Mugs did the leading and I did the motivating.

A steep snow slope led to the Cauldron, a steep, narrow venturi 260 feet long, which collected minute spindrift sloughs and amplified them into a blinding, freezing torrent of misery. I was appalled and impressed as Mugs led difficult 75- to 85-degree ice without protection through waves of gushing spindrift, a 15-kilo pack tugging at his shoulders. It was my turn and I secretly hoped for some respite, but knew I would get my justice, the justice I had already chosen like we all have. I was frozen when I reached the belay, fingers wooden as I fiddled with the camera and attempted to feed the rope out.

After another pitch we climbed together to the first traverse. It was steep powder snow covering sugar snow over rock. Scratchy to say the least, with imaginary belay anchors. Both leader and follower were in fact leading, each responsible for the other's life. Mistakes weren't allowed. The first traverse was three pitches long and led to a three-pitch calf burning ice slope, then onto another horrid traverse.

This was worse than the first one and longer. Near its beginning we heard a shout. Our minds must be askew, but it wasn't an alcoholic illusion. Some fellow mountaineers were ski touring up the Buckskin to the Ruth Amphitheater; we shouted back and carried on. The climbing was tenuous, thin powder snow laid over hidden patches of ice and steep rock. Protection was nearly nonexistent and the belays were the same. In places we were climbing 3 to 5 inches of snow over 60- to 65-degree rock; much to my distress, these pitches would often start with a downward traverse of 40 or 50 feet before going horizontal or upward.

Near the end of the day we reached a snow slope where it was just possible to dig a platform for sleep. Mugs fixed a pitch above for better anchors and we precariously nestled in. North Face had supplied me with a space-age sleeping system to test, and I was thankful for the pleasant success, being warm and toasty despite subzero temperatures, spindrift and all.

The morning was supremely frigid and we dared not move from our cocoons until the sun's rays gave some hope for life. Frostbite was our eminent host should we dare break the house rules, so we regulated our desires accordingly.

A steep chimney choked with ice rose up and out of our field of vision, and tested our abilities for the rest of the day. From below I judged it to be about five pitches long, but it turned out to be seven instead. This chimney and the headwall above would constitute the main difficulties of the route.

I led the first and least steep of these pitches before the white ribbon bulged abruptly so as to obscure our inquisitive gaze. Mugs pressed the attack up the 80- to 85-degree slippery gouge. In places he would encounter overhanging bulges, which the cold, dry winter had turned to airy unconsolidated granola. A desperate struggle ensued at these overhangs: Ice axes and hammers became useless, and we would be forced onto tiny edges for our crampons and shaky pitons for handholds.

Many times I had to use my ice-tool picks as cliffhangers on edges, or wedged in cracks nut fashion. The Forrest Saber hammer was especially useful for this and quickly gained favor on these pitches. This assault continued on through the day and into the failing light of evening. I started to become weak and nauseous from dehydration, as our daily consumption of water had been less than six cups per man. In those temperatures, man's devices cease to function as they are designed; the stove was by now an ineffectual nuisance that would only boil water after an hour of coaxing and shaking to warm it. We had penetrated the inhuman zone and were paying the price.

Mugs had fixed the last pitch, and I swung around a corner onto a small 65-degree ice slope, the only possible site for a bivouac. A precarious perch was produced after hours of ice sculpturing in the dark. It was nearly 1 a.m. before we collapsed exhausted in our sleeping bags. The morning of the third day started with a tedious struggle for liquids and ascending the fixed rope to our high point. Vertical ice reached upward, and once again Mugs valiantly met the challenge. He led two pitches up the icy serpent, then exited onto an easy 100-meter snow slope, which extended to a formidable headwall. Even with the telescope we had been unable to probe the secrets of this section of the climb. Intuition lured us to the right, up an ice runnel and onto a snow rib. I poked my head around the corner to be confronted by a steep rock wall. Its thin cracks were well armored with ice, and presented a chilling specter of extreme difficulty.

I tensioned off a nut I'd chopped a slot for; thinly gloved hands search for usable rugosities while crampon claws scratched at scaly granite. I laybacked a steep flake to find its top closed with ice. In quiet desperation I clung with one hand, perforating the ice overhead with the hammer, probing for a secure stick. Standing on the shelf of ice I caught my breath and looked for a possible route up the wall now confronting me.

I decided to move right into a groove, where mixed free and aid led to a point where it was possible to swing left onto my ice axe and climb up to a small ice ledge. I got some anchors in and brought Mugs up. Only a portion of the next lead disclosed itself, but things didn't look promising. Mugs moved off hooks onto the fragile thinness of precipitous ice; after 40 feet of slow, begrudging difficulties, he shouted down that it was blank above. The sky had clouded and snow began to fall.

To retrace our steps would be disastrous, we needed a bivy site and there was none below us for many pitches. We had to push on now, and quickly, for a night spent exposed and standing would be devastating to our bodies in their present weak and dehydrated condition. "Are you sure there is no possible way?" I queried. "Let me take a good look, I gotta figure this out," he replied. Mugs moved only occasionally, but some progress was being made.

What was he doing? I could only imagine the worst. He called down for the number 3 Friend, so I took out the belay anchor and sent it up. I hung in slings off a tie-off draped over a nubbin of rock, and continued my frigid vigil. The Friend went into a shallow hole, then a hook to a knife blade behind a half-inch flake, and it was working out. Several more technical aid moves, and after two hours of nerve-grinding climbing Mugs reached an ice tongue that led to easier ground.

I got to the belay and started the next pitch as quickly as possible. It was already late in the day, and we had to find some place to bivouac soon. The snow was coming down heavily now, and spindrift cascaded over us with increasing punctuality. The climbing was marginal; a traverse crossed a slab covered with 4 inches of snow. I had hoped that there would be ice, but no such luck. I splayed my feet duck style to attain the maximum surface area. I couldn't believe they held; it was like climbing a slate roof covered in snow. Once past this I entered a trough filled with bulletproof ice. By this time I was extremely sick.

Mugs came up and found me slumped over, weak and nauseous from dehydration. He led the next two pitches of steep mixed rock and ice, but it was all I could do to follow. It was dark and I had to use my headlamp to follow the last rope length, but we had found a place to dig a snow cave. A gift from heaven! After two hours the cave was completed, and we began brewing tea and coffee, two of the worst drinks possible for dehydration. At 1:30 a.m. we collapsed in our sleeping bags, secure from the storm.

Life came slowly the next morning. From my vantage point near the cave entrance I could see that the storm was breaking up, but I kept the vision secret from Mugs, as I wanted to rest just a little longer. Soon the sun was shining into the cave, and it was no longer possible to hide the obvious fact that the weather was turning beautiful. We crawled out from the cave and commenced climbing at 11:30 a.m. The problems were mainly in route-finding; picking the easiest but not always obvious way is a talent born of experience and often times luck. We were lucky, and by 3:30 p.m. we stood on top of the Tooth.

The vantage point was spectacular; it seemed that I took one photograph after another until two rolls disappeared. Soon it was 4:30 p.m. and Mugs asked coyly if I'd like to start down. The weather was clear in all directions; it was also fairly late and I was tired, but secretly I had been having subtle intuitions of foreboding about the descent. For you see, I had been thinking of the descent for quite some time. In reply to Mugs, I said a quick no. I felt a possible ordeal ahead, and wanted a full day to cope with any eventuality. Bypassing my suspicions, I offered a further explanation: The descent would be technical and potentially difficult, and we should give ourselves a full day as there would be no place to stop once we had started. We agreed and returned to photography.

Darkness came sneaking over the mountains while our stove begrudgingly produced two cups of hot tea without sugar. Our supplies were nearly finished, so getting down was imminently important. We burrowed deep into our survival cells as the cold became increasingly bitter. Temperatures plummeted to minus 30 degrees that night, and the wind decided to continue and wait for some exposed skin in the morning. It was truly torturous packing and getting ready to go. All manmade gadgets ceased to work;, just another wonderful quality of the inhuman zone. But the stove did manage one full cup of cold water each before it died.

We climbed down a snow slope and began rappelling over discontinuous snow and rock bands. As we descended rappel after rappel, the snow disappeared, leaving bare, flaking rock, the kind for which the Moose's Tooth is famous. Crumbling and rotten, the face steepened so that it disappeared below us, making it impossible to see where we were going or what we were going to do. I kept angling leftward as the couloir came upward toward our left. The rock had become blank of cracks, but there were a few scabs of very flexible rotten flakes.

The alarms went off in my head, activating my whole being into survival mode. I rappelled, passed an overhang and tension traversed left to a flake-like ledge, pounded two pitons into the compressed gravel behind it, and began wondering what to do next. Looking down I could see nothing to go for. I wished I had brought the bolt kit; Mugs had wanted to, but I had insisted that it wouldn't be necessary, and besides it was too heavy. Alpine style, you know: too much weight, count every match, and all that jive. My mind raced in all directions at once, as a cat might behave trapped in a corner by salivating Alsatians. The word *frantic* would best describe my reactions.

Computer-like, I made a decision and yelled up instructions to Mugs. I asked him to tie off one rope to his anchors and to send the other down so I could check things out. If I saw nothing, I would have to jumar 300 feet to Mugs, then we would have to climb back up to the summit, ten pitches or more, and look for another way down. It was a devastating course of action, which would require the rest of the day and part of the next.

I tensioned left again, and then climbed up and left, my crampons screeching on the rotten granite as I searched for tiny holds. Putting a number 3 Stopper in the only place available, I clipped in and continued rappelling. Near the end of the rope, a small but solitary flake came into view. I stopped and stared at it, hanging on the rope as a sad, sweet rhapsody of emotion washed over me. I remained there motionless with visions of people I loved and owed love to. It's sad that we don't appreciate the commonplace, yet wonderful and beautiful trivial duties of life, like saying hello or washing the dishes, without paying attention. I guess that you don't miss the water until your well runs dry.

These thoughts rustled over my mind, and I emerged slowly from the reverie, realizing that this was what we in California call a "heavy scene."

My intuition had been correct: We had come to meet our ordeal. I looked up and saw clouds beginning to prey the sky, then started back up the rope, turning for one last look at the flake.

Reaching the nut, I unclipped, swung back right, and continued up to the anchors. I yelled to Mugs to come down; I woke him, as he had fallen asleep from the excitement.

He could tell there was uncertainty in my voice. When he reached me, I explained the situation before we pulled the ropes so that he could partake in the decision. Once the ropes were down, we'd have no choice. He had an easy way of boosting my confidence while accepting my course of action, whatever I might choose.

Casino time: one roll of the dice for all the marbles. I said a prayer and started down. Retracing my traverse, I reached the Stopper I'd previously fixed and brought Mugs down to a minimal stance. He surveyed the anchor briefly, and then looked at me with wonder that was broken off by doubt. I shrugged my shoulders and said, "That's it." My heart was trying to escape from my mouth for the next 150 feet, until I secured a number 1 Friend behind the small flake I'd see. I placed another nut while Mugs duplicated the rappel; he later told me that he almost unclipped from the anchor, but quickly decided and realized that a fast death was more appealing than a slow and agonizing, yet inevitable, one.

After descending half the rope, I gave thanks to the merciful one. For, wonder of wonders, the ropes reached a snow-covered ramp. The chilling grip of death relaxed and a calming peace soothed my quaking soul. The descent became routine and within two hours we were galloping down steep snow toward the security of the tent.

Everything there was frozen. We immediately fired up the stove and began guzzling brew after brew of hot liquid. We laughed and joked until late in the night. We'd had five days of intense experience, and required some time to unwind. The cards were played and we had drawn aces. Finally I collapsed into prone paralysis; just before unconsciousness, the memorable words of French climber Jean Manassief came to mind, "This is the fucking life, no?"

SHAWANGUNK SOLO CLIMBS: FOOL'S GOAL

APRIL 1986, NO. 95

BY RUSS CLUNE

Though today everyone is familiar with Alex Honnold's mind-blowing June 3, 2017, ropeless ascent of El Cap's Freerider *(VI 5.13a; 3,000 feet), many don't know that free soloing at a high grade dates back several decades. Take Russ Clune's "Fool's Goal," in which he and his friends, cordless, worked up the grades at their local crag, the Shawangunks, New York—on lines they had dialed into near submission—with their eyes set on free soloing the ultimate prize: the overhanging 5.12c* Supercrack.

At the belay below the crux roof of *Fat City*, a Gunks 5.10, Jeff Gruenberg announced to his partners, "Someday I'm gonna solo this thing." But when he followed it, he popped off the down-sloping holds. Jeff dangled in the air and looked up at his friends.

"Well, maybe I'll make that a roped solo."

On a warm Friday evening about a year later, Jeff was again at the crux roof of *Fat City*; this time he didn't have his rope. It was an impressive solo. Soon afterward, Dan McMillan climbed *Erect Direction*, another 5.10, sans kernmantel. The feat had been attempted before by another climber; his efforts had left him stranded light-years off the deck, hanging by a single small Stopper in a corner below massive roofs. Dan had done the route a week earlier with a partner.

"It felt so casual, I just wanted to solo it."

A new game had come to town. Although nothing was overt, a third-classing competition had started within a small clique of Gunks regulars.

Jeff and I agreed there were three ultra-classic solos: *Foops*, *Open Cockpit*, and *Supercrack*.

Whenever we were at Skytop, we found ourselves doing the three routes again and again. *Foops*, a famous 5.11 roof, felt solid. *Open Cockpit*, a slightly overhung, 40-foot, 5.11 + face climb, was dicey. *Supercrack*, a 5.12 finger-wrencher, was out of the question: We still fell on it.

A sunny autumn afternoon brought me out to Skytop. I decided to give *Foops* a look. No one was around and I enjoyed the solitude. I climbed the 50-foot 5.9 wall to the base of the 'hang and contemplated the chalk marks extending to the lip. After testing the first couple of holds, I returned to the rest and thought some more.

I heard boisterous conversation—a small group of tourists appeared in the talus below. Someone exclaimed, "Look!" I glanced down and saw a finger pointed at me. They became silent and sat down among the boulders. I imagined I was in an auto race, the spectators just waiting for me to crash and burst into flames. I waited them out. It felt an eternity. After they bored of watching paint dry, they left. I down climbed; the mood was shattered.

Once again, it was a warm Friday evening when Jeff found himself alone on *Foops*. Once again, it was a momentous accomplishment: He'd ticked the first of the masterpiece solos.

That stirred the scene up. All the talk was becoming action. Naturally, we denied there was any competition involved. After all, what's the fascination in soloing something that's been unmercifully wired? But while we said, "No big deal," we thought to ourselves, "Holy shit!" Nothing much was said about coming attractions, but the clique knew what was bound to happen, sometime in the foreseeable future.

Jeff and I were on *Supercrack*. I redpointed it, set up a toprope and lowered down. Jeff waltzed through and belayed me from the top. I did another lap, removing the gear along the way. "This is really getting easy," I thought. Jeff had a smirk on his face when I pulled over the top. "So, when ya gonna solo it, Spencer?" he asked expectantly. "Oh, never. What's the point? What would it prove?" I said. "I have it so wired. Now, if somebody third-classed it onsight, that'd be impressive." Regardless of what I told Jeff, the idea of soloing the thing became a goal.

Jeff pulled another coup when he broke from the sacred three. *Open Cockpit* was the natural successor to *Foops*. Instead, he opted for *Yellow Wall*, a 5.11 that weaves through forbidding overhangs on less-than-the-best rock. It was a brilliant solo.

On a cloudy day midweek, I meandered out to Skytop with just my shoes and chalk bag. I told myself I'd look for friends and climb whatever people were doing, but I knew the place would be deserted. Well, it almost was. John Harlin and his wife, Adele, were climbing a route in the vicinity of *Open Cockpit*.

"Hmm, *Open Cockpit*," I thought. I stood below it, then slipped my shoes on. Adele came around. I started up, chatting with her. Somehow her presence made me feel at ease. Whether it was because it kept my mind off what I was doing or it was just nice to have company, I'm not sure. I kept going; we kept talking.

When I was three quarters up the face, Adele made a concerned inquiry. "Are you going to solo it?" "Well, it'd be easier going up than climbing down at this point," I replied.

Three days later, Barry Rugo soloed *Open Cockpit*. He knew nothing of my undertaking and thought he'd bagged the first solo. His inspired ascent produced an ironic situation.

The heat was on: two down and one to go. *Open Cockpit* had been somewhat spontaneous; *Supercrack* was totally premeditated.

Dick was home. My headlights flashed against his car as I pulled into the driveway. It dawned on me that this was the end of the summer. Tomorrow would be my last day in the Gunks before classes started. Tomorrow would be it.

I had been housesitting in New Paltz for Dick Williams and Rosie Andrews while they visited Britain. Exceptionally fine August weather allowed for daily rituals of pulling, pumping, and tweaking on solid quartzite. The result was a confidence, which only comes from familiarity. Once my attention turned to school, the spell would be broken.

I greeted Dick in the living room and we talked about his trip. My attention was only partially on the conversation. Whisks of tomorrow's plan swept through my head and I felt like a kid with a secret.

Dick went to bed and I slouched down on the couch, draping my bag loosely over me. The night was warm, the insects noisy. I closed my eyes and saw *Supercrack* in front of me. I envisioned my hands and feet on each move until I stood on top. Back at the base, I climbed it again. Perfect. Again. Perfect. Again . . .

The aroma of freshly ground French roast coffee filled the house at an obscenely early hour. Dick, unable to sleep well because of jetlag, joined me for a cup as we exchanged good-byes. He thought I was headed directly home. I knew better. My truck puttered uphill toward the Trapps. I parked, pulled my bike out of the back, strapped my pack to my back, and turned on the Walkman. Cool air rushed against my face as The Smiths blared through the headphones.

I pedaled fast toward Skytop. At the base of *Supercrack* I was sweating and breathing hard from the ride. The crack looked long. I pictured myself on it; watched myself climb it from the perspective of an observer. Then I mentally climbed it as the climber, watching my feet and hands on each hold.

My breathing slowed down. Now the climb looked short. I liked that. My Walkman was off, but The Smiths still swirled in my head. I pulled my shoes on and laced them with the care of a diamond cutter, letting each toe find its favorite indentation before locking it into place. I squeezed my full chalk bag a few times, breaking the chunks down to the right consistency. I started up, went several moves, and came down.

I had to erase every iota of doubt. I went back to my pack and pulled out a rope and a couple of units. I climbed around the back of the pinnacle and anchored the toprope. At the bottom, I rigged a jumar to my harness.

I shot up the crack. It felt good and secure; just right. I dropped the rope and pulled the anchors. Back at the base, I sat and rubbed the soles of my shoes clean.

Automatic pilot switched on. The crack had the feel of a well-worn glove, every rugosity clicking into place. Footholds appeared with acute clarity, looking overly large. Thumb pinch with the right, index finger down with the left, feet stemmed, butterfly jam with the right, right foot pebble, left foot edge . . .

Internal dialogue made an uninvited appearance when my left hand clutched the jug above the roof. "What the hell are you doing?!" it exclaimed in shocked horror. I squashed the thought like a troublesome insect, and with a surge of adrenaline laybacked to the stance. A wave of relief washed over me. I chalked each hand thoroughly and continued up on steel-solid locks. On top I looked out over the valley toward town. My heart thumped audibly and a tumultuous shudder ran the length of my body. Internal dialogue returned with two thoughts: "God, I love this place" and "I'm retired."

I met Jimmy Surette in North Conway the next day. Jim is a talented 17-year-old climber with a bright future. He glowed in delight when I told him about *Supercrack.*

"Wow, awesome!" he said. "I'm really glad you did that."

We went to the *Airation Buttress* on Cathedral Ledge for the day's climbing. Jimmy silently put his shoes on. Next thing I knew he was soloing *Airation,* a 40-foot 5.11 finger crack. I watched in concern, but he had it in control. A few words of encouragement were all I gave.

Even as I worried, the competitive streak in me said, "Go for it." I squelched it. I realized my following would only spur him on. We had a talk when he came back down.

"Good job, man."

"Thanks."

"Listen, I don't want to sound like your old man, but it concerns me you did that right after I told you about *Supercrack*.

I told him that soloing was great, but asked him to keep it in perspective.

"Don't do it to impress anyone but yourself, it's not a shortcut to grandeur. It's a shortcut to nowhere." Jimmy listened, then assured me it was no problem. He'd been wanting to do *Airation* for a while. I felt responsible, but could hardly say much more, being the pot calling the kettle black. I remembered "Noddy," a British climber, a Moffatt groupie, who decided that soloing was the hot ticket to fame. It wasn't. John Kirk wrote in Noddy's obit: "He will never be famous. He was the guy who held Jerry Moffatt's ropes. . . . Another life finished before it had really begun."

As people started hearing about *Supercrack*, the compliments and congratulations flowed thick and fast. It bothered me a little then and still does. What I did was not glorious, was no amazing feat of derring-do. I had the thing wired into submission. It was simply the proper state of mind.

About a month later, I was at *Supercrack*. Todd Skinner had just led it and offered a toprope. I thought about what it would be like to fall off it. Last time I was here, falling had never entered my head. I tied in and started up. The butterfly jam popped out; I was off, and everybody screamed.

I'm definitely retired.

I think.

KISS OR KILL

OCTOBER 1986, NO. 98

BY MARC TWIGHT

*Angst-ridden, unfiltered tales from the alpine backed with lyrics by the electro-indus-
trial group Skinny Puppy and the goth band Joy Division—that's Marc "Dr. Doom"
Twight's modus operandi. "I'm a self-centered asshole, but being possessed is something not easily shared, nor is it often appreciated," he writes. First in* Climbing *magazine and later republished in his book by the same name,* Kiss or Kill: Confessions of
a Serial Climber, *Twight accepts an invitation from the legendary climber Jeff Lowe
to visit the Himalaya and climb Kangtega and Nuptse. The trip doesn't go as planned.*

I've always dreamed that I would die being eaten by rats. Perhaps I've read George
Orwell's *1984* once too often. Indeed, 1984 was the beginning of my descent into
the black depths of extreme alpinism. This obsession has destroyed my relationships, driven me into depression, and changed me from a happy, future-hopeful
young man into an embittered cynic.

In 1984 I went to the Eiger because it was the most radical, dangerous climb I
could imagine myself doing. To prepare, I backed away from everything except the
mountain and my ambition; they were all that mattered. Relationships that were
incomplete or inconsequential were cut away. I consolidated my power by not
sharing it. Sure, I'm a self-centered asshole, but being possessed is something not
easily shared, nor is it often appreciated.

I suppose it came from the music to start with. Joy Division taught me that
cynicism is OK. Ian Curtis, the band's vocalist, was so consumed by it that he hung

himself as a solution. Johnny Rotten stated that the future is a "pointed stick," so why bother? The young punks and the music generated in me such vehement intolerance of stupidity and mediocrity that extremism became *my* solution.

Kiss or Kill.

The Eiger wasn't enough. Alaska was not enough. The wild soloing didn't do it either. No matter what I did, the suffering I experienced did not satisfy me. I had to have more . . .

Then I met Jeff Lowe.

Jeff is ten years my senior, he's not into my scene. In fact, he used to be a hippie; being so young, I don't know exactly what that means, but I suspect that hippies were basically punks that weren't angry. Mind you, Jeff is intense, although not with my kind of dark intensity. He wouldn't have a birthday party where all the guests wear black.

Jeff invited me to Kangtega and Nuptse: "New routes, Marc, hard, high, unknown ground. . . ." I'd met Jeff once before, I knew he was good, I accepted. With only ten days' notice, I cut off everything that might hold me back. I am very good with the knife now.

Twelve days after Jeff's call I was in Kathmandu, which is a third-world cesspool no matter what the travel books allege. I hated it and couldn't wait to get out. But I had to wait, because there are no schedules, there are no exceptions made for climbers, and the bureaucrats do not understand ambition which one does not profit from, which they do not profit from.

I hated Kathmandu, but I understood it; the crying souls, the poverty, the futurelessness. This condition disgusts some, enlightens all, and inspires others to join the Peace Corps to "help." As I trudged through the filth, I understood it.

Entire chapters of expedition tomes have been devoted to the approach toward the Khumbu; that horse is well flogged. But it's no longer necessary, because the approach has been modernized. Now, we fly to Lukla, above the leeches, above the wasted landscapes, above the porter hassles.

Both Jeff and I came down with amoebic dysentery in Lukla and spent three days weakly laughing at each other as we alternately vomited and shat without control. Feverish, shivering, always hoping it would end. Two macho, high-altitude athletes driven to their knees by something microscopic—too poetic. Now that was suffering.

"Basecamp was languorously pitched at 14,000 feet among blossoms and boulders, with waterfalls that lulled us to sleep at night and birds to wake us at dawn." Waxing eloquent? Lying. Basecamp was at 14,000 feet, but we'd come too high too fast and headaches shrieked like jackhammers, our stomachs hadn't adjusted to the food, and the only birds to be seen were crows the size of baseball mitts. We gave them anything they wanted.

We wasted no time at Kangtega basecamp, but immediately moved up to Lobuche village, beneath the mighty Lobuche Peak. We intended to acclimate. "Skoage village," as Nancy christened it, awakened new states of disgust in me. A trekking group had pitched their toilet tent over the water supply, raw sewage polka-dotted the few campsites, and Western garbage, American garbage, was piled high everywhere. Yeah, I felt like a gringo. Yeah, I felt sick.

After climbing the peak I left the others behind and ran away. I ran 10 miles back to Kangtega basecamp. I couldn't embrace what our presence had done to that awesome place. I had to escape. I had to forget. So I drank. I drank all that I could. I crawled semiconscious from my tent on hands and knees, and I vomited long and hard. Morning found me half-in and half-out of my sleeping bag; I was hung over, but I felt cleansed. The same morning we started up Kangtega, an epic that lasted through ten long and hungry nights. I knew I'd get up the mountain, but a voice inside sadly assured me that it would not be enough.

I returned to basecamp lean and wasted; the warm-up climb had worn me out. I needed rest but never got it; on May 7 we began trekking toward the apocalypse.

At anxious last I saw it: The southeast spur of Nuptse was terrifyingly beautiful. It has the elegance of a Halston dress and the abruptness of a metal-studded dog collar. There was a hollow feeling in my stomach; it became an ache, the ache became a stabbing pain. I fell to the rocks clutching my frightened head in my hands . . . I wanted like I had never wanted before.

Oh precious ambition that feeds me, I worship your power with emotional violence. I am struck down by watching angels and paralyzed by haunting fear in the final hour. I must go to the wall, driven by anger, by anguish, by anxiety. Oh precious ambition, I just want to die with a smile on my face.

I tried to use music—Joy Division, Skinny Puppy—to prepare myself for the suffering ahead, but all I found in it was my own insignificance.

"You never run out of batteries for that thing, do you?" Jeff pointed to my Walkman. It'd be poor style to run out of batteries; besides it's my survival mechanism. When the going gets tough, the tough turn up the volume.

The avalanches have a tremorous effect on my bowels. The sustained primal groan excites my fight-or-flee reaction even when nothing could be achieved by either. We are quite sate out on the spur. We continue upward day after day. It is enjoyable. It is horrifying. Always, it is painful. I am a drowning man and I climb desperately; pushing, demanding, trying to lose my mind within my body. I may be possessed, I may be obsessed, but I can feel, I can love just like the rest of you. I don't have a Walkman with me, so I sing, and I suffer when Jeff does.

The storm hissed like a serpent, we were burned. It couldn't kill us, but it was fierce enough to stop us. We'd climbed 4,000 feet toward clear skies until the seventh day, when it began to snow. I pushed one more pitch into the spindrift and wind on the morning of the eighth day. At the top, I set up the anchor to rappel from and dropped back to the cave for a decision. At 1 p.m. we began descending. Six p.m. the next day found us walking into basecamp with no hardware left, no food or fuel, no bivouac gear and nothing material to show for our desperate act of volatile ambition. All we had was a resolve to return in November.

There is a damp smell in my tent. I stare at the waxy yellow ceiling and turn myself inward, introspection that eventually ends in pain.

Back in the city the darkness stalks me with cold skill. I dash down bombed-out streets through a hard and dirty rain. Pavement scatters as my feet pound beneath cliffs of buildings that soar up into the filthy mist. I see faces that carry the marks of strain, faces that wear weariness like lumps of clay; tired, danceless faces. I see people who are stained and damp, with ashtray breath like the smell of decay. Everywhere I look I see hope that's been smothered by deadly routine. And I see the rats hunting.

I remember the mountain from a distance and I try to convince myself that the rats will not catch up to me. At long horrible last, I am truly suffering.

And long hearses without drums or music drag in slow file through my soul; hope vanquished weeps, and atrocious, despotic anguish plants on my bowed head her black flag.

WOLFGANG GÜLLICH

JUNE 1987, NO. 102

INTERVIEW BY BETH WALD

One of the finest rock climbers of all time, the German Wolfgang Güllich (1960–1992) developed cutting-edge training regimens that today have become commonplace, including campus boarding, which he invented in 1988. As a testament to his incredible strength and forward thinking, in 1991 he fired the first ascent of the world's hardest sport route, Action Directe, *a wicked-steep sixteen-move line in Germany's Frankenjura rated 5.14d. To put that grade in perspective, it took ten years for climbers to realize the next rung on the ladder, with Chris Sharma's first ascent of* Realization/Biographie *(5.15a) in Céüse, France, in 2001.*

The name and frame of Wolfgang Güllich was made known to American climbers in 1982 with his first visit to the States. The coveted second ascent of *Grand Illusion* (5.13c) is certainly the most famous result of that masterful tour, which also included ascents of *Equinox* (5.12d) in Joshua Tree, *Cosmic Debris* (5.13a) in Yosemite, and the bold *Bachar-Yerian* (5.11 R/X) in Tuolumne.

In 1984, Wolfgang visited the Shawangunks, which seemed to be created especially for his powerful style of climbing and impressive endurance. His quick ascents of such testpieces as *Intruders* (5.12+) and *Project X* (5.12+) were a prelude to a virtuoso performance on another continent.

In 1985, Australia's Arapiles offered the endlessly overhanging raw material for his new route *Punks in the Gym*, which rated a 32 on the existing Aussie scale of 1 to 30. With his subsequent ascent of *Wisdom of Body* (30/31), Wolfgang had established the first and second hardest routes in Australia.

A climber is more than a list of routes, however, or a few shots of flexed muscles cranking through roofs. Little news seems to have filtered into the American magazines about German climbing, its traditions and ethics, or about Güllich's progress and accomplishments on home turf. From Teutonic rock warriors campaigning in the Valley, Joshua Tree, and the Shawangunks, I first began hearing of the vast limestone gardens of Germany's main area, the Frankenjura. Their list of extreme German routes was usually dominated by Wolfy's creations.

Inspired by these lists and armed with addresses, I made a long detour to Nurnberg while on my way to the 1986 Speed Climbing Championships in the U.S.S.R. I arrived at the twin doorsteps of a pair of houses by the core of the Frankenjura climbing scene: Kurt Albert, Norbert Batz, Norbert Sanders, and Wolfgang Güllich.

Wolfgang has lived in the Frankenjura since 1981 when he moved from the sandstone area of the Sud Pfalz, where he started climbing in 1977. Standards in the vast limestone area of the Frankenjura started to rise in about 1982, due in large part to Wolfgang, but also Kurt Albert, Norbert Batz, and the peerless boulderer Flipper Fitz. In 1983, Güllich did the first IX- (5.13a) *Mister Magnesia*, in South Frankenjura, just edging Jerry Moffatt, who added *Eckel* (IX+) a few weeks later in the North Frankenjura.

Standards have continued to jump. The latest leap was Wolfgang's 1986 ascent of *Ghetto Blaster*, the first X+ (5.14a) and a wordless testimony to years of motivation and hard work. During my visit, Wolfgang also managed to establish a new X- (5.13b/c), just one month after grounding off of *Master's Edge* in England, followed by two weeks of inactivity.

Not content to just physically push the outside of the envelope, Wolfgang has embraced the sport intellectually, developing advanced and radical climbing techniques. Many of these are discussed in *Sportklettern heute (Sport Climbing Today)*, a 1986 book coauthored with Andreas Kubin, but unfortunately with no English translation. When not traveling, he studies sport science at the University of Erlangen.

His intellectual journeys have led to globetrotting in search of diverse experiences, climbing in exotic areas such as Egypt's Sinai Peninsula, competing in the U.S.S.R. Speed Climbing Championships in the Crimea, and most recently exploring the climbing potential of China. This fall he visited Yosemite and Australia with a film crew. For the benefit of German television audiences, Wolfgang climbed such classic routes as *The Rostrum Roof, Alien*, and the *Phoenix*; desperate boulder problems such as *Midnight Lightning* and *Thriller*; and a spectacular solo of *Separate Reality*.

Wolfgang remains somewhat of an enigma to both the American and European scenes. After two years of continuously brilliant performances on three continents, he disappeared to spend the winter in Oberschollenbach, rebuilding motivation and muscles, then burst back on the scene in the spring of 1986.

After experiencing the hype and pressure of one organized competition, he shuns the glitter and financial lure of the French competition circuit. Ironically his early repeats of French testpieces helped inspire the French climbing scene to become world class, which has since led to climbing competitions as intense as any big money sport. He is a private climber, who will express dismay at the crowds descending on his favorite bouldering area, while his photogenic image is plastered all over the world, promoting Fires and Edelweiss.

His hardest routes are done in the classic European "rap and drill" bolting style, but he also revels in repeating the hard, scary routes in East Germany's Saxony, or creating his own routes protected by marginal nests of RPs. He is one of the most powerful climbers of the modern scene but has spent almost as many hours studying the sport as he has in the gym.

This interview developed during two rather disorganized evenings in Wolfgang's kitchen, over a table cluttered with numerous coffee cups and kuchen crumbs. Our conversation, which was often interrupted by visiting climbers and frequent trips to the gym for demonstrations, revolved around training and techniques. We discussed the development and future of climbing in Germany and Europe, and Wolfgang's unique approach to the sport, with only brief ethical asides. The ethics issue, so hotly debated in the United States, only smolders in Germany, with occasional flare-ups over chipped holds.

Wolfgang's mastery of the sport was evident on the rock, and I watched him do repeat laps of a IX+ (5.13a) for the pump, and later read the frequent signature of "Güllich" on climbs listed in the Frankenjura route book, carefully sequestered in a cafe. My most vivid impressions, however, were of his focused enthusiasm as he paced the kitchen, talking of the direction of extreme free climbing, or the obvious excitement of discovery as he demonstrated new theories of movement in a chalk-dusted gym.

Ten years ago you started climbing in a sandstone area, the Sud Pfalz. Why did you relocate to the limestone of the Frankenjura?
The Pfalz is too loose for an extreme area and there aren't as many types of routes as there are in the Frankenjura. Most hard routes in the Pfalz are shorter—boulder problems between ledges, with no endurance routes.

Rock in the Frankenjura is very solid and there are so many cliffs and so many sustained routes. Limestone has a wider variety of climbing than any other type of rock—finger cracks, roofs, face climbs through bulges and steep slabs, et cetera.

Limestone also has the most technical climbing, because of the wide variety of moves. What interests me most about climbing on limestone is the "coordination system," in which one must analyze a section of rock, come up with a solution, and put it into practice very quickly. This process is very difficult with pocketed limestone and it becomes more of a challenge because a pocket can be used in many ways. You can pull down, to either side, or up—the solution to the problem is more complex and more interesting.

Several years ago, the Americans and Brits came to the Frankenjura and supposedly impressed the locals with their ability. But now, you and other Europeans have left quite an impression on the United States. How much did the Americans influence the development of extreme free climbing in Germany?
At first, there were harder routes in the United States. *Grand Illusion* at IX+ was done in 1979. The first IX+ in Germany was done in 1983, soon followed by an X-. The most important point, however, is that free climbing started in West Germany in 1975 in the Sud Pfalz, and was influenced by East German climbing and not by American or British.

Free climbing at high standards has been practiced in Saxony (East Germany) since 1910, most recently by Bernd Arnold. Many of the best German climbers visited this area a lot. I have gone (to Saxony) almost three times a year since 1977. The rules there are different and there are no 5.13s, but there are very difficult boulder problems between bolts.

You have said it is important to travel. Why?
It is important to go to different areas to get a treasury of movements. If you don't ever travel, it is possible to become a "stupid" climber. A person who climbs only in his own area is very limited and often climbs like a computer.

With your ascent of Grand Illusion, *there is no doubt you have mastered crack climbing. What kind of face routes have drawn you?*
Arnold's routes in East Germany, of course, and since 1980, I've gone to France every year, always repeating their hardest routes.

Back then I was always happy to repeat the testpieces—I was totally satisfied. You can always be busy doing second ascents, especially in France, where they claim they have established the hardest route in the world every other week. But then I changed my mind, and began to think that creativity is what makes climbing special. I thought I should expend energy on my own projects.

In 1985, I decided to go to Australia, instead of spending the winter in France. After I did the existing testpieces at Arapiles, I went looking for something harder, and eventually did *Punks in the Gym* and *Wisdom of Body*. I was so much happier with the result.

I think it is important to repeat other people's routes to have a comparison, but only the creative potential makes a climber unique, not the record of repeated routes. "New" is the byword for the creative challenge, although always in the context of the rules of free climbing: new, harder routes at a higher grade, new, better style to repeat-flash, solo, et cetera; to explore a new area, and maybe a whole new country.

Was this the idea behind your trip to China?
Certainly everything we did in China was new. Free climbing is completely unknown there. We climbed in Southwest China, near the Great Wall, Near Gui-lin, and on a tropical island in the South China Sea, and never saw or heard anything about (Chinese) free-climbing activities. We got our information about rock formations from travel guides or landscape books.

Since we knew nothing about the area, it was always exciting to explore. We could pick all the best lines at a high standard. In China we had all the aspects of pioneering, not just doing a new line on a cliff you have seen a thousand times before. If you are trying to climb with very little knowledge like we did in China, everything is exciting. It's the same emotional situation as when you were learning to climb.

From your travels, would you say the United States is behind in extreme free climbing?
To say "behind" is perhaps deceiving. What is important is the route. A route, even a very hard one, only counts in comparison with other routes at the time it was done. That point in time will inspire the climbers to excel, and in this way climbing builds on itself. Behind is not so important.

Your new route Ghetto Blaster *(X+) would certainly be 5.14 in the United States. Do you think rating systems can be compared?*
At the higher ratings, yes, because each grade is such a clear step. The difference between IX+ and X- is that you can train on a IX+, but a X- or harder requires so much motivation that I never do them again. For example, there are ten Xs in the Frankenjura, and all have very hard coordination moves, combined with highly powerful moves. To do them, you must be totally fit, concentrated, and motivated.

In contrast, when you were in the Gunks, you did Intruders (5.12+) with just one fall. Your famous quote describing that route was, "It would be hard if there were any hard moves." Intruders was only a fitness problem. On *Punks in the Gym*, even after 65 feet of strenuous climbing, you still must have the exact crux moves and muscle coordination ready in your brain. On an extreme route, you must have an incredible amount of information organized in your mind before you start. It is a big mental problem as well as a fitness and motivation problem. To flash a difficult route, you need to get the information, analyze it, and execute the moves while you are climbing.

This is not possible on extreme routes. All Xs have B2 sections. Say on a very hard route, above X-, you try it in the autumn and find one specific crux move, which you simply cannot do without training all winter for it in the gym. Even when you are incredibly fit, you are not able to execute the move without specific training. But, of course, as climbing progresses, there will come a time when climbers will have more complete strength, and, quicker ascents, perhaps flashes, of these routes will be possible.

What is most important in your training?
Bouldering is a very important training device, especially since the hardest routes are extended boulder problems. I also concentrate on repeating routes from IX- to IX+. I train my coordination and timing by studying and practicing moves in the gym and on the rock using the "deadpoint."

The deadpoint is the point on an arc of movement or a jump in the air before the body starts to fall and is weightless and motionless for a split second. Free, precise movement is possible at this point. We studied the deadpoint and its potentials at the University of Erlangen with basketball players who are specialists in the deadpoint, making most of their throws from that point. Applied to climbing, one can use the deadpoint to increase efficiency.

Wolfgang hangs from a small edge, and pulls up on it in one quick, controlled motion. At the precise moment his body stops moving, his left hand shoots out for the next higher edge, easily grabbing it and sticking. A simple exercise with profound applications.
It is much easier to grab a small hold at the deadpoint and more efficiently move off it. In the future, with total training of your coordination and timing, it may be possible to grab and move off a one-finger pocket that you couldn't even hang on statically.

I've written a book about climbing and training methods, which explores these techniques. It is very popular, but I would like to write one on training exclusively, because there is so much to learn.

Techniques such as the deadpoint have obviously allowed you to stay at the forefront of German climbing for years, especially in the Frankenjura. There are an incredible number of very hard gymnastic routes there.
But I think that there are too many bolts in the Frankenjura. I also enjoy doing hard routes where the protection is difficult to place, because it is another technique to master and involves the head. I am doing more of these routes in the Frankenjura. For example, I think the climbing in the Gunks, with their no-bolt ethic, is good.

Don't you think that kind of climbing is much more restrictive?
It is more of a challenge; if there were a bolt, it wouldn't be so interesting. It is good to master different styles of ascent.

But for the most extreme routes, which seem to be limited to limestone, don't you rap to place bolts?
Yes, because in general, limestone doesn't take protection well.

The French seem to accept "improving" holds as well as placing bolts on rappel.
I don't believe this is a good practice, but it is a tactic sometimes used in Germany on routes I won't name.

So what is the acceptable style of first ascent in Germany?
A route is considered established when a climber leads the route from top to bottom without falls, either placing all gear (redpoint), or with the rope through a high piece (yoyo). I think a yo-yo ascent is fine, because a redpoint only means you have practiced the route more. Anyone who yo-yos a route could eventually redpoint it.

Is climbing a mainstream sport in Germany?
It is starting to become very popular—over the last couple years, TV, film, and newspapers have become interested. In the German Alpine Club, mountaineering is considered an almost cultural thing rather than a sport, and they have always held free climbing very low. Before, free climbers didn't fit into the brains of the Alpine Club; they were considered freaks that didn't want to be organized.

The youth organization in the Alpine Club was even more against free climbing as a sport. Germans tend to be conservative and think free climbing has a bad influence, especially on young people; they think rock climbers don't work.

But now the club is discovering how popular free climbing is becoming and that it can be considered a mainstream sport. They see that if climbing is a true, popular sport, the club, which represents this sport, is entitled to a lot of money from the government—for development of the sport. Plus, they would get a lot of new members. So suddenly, they are very interested in free climbing and eager to help. They supported our rock climbing expedition to China.

Do you think that climbing competitions may help promote climbing?
I don't think they are good for the sport; the intention of climbing is something different. A climber can go in two different directions. One is to go out and earn money, which is possible in competitions. But I go out to do a route, not to burn off a competitor. When you go out to do a route, you only have eyes and mind for the route, but at a competition, you are looking at everyone, seeing how they perform, and hoping they aren't as strong as you.

At competitions, it is nonsense if someone says to you, "Go, go!" People at competitions change so much. People you have known for a long time only want to know what shape you are in, and when you will start. I want to climb when I feel for climbing, not when they call my name.

At a climbing area, there is competition, but it is indirect. For me, climbing is creative. I want to do new routes or a route with a name and an identity—you hear of a route and have a dream to do it. At a competition, you have nothing in mind, only a chipped track on a piece of rock in front of you. If you go, you go only for the money.

Do you think competitions can distinguish the "best" climbers?
There can be no such thing as a "best" climber. You can say someone is a successful climber, but not the best. A "successful" climber would be someone who has done many hard routes in many areas, not a local specialist. There are many disciplines in free climbing and a successful climber should be able to do all: be able to flash hard routes, do some solos, do routes with difficult protection, do extreme routes, and do new routes, be creative.

Competitions are good for earning money. I see it as nothing more.

Why have you chosen to be successful at climbing, rather than at another sport?
If you see sport as a combination of body and psyche, climbing allows you to choose which to concentrate on. For example, on total-limit routes the body dominates, versus scary routes or solos where the mind dominates. Climbing also gives me a goal for travel. I see discovering exotic areas, such as the Sinai in Egypt, or our expedition to rock climb in China as another discipline in free climbing.

You can also use the mind to study the scientific aspects of climbing, like movement, training, or the dynamic aspects we talked about. In other athletics, you start from the beginning; you learn the game or the specific motion, and then you perform. But in climbing, you are always faced with new problems in which you must perform using intuitive movements, and then later analyze them to figure out why they work, and learn from them.

In the study of free climbing there is so much new to discover. I can't see this in other sports. Everything you discover about training, about techniques, about movement, is new.

After you have climbed for a long time, you get to the point where you want your ideas on the sport to materialize by establishing new routes, new areas—even in another part of the world. To do a new hard route is such a challenge, because you have to do everything on your own; learn the mental and physical coordination and come up with the motivation to continue a project, which may be impossible.

When you just repeat a route, that burden is much less, because someone has climbed it before, and you know there is a way to solve the problem. But on your own route, you might not see the way for a long time, and quit because no one could help you to realize the possibility. And it's only natural that the more effort you put into something, the more you are satisfied when you succeed. Your creation—made up of the line, the difficulty, the protection, and even the name, expressing all the emotions about the route—has a special, unique character. If climbing is an art, then creativity is its main component.

SALATHÉ WALL: 1988

OCTOBER 1988, NO. 110

BY PAUL PIANA

Accomplishing a "first" in climbing doesn't come easy—the unknowns are often the biggest hurdles: "Can it be done? If so, how long will it take? Will we die trying?" Take the first ascent of Everest, on May 29, 1953, by Tenzing Norgay and Sir Edmund Hillary, a climb requiring legendary courage and perseverance. In many ways, the first free ascent of the Salathé Wall by Todd Skinner and Paul Piana is no different—it took a futuristic vision, total confidence in that vision, and total commitment to realize. And just like the saying "When you reach the summit of Everest, you are only halfway there," the same rang true for Skinner and Piana. As they crested the top of the 3,000-foot wall for the Salathé's first free ascent, tragedy struck and the two barely made it out alive.

After more than thirty days and nights on the *Salathé Wall*, we were able to read the shadows and tell the hour of the day to the minute. It was 8:45 p.m. and across the valley the Cathedral group had lost its cap of alpenglow. Only an ambient glimmer lit our little world on the wall.

To the casual observer, we might have been the average team aiding toward the security of a bivy on Long Ledge. But as Todd neared the belay his movements became less fluid, his confident swimming motions from jam to jam turning stiff and choppy. In the growing darkness, I thought I could see his forearms glowing. Arms pumped to the point of fusion provided enough light to see, but Todd couldn't crank the last few moves, or even swear during the inevitable

30-foot plummet. Dejected, he slumped at the end of the rope, then swung back in to the rock.

We hung on the belay anchors, sapped. The ground was some 3,000 feet of giddy drop away, and here we were, perched in the middle of an overhanging sweep of granite. We pulled the rope and slid down into darkness as black as our fatigue and as deep as the herculean task we had begun. Our portaledge camp under the Great Roof was a secure hang, but tonight it was not a home. The *Salathé*'s Headwall remained, taunting and smug in its glorious position.

People had been climbing big walls in Yosemite for several years, but the first ascent of the *Salathé Wall* in 1961 was a real breakthrough. The year before, Joe Fitschen, Tom Frost, Chuck Pratt, and Royal Robbins had made the second ascent of the *Nose* in six days without the use of fixed ropes; it was the first time a major El Capitan route had been done in a single, continuous push, but this adventurous climb was just a precursor of what was to come. Frost, Pratt, and Robbins had an even more ambitious plan: their proposed *Salathé Wall* would link a series of cracks with far fewer bolts than the 125 that the *Nose* had required. After fixing the first third of the route, the trio dropped their ropes and pushed on to the upper 2,000 feet of vertical to overhanging wall. At the end of the sixth day, they topped out, having used just thirteen bolts for the entire route.

At that time, the *Salathé Wall* was the state of the art in technical difficulty. This supremely talented and bold team created pitches, both free and aid, that were as difficult as anything that had been done previously. If they blew it, they would have had to rely on themselves alone for a rescue. And in 1961, being 2,000 feet up on a Yosemite wall was a lot farther off the deck than it is today!

In many ways it is logical to use aid on a big wall. The prospects of falls, or of trying to keep it together on a very thin crux way off the ground, seem too frightening to consider. But for Todd Skinner and me, free climbing high up on a big wall was the stuff dreams are made of.

For us, this dream was brought to life by an article in *Mountain 79*. In "Long, Hard, and Free," Mark Hudon and Max Jones described their free-climbing efforts on the big walls of Yosemite. We marveled at their audacity and boldness, and began to think that it was possible for us to climb long, hard, and free as well. Soon, the *Salathé Wall*, the "greatest rock climb in the world," was lodged in our minds.

Todd spent spring 1985 in Yosemite, and this was the practical beginning of our quest. While Todd was working on free climbing *The Stigma*, John Sherman mentioned that if that would go, then maybe the *Salathé* would go as well. After completing *The Stigma* Todd phoned, but I was unconvinced and remained in Laramie. Not yet dismayed, he packed five days' food, gathered a team, and assumed the *Salathé* was his.

According to Todd, they were lucky to aid the route, much less free climb it, but what he saw inspired another look. A year later his second attempt encountered a similar fate, and was stopped again by the pendulum to Hollow Flake. They didn't take the time to search for an alternative, but free climbed the pitches that went easily and quickly, aiding those that would be cruxes.

Curiously enough, on both attempts, the teams were so inexperienced at aid climbing and so terribly slow that they often encountered the pitches they most wanted to case well after dark! So, after a total of about ten days on the route, Todd was only a little more convinced of the feasibility of freeing the *Salathé*. Even though there were sections of the climb that he hadn't looked at with an eye toward free climbing, the vibes felt right. Todd was confident that a free line could be found somewhere on the face.

Within a few days of this last reconnaissance, Todd and I were scheming in Boulder, frantically drawing topos, examining photos of the wall, and looking for free-climbing options on adjacent routes. Fearful of rival teams, we allowed no one to sit in on these planning sessions—even girlfriends. The knowledge was committed to memory and the topos we drew were shredded and burned. The ashes were mailed to parts of the world where English isn't spoken. To the outside world, we hoped it would appear that the *Salathé* was not free climbable.

Since neither of us owned watches, we synchronized our calendars. A pact was made: We would be in the Valley May 1st, and we would gamble our health, our esteem in the eyes of our families, and what little wealth we could command to arrive on time at the gate of dreams.

The ensuing months were spent in the gym, utilizing a secret training system devised from all we could learn from the French and Soviet climbers. Endless mornings on the boulders fed our desires. As our strength increased, so did our phone bills. But the long-distance psyche sessions from Hueco to Boulder made possible many more lat pulls and forced one more lap on the bouldering circuit. "The Winter is long—yet the robin has a song to sing," says the proverb. While we weren't too concerned about singing on key, we wanted to be able to sing loud.

We learned from the grapevine that Stefan Glowacz had joined a little-known fraternity of Europeans including Heinz Mariacher and Manolo, who had tried to free the *Salathé*. After ten days of effort, he had come away with the prediction that it would not go. Several pitches could not be bypassed and according to Stefan, the pitch above the Great Roof, if it could be done at all, would resist attempts for at least ten years!

While at the competitions in Europe in 1987, Todd tried to get as much beta out of Stefan as possible without giving away our plans. What we learned was disheartening, and we suspected that he too was "playing the game." But we were happy to discover that he had found a way to bypass the pendulum to Hollow Flake, via a 5.12b traverse 60 feet lower.

Our arrival in Yosemite was almost not to be. Racing north from Hueco Tanks, Todd blew an engine in Raton, New Mexico. He broke the news to me in a midnight call. We were hosed—my bus hadn't run in five months. With help from his brother Orion, Todd arrived in Boulder. Miraculously, my bus started and we traded a dead horse for a dying one and rode north into Wyoming.

The spring blizzards waited until our ailing bus tottered across the howling, windswept eternity of I-80. The geriatric VW could manage 40mph downhill and got 8 miles to the gallon. At every gas stop, and there were many, the starter refused to work, so I was underneath with a screwdriver to short the connection. As if deep slush, mud, and cold weren't enough, ten minutes were spent at each stop chipping away the massive accumulations of ice in order to reach the starter.

We arrived in Pinedale, Todd's hometown, at 3 a.m. in a second-gear headwind and slept furtively, dreaming that the bus would never start again. In the morning, after a quick overhaul, we had a vehicle that raced along at 50mph and got a stunning 12 miles to the gallon. On the road again.

We knew that we wouldn't be able to just walk up and climb the route free. It would involve an unheard-of amount of continuously difficult climbing, and from Todd's recon efforts and those of others it was obvious that the *Salathé* couldn't be touched without a lot of preparation.

We decided that a series of "camping trips" would allow us to gain the necessary knowledge and to become accustomed to life far off the ground. Our strategy was to spend six or seven days at a time working on different sections of the wall. These trips were also used to cache water and the occasional can of beans at critical sites. During this stage we often camped in the Alcove, the large and comfortable ledge at the base of El Cap Spire. We preferred its sheltered nature to the more famous and aesthetic bivouac on El Cap Spire. This also allowed other parties the unique experience of sleeping on top of the spire.

After our work low on the route—that is, up to pitch 24—it became difficult to haul enough water and food to points higher on the wall. Our tactics changed and we drove toward Tamarack Flat Campground. The entrance was locked at the highway, so we began our hike to the top of El Capitan from there, enduring huge loads of food, ropes, and gear over almost 12 miles of very hilly trail.

Near the summit, we located a nice spot for our recon camp and began the outrageous rappels off the rim. I couldn't help but laugh at the ridiculous nature of rappelling down El Capitan. What had seemed like hideous exposure on pitch 24 suddenly seemed no worse than the void experienced on short free climbs. We went as far as Sous le Toit ledge, leaving fixed ropes that were ultimately anchored to a big block just over the rim. We then climbed back out to a stance just at the lip of the Great Roof and began work on the crack in the Headwall.

Several days were spent on these Headwall pitches as we toproped or led them, or sussed out the protection, and just got used to being in such an exposed place. We were continually impressed by the boldness of Frost, Pratt, and Robbins, who had dared to risk it all and were there first in 1961.

We also marveled that at each impasse there was a sequence that worked, even if just barely. But we were appalled by the inhuman amount of difficult climbing that faced us. We were haunted by the specter of injury. Damage to a critical joint or tendon would finish our bid. A turn in the weather could be equally demoralizing. Occasionally the mental strain of so many difficult sequences and unrelenting crux pitches became a burden that threatened to crush our dream.

Every working day on the Headwall ended in a multipitch jug to the rim and a joyous campfire at our summit camp. One of the most enjoyable nights was spent with a group of Kiwis who had topped out late in the day and had brought along a celebratory bag of marshmallows! Toasting marshmallows on the summit of El Capitan with good friends is a night I'll long remember.

We were chased off the summit twice—once by snow and once when we ran out of food. The latter posed a serious problem, as we were also out of money. I had survived the past two weeks on forty-seven cents and Todd was the rich man of the team with twelve bucks still in his pocket.

We really needed to perfect the pitch that exits the Headwall onto Long Ledge. During our recons, this area had been a bottleneck as we sat on Long Ledge waiting for parties to aid past. We desperately needed another camping trip to figure out this pitch, but hadn't the greenbacks to spend even another day on the wall. However, we knew we would stay no matter how hungry we became, and often commented on how trusting the deer were in Yosemite.

To fund our *Salathé* quest we had a yard sale in the Camp IV parking lot. We auctioned everything we thought we could live without: a brand-new pair of rock shoes, slippers, Friends, a Metolius Simulator, virtually everything except our souls. Each sale saw our feedbag swelling not just with beans and tortillas, but with treats that would keep our morale high. Pop-Tarts were morning essentials, and Snickers and raisins were great for lunch. Eventually we had enough cash to fund either another recon or a final push, but not both. We chose the latter, as there was little else we could sell. We knew we had a good chance of pulling it off if we could stay together physically and if the weather stayed cool and dry.

We bought four extra cans of tuna in case we had to spend four extra days on the wall. Photographer Bill Hatcher and our "Wall Master" Scotsman John Christie would climb just ahead of us. The plan was for John to lead, allowing Bill to lower back down to take photos of Todd and me. From the Block, John and Bill would punch it to the top. Then Bill would fix ropes back down for photos, while John would go down the East Ledges, thus sparing precious rations.

The route had been steadily whittling away at our fingers, so we agreed that we wouldn't follow the crux pitches free and would jug them instead. We knew this might make the difference between success and failure. We also felt that we'd need a rest day up high, but were concerned that the weather might not allow one. We were very fortunate to find that "Mad Dog" Bob Boehringer, a veteran of Todd's 1985 recon, was in the valley. We recruited Bob, this time as Radio Free *Salathé*, and every evening at 9:30 we would receive a current weather report.

Armed with a month of recons, food and water, radio support, and a super photo team, our final push was ready to get off the ground and onto the Big Stone. We had done our homework, but the magnitude of the final fight was still a heavy burden. Yet without the burden there would be no appeal. We looked upward and vowed to take no prisoners!

The *Salathé* begins with ten pitches known as the Free Blast. The first three are wonderful, but the fourth and fifth are so trashed out that we were ashamed they were in America. The wall is pasted with huge, useless, saucer-size blobs of aluminum that have been beaten into old bolt holes. Faded and tattered runners hang from everything, and the belays are of the same poor quality. The Free Blast could be repaired and become the quality climb it once was, but until that happens it remains an embarrassment to the hypocritical ethic that we care about preserving the rock, the experience, and our image.

After the Free Blast and a 5.10a downclimb to Heart Ledge, we were happy to climb Stefan's traverse to Hollow Flake. After this desperate pitch the infamous Hollow Flake must be dealt with, and I was horrified to learn that a 50-meter rope isn't long enough to enable the leader to reach the top of the flake. Todd struggled higher and higher on this completely unprotected pitch as I quickly untied the belay and simulclimbed with him. I figured that only one of us needed to be freaked out, so I neglected to mention this to Todd until I had reached the top of the flake.

Our original plan called for avoiding the aid pitch above The Ear by climbing an offwidth just to the left. Steve Schneider had run these 5.10d pitches out during the first ascent of Bermuda Dunes, but we both doubted our offwidth skills and wanted nothing to do with such a loathsome technique. Since we were aesthetically repulsed by this vile crevice, we decided we would have our way with the original aid pitch or else abandon the climb.

This 5.13b pitch turned out to be a beauty. Were it on the ground, this tight dihedral would be a much-tried classic, but the 1,700-foot approach will deter many. This was the first crux, and it required a wide variety of crack techniques. We found power flares, 5.12+ dynos from them into pin scars and back out again, and thuggish laybacking—and then we found the crux. Searing, fingertip pin scars, laser-precise edging, and postdoctoral skills in body English were the ingredients of the last 20 feet of this pitch.

Two rope lengths above El Cap Spire we reached an impasse at an A1 pitch. Several days had been spent here on our recons trying to find something that worked. While the first half went relatively easily at 5.12a, the second half resisted everything we threw at it.

We had spent days trying to toprope three possible variations to the right. Faces that looked as though we would have them at a glance slapped us around like dumb blondes. We would try one and get slapped. We would try another and get slapped. We were tired of being slapped.

We left the pretty faces for a glassy open book to the left. It looked impossibly smooth so we put the moves on the arête in between. Todd soon found it was smoother than our moves. I lowered down and tried all my best lines. The smoothest refusal we had ever received met me in that corner, and I was overjoyed that on the final push, Todd won the 5.12d pitch with powerful stemming, several more-than-playful slaps, and no falls.

And then it was on to the Block, a perfectly situated but hideously sloping balcony from which we could lounge in relative comfort and gaze at the sweeping perfection of the Headwall. The rope length below the Block was the bad neighborhood of the Salathé, a slummy pitch hung with moss tendrils and streaming with water. It is as ugly as the Headwall is beautiful— as if someone had diverted a sewer through the Louvre. Climbing it was not a pretty sight and invective flowed as freely as the mud in the jams.

Once on the Block things got better. The rock above was dry and clean. The bivy on this sloped perch was the last grand floor to walk around upon; we could drop gear and get it back. Here we spread out the picnic and glopped stolen Degnan's condiments on bean-smeared "Manna from Hell," the petrified, jerky-like tortillas that Todd learned to make from an ancient Mexican woman. We ate until we were full, or until our jaws cramped from chewing. We paced in little circles. We dropped things just to see them stop falling. We slept.

The morning saw us moving toward the Great Roof. The pitches were increasingly difficult—a portent of rope lengths to come. The pitch below the Great Roof was especially memorable. Powerful, openhanded laybacking and technically desperate stemming was protected by horribly frayed bashies and an unwillingness to fall. Our aching backs called this flaring dihedral 5.12b.

The pitch ended at a dangling stance below the amazing Great Roof. This bold feature stair-steps over and out for 20 feet, and with the walls of the corner below, cocooned us from the wind. We hauled our bags and set up our portaledge camp.

The first night of several was spent here, lives and gear tangled across the hanging corner like some giant cobweb. Our little world was quite secure, but we could never truly relax. The position was too spectacular. Dropped gear fell a long, long way before we lost sight of it.

We had to be careful to keep everything tied in and only failed this test once. Todd and I had taken as many Louis L'Amour novels as we could scrounge. We had finished the batch and had poured through Edgar Rice Burroughs's *Martian Stories* as well. Todd was well into *Thuvia, Maid of Mars*, but I was left with a romance novel that Bill Hatcher had fought through, complaining with every page. It accidentally slipped from my ledge and became the fastest read of the climb. I started rereading *Hondo*.

The next morning I awakened slowly—I must have been dreaming of Mars. As the sky brightened, I thought I heard the faintest clash of sword on sword. I peeked cautiously over the edge of the suspended cot and glimpsed Todd, still asleep, scything and parrying with some dream-induced, green-skinned Martian warrior. On his face was a confident fighting smile.

The next pitch was a stiff cup of coffee. From the top floor of our camp, the route moved out right with lots of cool morning beneath our heels, an easy but spectacular traverse leading to an attention-getting series of deadpoint surges to sloping buckets. From here it is possible to brachiate wildly to the right, feet swinging, and then to throw your leg up over a huge horizontal spike in the same way a L'Amour hero would mount a galloping horse.

What a place! Halfway out a huge roof a hundred miles off the deck is this amazing saddle-like peninsula so flat and comfortable that we could have served coffee on it—not that it was still required.

From the saddle, it's all rounded buckets to the lip and a terrifying heel-toe above the head and crank to a shoulder scum, but if I fall I'm going to scream. All the while my heart was slugging away, doing Mike Tyson imitations while I made the tenuous step up onto a hands-down rest. We decided to throw in a belay here since we had the stance.

Stefan Glowacz had told Todd that he didn't think the pitch above the Great Roof would ever go, but fortunately, years of climbing Vedauwoo's flares served us well. From the belay it looked pretty grim. Scarred by pitons and scabbed over with useless lumps of ruined bashies and one sad fixed piton, this short pitch was one to be feared.

The first 5.12+ flare moves were harder than any I had ever experienced and were unprotected as well. How the jams felt meant nothing—they were so bad that Todd had to visually monitor his hand throughout each move. With his Megas 15 unprotected feet above the belay he had to pull up slack to clip a tied-off peg. So flaring were the jams that it was impossible to downclimb, and the slightest error, even a change in the blood pressure in his hand, would see the *Salathé* flick him off and send him screaming far below the roof, until the force of the fall crashed onto my belay anchors with Todd wild-eyed and spinning thousands of feet off the ground.

We were both glad that he didn't fall. The flares ended with a thankfully short but tremendously difficult face sequence. Power, grace, tremendous skill, and the essence of boldness were some of the practices Todd pulled from our cheat's repertoire. Even a bitter has-been would have cheered the brilliance of Todd's lead. We were ecstatic that the second 5.13 pitch was done, but sobered because two more were just above.

The Headwall must be the grandest climb in the universe, a beautiful and inspiring crack system splitting the 100-degree sweep of the golden wall at the top of El Capitan. The essence of the *Salathé* is distilled in this one incredible fissure. To be here, whether free climbing or aiding, is one of the most overwhelmingly good experiences a rock climber can have.

It is indeed a beauty, one that cannot be wooed with mere technique, but a prize to be fought for. Todd and I feared the unrelenting pump of this pitch. The Headwall Crack became the object of Todd's desire. He wanted to free "the most beautiful crack I've ever seen" in the most impressive position either of us could imagine.

This day it was not to be. Todd gave it his best, failing twice just a move away from the anchor. In the last of the day's light, I thought he had it when his left foot rocketed off the wall as a little flake snapped. He fell 30 feet, too flamed to even curse. He hung a few moments, toes brushing the wall, then I belayed him to his highest piece so that he could unclip and down jump far enough to be lowered to the belay.

Against all hope, Todd went up again, but even 10 feet off the belay, it was obvious that he was too tired to succeed. Still he gave more than his best. Violent karate chop jamming, frantic foot changes, and missed clips, then at 90 feet out, a dejected murmur in the gloom—I was yanked upward and into the wall as Todd hit the end of the rope.

Rappelling over the roof in the darkness was scary. We would get to the bottom of the fixed loop and yard ourselves into the hanging camp. The valley was dark, the highway a thin stream of yellow light as cars flowed into Yosemite. Dinner was a quiet affair. At that moment we felt like we were too far off the ground, the gloom altogether too black. The night was long.

The half-light of dawn was the same monochrome gray as the ceiling above and I might have been staring at it for hours when Todd's voice announced that he was still really beat and needed a rest day.

By this time, we both could have used a rest week. Neither of us could close our hands and our critical forefingers had been brutally bludgeoned by the many cruel pin scars. Our knuckles were swollen to a shocking size. We were concerned that we would tear ourselves apart before we could finish, but that wasn't the game we could afford to play.

By this time, Bill and John had topped out, and Bill had fixed lines back down to take photos. Rather than waste a day resting, we decided that we would jumar their ropes to the pitch that exited onto Long Ledge. I had been having better success on it than Todd, so we figured that I should work it some more and then Todd could still have the Headwall Crack.

We spent a frustrating day on this exit crack. I could almost do it, but would fail a few feet short every time. I must have fallen a nautical mile that day, but we gained valuable knowledge about subtle foot placements, and Todd did get a little rest. Even so, I was afraid I wouldn't be able to do it at all. After hours of failure, my severely gobied fingers would ooze quickly through super glue and tape, so we retreated to our hanging camp and worked at repairing my fingers.

It was my night to be depressed. I tried to relax and sleep but couldn't. I climbed that pitch a thousand times in my mind. Todd slept deeply, dreaming once more of defending the honor of the most beautiful Martian woman, swords glinting in the sun.

Morning brought apprehension and a slow, stalling breakfast. Having put it off long enough, we started up the fixed lines to do battle with the Headwall. Todd clipped his ascenders onto the thin, red arc that swooped out and disappeared over the lip.

From his spectacular dangle he looked back just as I was "buried at sea." This was the term we used to describe the frightening and amusing fall one took when unbalancing a portaledge. I had weighted the ledge a little too close to one end and dramatically slid off and fell to the end of my tether. Todd's laughter faded over the lip and after calming down I joined him at the start of his pitch.

Todd felt a bit hesitant so early in the morning and needed to clear his head. He climbed 15 and then 20 feet above the piece he hung from and dramatically hurled himself into the void. He repeated this six or seven times, until it became fun and the reluctance to go for it was completely gone.

Back at the belay we looked down at the still-dark valley floor. The sun hadn't hit the face and the winds of the Headwall were still. Todd flowed through the stillness and all the difficulties, slowing at the last few moves, taking care to make no mistakes. And then all the fears we had for this pitch were laughter as he clipped the belay and I started up to join him.

I was happy that the beauty had been won but afraid of what was just above. Todd and I spent at least an hour cleaning my hands with alcohol, super gluing the rents in my fingers, and then carefully applying a wrap of tape over the glue. Before starting, I torqued my fingers in the crack to numb the pain.

The morning's lethargy became adrenalin as the thin jams were suddenly below and I found myself wedged into a podlike slot. Exiting the slot seemed particularly rude to my tattered hands, its flared jams as painful as backhanding a wire brush. After clipping the highest piece, I lost my nerve and decided to downclimb into the pod to rest. I was afraid to fall again.

This wasn't the usual fear of falling—the gear was good and we had lived so long up here that the drop was not the rope-clenching horror it had been more than thirty days before. My phobia was failure. I couldn't bear the agony of another day without succeeding on this pitch. I fell while downclimbing.

The next try was as solid as could be. The pitch seemed to flow together until I found myself staring at the dyno target. Todd was screaming, "Hit it! Hit it! Hit it!" Long seconds passed while I pondered failure, either from missing the dyno or from a lack of trying. A deliberate lunge and I pinched the knob so hard that Arnold Schwarzenegger would have been proud. I cranked to the belay, laughing and waving my arms like a lunatic. We had it in the bag now.

We spent the rest of the day rapping back down to the camp under the Great Roof and packing our gear. We slowly hauled it up to Long Ledge and enjoyed walking back and forth. It was late, but we yearned for the prize, so leaving the haulbags, we climbed for the top.

The next pitch is one of the gems of the climb. From the extreme left end of Long Ledge an overhanging, knobby wall rolls and bulges upward. Todd reveled in the delicate foot changes, long reaches between knobs, and deadpoints to crisp side pulls. After he had danced up this 5.12a Hueco-esque wonder, I enjoyed a superb 5.10 thin hand crack, which put us only one pitch from the top. Todd made light work of the last bit of 5.11 and the *Free Salathé* was done.

Our long, hard work had nearly ended and we were indescribably happy as we raced the sunset back down to Long Ledge to radio John Christie and our other friends in the meadow that the *Salathé* was ours! We spent the most satisfying bivy of our lives eating extra Pop-Tarts, drinking lots of water, singing funny songs about John Long, and discussing the finer quotes from Louis L'Amour. Tomorrow would be a grand celebration!

The next morning was perfect. We breakfasted and started hauling freight to the rim. We joked about being extra careful, as most fatal auto accidents occur within 2 miles of home. I was first over the rim and selected the best anchor I could find. We had already used this huge block, as had years of *Salathé* climbers.

Off to one side there were a couple of fixed pins that I anchored Todd's line to. I plugged in a number 1 Friend to make sure. While Todd jugged the pitch I used the block as a hauling anchor and as my tie-in as well. When the bags reached the lip, I was unable to pull them over myself and waited for Todd to arrive.

While waiting, I decided that I might as well be embarrassingly paranoid and clip the fixed pins as well. Todd reached the rim and I made him pose for pictures like Layton Kor at the top of the *Salathé*. Since he was on top and pulling up an extra rope, I began taking out the anchor. I removed the Friend, then turned and started lifting the haulbags. We heard a horrible grating noise and, turning back, were horrified to see that somehow the block had come loose!

I'm not clear about exactly what happened next. Todd remembers me putting my hands out at the block and yelling, "No!" I do remember the two of us being battered together, and the horror of seeing my best friend knocked wildly off the edge, and then a tremendous weight on my left leg as I was squeegeed off the rim. I recall a loud crack like a rifle shot, and then more pummeling, and suddenly everything stopped spinning and I could just peek back up over the edge.

Everything was in tatters, ropes pinched off and fused—it appeared that they had all been cut. I was afraid to touch anything, and sick with the knowledge that Todd had probably just hit the talus. Suddenly, a startling bass squeak sounded below me, followed by a desperate "Grab the rope!"

I hauled myself over the top and soon a bloody hand on a crushed ascender slid over the rim. I helped Todd up and we lay there for a long time. We were terrified because Todd was having trouble breathing and his pelvic area hurt very badly.

My leg was in a really weird position and reaching a crescendo of pain.

I don't know how long we were there, afraid to move for fear of fainting and unraveling the braid of cut ropes that held us. When we did get up we discovered that Todd's line appeared to be OK. He had been held by one of his CMI ascenders.

Apparently, the rock had scraped over the ascender and miraculously that small, gouged, and bent piece of metal had kept Todd's rope from being cut. I had been held by the loop I'd clipped to the fixed pin. The 11mm rope I had tied into the block with had been cut as easily as a cotton shoelace. Two other 9mm ropes were in eight or nine pieces and the haulbags were talus food.

We coiled the remaining rope and slowly started down the East Ledges. A descent that usually took us just under two hours required almost seven, and we arrived at the base of Manure Pile Buttress looking much worse than the average wall climber who staggers down that trail.

We had dreamed, we had trained, and we had struggled. Even though the climb ended with a bit of a nightmare, we had triumphed. I'm sure that the ecstasy we feel now will live inside us forever.

Sometimes at night, as I'm drifting off to sleep, I suddenly hear that big block move and I see Todd tumble off the rim. I think about how difficult it would have been for our families if we had been killed. I shudder at the remembrance of being dragged off the summit of El Capitan and knowing that we really were going to die. For me, the definition of "horror" is now an emotion.

Now that several months have passed, and Todd and I have almost healed, I'm even more pleased with our climb. We worked harder than anyone else was willing to work, harder than we thought we could. We were willing to risk seeing our most shining goal become a tormenting failure. Yet we were prepared to fail and fail and fail until we finally could succeed.

Todd and I are still awed at the difficulty of the *Free Salathé*. The climbing is unrelenting in its severity and the logistics are staggering. We are confident that unless a team is willing to put in a comparable amount of work, the *Salathé* will not be climbed again as a free route. In fact, we suspect that the *Free Salathé* will not be repeated for many years. We are very happy, very proud, and when we're no longer sore, you will see us back on the crags. But I keep wondering, what is *The Shield* like?

UP AGAINST IT

APRIL 1989, NO. 113

BY ED WEBSTER

"Four against the Kangshung? You're mad!" a friend told Robert Anderson, Ed Webster, Paul Teare, and Stephen Venables before they attempted Mount Everest's 11,000-foot Kangshung Face. The men chose to climb without support, meaning no radios, Sherpas, or bottled oxygen. Though Venables reached the summit, the author, Webster, collapsed before reaching the top. There he visualized "colorful fabric . . . in the wind [and] several Buddhist monks." Additionally, he sustained frostbite to his toes and fingers, leading him to wonder if he would be able to sign his name again, much less climb.

The sun's first rays bathed Everest's East Face in a bright white light. We heard the serac explode a mile above us. "Here comes the big one, down the Lhotse wall!" screamed Robert. Our hands tore madly at tent doors as we watched the wave of snow and ice roar down the vertical precipice and explode across the amphitheater.

"Good, it didn't clobber our route," said Stephen as he prepared to depart for the climb.

What a way to begin the first day on the hill, I thought. April 3, 1988 began like every other morning for the next six weeks—with another symphony of destruction pouring off the surrounding mountain walls, avalanche after avalanche thundering to its final crescendo onto the Kangshung Glacier.

Americans Robert Anderson (30) and I (32), Canadian Paul Teare (28), and Englishman Stephen Venables (34) intended to climb a new route on the most dangerous side of Everest, the Kangshung Face. We would climb without Sherpas, radios, or bottled oxygen.

Mimi Zieman, MD, and Joe Blackburn, our photographer, were both Americans and provided invaluable support at our advanced basecamp. Tenzing Norgay's eldest son, Norbu Tenzing, organized our logistics; Kasang Tsering came as a cookboy; and Pasang Norbu was our sirdar, cook, and Tibetan interpreter. Lord Hunt, who led the first successful British Everest expedition in 1953, was our Honorary Leader (consulting us from England). In keeping with our thirty-fifth anniversary climb, Hunt had wisely recommended Stephen as a member.

While approaching basecamp, three weeks of winter storms had frustrated us to the breaking point. In the mountains, you know to expect bad weather. But in Chinese-occupied Tibet, people delays are equally certain due to their slow cultural clocks. When the weather finally cleared on March 24, we cajoled 130 ill-clad villagers over the snow-bound Langma-La; the 12,000-foot East Face was a dozen miles away.

In 1921 George Leigh Mallory and G. H. Bullock searched for a viable approach to the North Col and became the first Westerners to trek to Everest's East Face. Of our route, Mallory wrote, "Other men, less wise, might attempt this way if they would, but, emphatically, it was not for us."

"Four against the Kangshung? You're mad!" said Charles Houston, whom we met in Bombay. Houston later added that there was some small chance we might succeed. We agreed that Everest was the only mountain for which we would work so hard, and suffer so much, to climb.

Our route had probable wind slab snow below the South Col and avalanches from the huge hanging glaciers threatened our proposed line. However, the route seemed perfect for a small team. The logic behind our route selection was that all the technical climbing was at a relatively low altitude, then easier snow slopes led to the col—where oxygenless climbs to the summit had already been completed.

Our advanced basecamp was 2 miles north of the immense Lhotse headwall and a mile from the base of our buttress. We had found a route separating our buttress from the Lowe Buttress (climbed in 1983). We hoped to circle left around the bottom icefall, diagonal right across two lower snowfields, cruise a short rock headwall, then jog up the narrow rock-walled Scottish Gully into Big Al, the huge avalanche funnel separating the two buttresses. Escaping from Big Al onto the crest of the buttress looked quite doubtful; escaping an avalanche coming down Big Al, or collapsing seracs off the Cauliflower Ridge above, would depend entirely on luck and karma. Pasang promised to burn sacred juniper and pray for us. We would need it.

On the first day, Robert and Stephen made rapid progress fixing ropes. Paul and I played packhorse and hauled additional ropes. Stephen led the 300-foot headwall and found fun 5.8 face climbing on sharp edges; he apologized because he knew I had wanted the lead. The beauty of four climbers, however, was that we would each eventually do plenty of leading.

Robert led the Scottish Gully the next day, then Paul embarked across the traverse into no-man's-land, crossing the left side of Big Al. While overhanging rock in the Scottish Gully gave a vague security, there was constant avalanche danger on the traverse above. I likened this section to climbing up a nuclear accelerator tube; the idea was to avoid becoming the smashed atom.

Stephen and I handled some steep mixed climbing to the Terrace, a narrow platform beneath overhangs. The next day we watched Robert and Paul through a 600mm lens as they climbed steep ice at 21,000 feet. Paul had recently soloed the difficult Silver Strand in Yosemite, but he called his 300-foot, 75-degree effort on Everest the hardest ice pitch of his life—it overhung for the last 15 feet. Nonetheless, he was upset at having to rest on an ice screw! This escape from Big Al onto the crest of the Cauliflower Ridge was one of the climb's cruxes.

At 2 a.m. Stephen rose to light the stove and make tea and instant oatmeal. I had never met a climber with such unbridled zeal for alpine starts. His life had already encompassed a dozen Himalayan expeditions. Stephen's quest for perpetual movement occasionally ran against the grain of "the Yanks'" habit of dozing an extra hour or two. Whether it was an alpine start, setting a new speed record up the ropes to Camp I, or rushing back across the glacier for a cup of tea, Stephen relished his role of rousing the troops to action.

On the other hand, Paul's spontaneous humor was a perfect complement to Stephen's steamy intensity. Paul was our relaxed Californian, always quick with an absurdly funny joke, or odd but true observation. He loved David Lee Roth and the Rolling Stones at full blast, and he was exceptionally altruistic and emotionally sincere—altogether an essential team player.

I knew Robert better than anyone on the team. We had taken a trip to Everest in 1985, had suffered together during a winter ascent of the Notch Couloir on Long's Peak, and had later climbed a new route on the Diamond. We possessed that combination of easy communication and unspoken trust in the other's capabilities that is so vital for Himalayan success. Robert's good-natured attitude, his stubborn vigilance over the Chinese bureaucracy, and his personal drive to climb Everest helped turn all our aspirations into a reality. He was also strong as a bull and an expert at high-altitude snow wallowing.

Robert and I had met Mimi, our doctor, in Nepal in 1985. She added warmth and a civilizing influence to an otherwise cold and bleak existence. Her bright smile cheered any day, she could dance in tap shoes or double boots, and after six weeks of wondering what she was doing on our expedition, she treated our subsequent injuries round-the-clock, like a concerned angel. Being the only woman among seven generally unwashed men was not an easy job.

Joe had been the official Yosemite Park photographer and a personal student of Ansel Adams. Joe was hardworking and a diligent photographer, and he had the distinction of being the slowest member of the expedition—even behind me! He took pride in wearing both his Rolex watches (one on each wrist), yearned to follow us up the climb, and made mouthwatering instant cheesecake. He and Mimi also welcomed us back to camp on all-too-numerous occasions with hot meals and tea.

Pasang was a widely traveled Sherpa and became our combination sirdar/chief cook/Tibetan mediator. I had met him when I accompanied Roger Marshall on his first Everest solo attempt in 1986, where Pasang proved that he was the only cook on Earth who could prepare perfect al dente spaghetti at 17,000 feet in a pressure cooker. He imparted a tremendous energy and sense of duty to his various jobs, and without his linguistic and diplomatic skills with the Tibetan porters, we wouldn't have reached basecamp.

We had met Kasang in Kharta while looking for a cook tent to replace the large, luxurious Coleman tent that had vanished en route to China (it later reappeared, fortunately). Kasang volunteered not only the tent—but himself, all for two dollars a day. His first words of English were "Goo' Morning." It might be 5 p.m., but if you heard those memorable words, you knew it was time for dinner. By the expedition's end, Kasang was utterly corrupted by Western ways and fluent in Californian slang.

Back on the mountain, after jumaring a dozen 100-meter ropes below Camp I, I shuddered. It was my lead. The two worst-looking Cauliflowers, including the notorious "Greyhound Bus" (which I hoped would stay parked), loomed directly overhead. Separating them, luckily, was a col. I frontpointed up near-vertical boiler plate ice, my breathing and heart rate shooting out of sight. I used up my ice screws while pigeonholing across steep sugar snow below the Cauliflower, ran out 80 feet of rope, and collapsed on a terrace on the ridge crest—the site of Camp I.

Above was an 80-foot overhanging serac. Stephen was feeling the altitude, so I continued up perfect hard névé. I free climbed the 95-degree wall, then surmounted the final sugary edge by aiding on snow pickets. Stephen whooped below.

More shouts greeted our return to advanced basecamp. Momentum was building. We had reached 22,000 feet.

The next day Stephen returned with Robert and Paul to do battle with the buttress. Topping out of a runnel, he grabbed the sharp edge of a hidden 50-foot-wide crevasse, which split the width of the upper ridge. Easy snow slopes lay just beyond. A Tyrolean traverse appeared to be our sole option, but none of us had ever rigged one. After resting for four days at basecamp through bad weather, upset stomachs, and lethargy, we returned. We erected two Bibler tents at Camp I. Robert and I moved in for a three-day effort to cross the crevasse. We slept horribly, pounded by headaches.

Two days later, after an initial reconnaissance, Robert and I rappelled back into the gloomy crevasse. "This is the freakiest place I've ever been in," gasped Robert. "We're inside Everest."

The crevasse was sheer-walled and 100 feet deep. Horizontal dust layers striated the eerie blue walls; the base of the secret passageway was smothered in powder snow. After squeezing through a body-wide passage, I entered a new chamber where a 40-foot ice chockstone was wedged between the two crevasse walls 30 feet up. The chockstone looked large enough to be stable. I advocated aid climbing out of the crevasse, but Robert felt we should explore beyond the chockstone first. He put me on belay.

Twenty feet from the chockstone, I stopped to place an ice piton. The ice was rubbery, so I pounded with all my might. Suddenly the chockstone blew up—I thought a bomb had gone off next to my right ear. I ran—at nearly 23,000 feet—back to Robert. Ice crystals blasted us in a continuous wave, shimmering in the sun; the sky was falling on our heads.

The vibrations from hitting the ice piton had caused the chockstone to disintegrate. When at last the air settled, Robert looked at me with a wry grin. "Well, it's safe now." That afternoon I aided up the far wall on ice pitons and snow stakes, then we rigged several ropes for a Tyrolean traverse. The route to the South Col was open.

On May 1 we carried through knee-deep snow for seven hours until we reached Camp II at 24,500 feet beneath a large bergschrund. The snow was perfect for glissading, and we returned to Camp I through a whiteout in one hour. After six weeks of acclimatizing, a dozen trips up and down the buttress, and one trip to Camp II, we were ready for the summit. None of us had been seriously ill for even a day.

Two days later, a snowstorm brought an abrupt halt to our first summit bid. Early monsoon snow hammered the East Face. We retreated from Camp I in deep snow. Early the following morning, a monstrous avalanche swept Big Al clean.

We finally left advanced basecamp on May 8, made a routine ascent to Camp I, and continued to Camp II the next day. The twelve-hour haul through waist-deep snow to 24,500 feet tired us considerably.

Early the next morning, a half-moon hung over the west faces of Chomo Lonzo and Makalu. The day was picture-perfect, a dream. There was even a little névé. We skirted the right end of the dramatically overhanging bergschrund, then happily trod new ground toward the South Col, diagonalling left into the large, upper basin.

The morning ecstasy faded as we waded up deep snow, gaining safer ground beside two rock outcrops. A capricious wind now ripped over the Col, threatening to dislodge us. We quickly donned our expedition suits. Leading the final 100 meters to the South Col was just my luck. The snow steepened to 60 degrees for the final 30 feet. Plunging my ice axe in, I hauled myself over the edge.

The scene was the most desolate imaginable: a subzero wasteland of snow, ice, rock, and terrific wind. Plumes of snow streamed from the summits of Everest and Lhotse. One hundred mile-per-hour gusts tore at our clothing and faces until we set up two small tents and crawled inside. In case the winds increased, we stacked rocks inside each corner and anchored the tents to boulders with rope.

At 8,000 meters, we gasped for precious breath, struggling against the debilitating effects of altitude. We prayed the flapping tents wouldn't rip. We forced down some soup and tea, but sleep was nigh impossible.

Early the following morning, Robert announced that Paul had thrown up. He might have cerebral edema, and needed to descend immediately. I thought I should go with him, but Stephen and I were both healthy and relatively strong. Descending would mean that one of us wouldn't have a chance at reaching the summit. Stephen was silent.

Before we could decide, Paul crouched at our tent door. "I don't want either of you to come down with me. We've all worked hard for this climb," he said. Then his voice cracked with emotion.

"I can get down on my own," Paul said. "Just make me proud, OK? Get to the top." He started down the 8,000-foot face to advanced basecamp where Joe and Mimi were waiting.

Luckily the wind diminished that afternoon, and at 11 p.m. on May 11, Robert, Stephen, and I started for the summit. To save weight we climbed unroped and without packs. Two hours later we veered slightly off-route and found ourselves too far left, climbing broken slabs near the edge of the Southwest Face. One slip would have meant falling thousands of feet into the Western Cwm. Fortunately we navigated this unnerving section and by sunrise had reached 27,500 feet.

At 5 a.m., finding a Japanese tent left by the expedition a week earlier, I stopped for a rest. I turned around; the rising sun had turned Lhotse's upper wall into a sea of pinkish-orange alpenglow. It was like watching the sunrise in heaven. As long as I lived, I thought, I would never see a scene like this again. Here in the shade the temperature was 30 or 40 degrees below zero. Dulled from the lack of oxygen, I tried to think: Could I get frostbite? The colors on Lhotse were fading.

I yielded to impulse and removed my bulky down mittens to pull out my camera—the metal felt like dry ice and burned my fingertips through the liner gloves. Grimacing, I cradled the camera and took several pictures in less than two minutes. I hoped no permanent damage had been done.

My fingertips were numb. There was no pain, just a cold dull ache. I saw no reason to descend, for I was convinced that we would summit.

We climbed on automatic pilot, without talking. Two hundred feet below the lower South Summit (28,750 feet) the last shreds of reality slipped through my fingers. Snow swirled off the ridge, creeping around me. I glanced up. Colorful fabric fluttered in the wind and I noticed several Buddhist monks. The rock outcrops along the ridge were carved and brightly painted like a Mani wall. Prayer flags hung between the crags, and the chanting purple-robed monks paced back and forth.

Nothing seemed particularly unusual or out of place. Stephen sat resting in the snow to the right of the monks. He looked at me, but didn't speak.

Suddenly a wave of sleep and exhaustion washed over me and I could not stay awake a second longer. My head slumped forward and my mind went blank. Time passed. I awoke with a start to find the monks gone. "I'm on Everest," I thought. "I've got to get in control!"

"Will you help me break trail?" Stephen yelled. He was frustrated at having to do all the work himself. I didn't blame him, but I couldn't catch up. "I keep on falling asleep!" I shouted. With that, Stephen stomped his way to the South Summit directly above. A second later, he disappeared toward the real summit, still an hour away.

I still thought I could reach Everest's summit, but 30 feet higher the angle steepened to 60 degrees. I began to feel very vulnerable without the rope's security. What if I passed out again, and slipped? The 12,000-foot fall would be decidedly fatal.

It was 3:30 p.m. If I continued up at my present rate, I was risking an open bivouac with no tent, sleeping bag, or oxygen. I could still grasp the deadly outcome of that plan. If I descended immediately, I might reach the South Col before dark.

I thought of Mick Burke, who disappeared on Everest's summit ridge in 1975. To continue would have been to court death, and I had other equally important goals in life besides climbing Everest. I was happy to have reached 28,730 feet, a point higher than the summit of any other mountain on Earth, by "fair means," without oxygen or Sherpa support. I turned around with only a trace of regret.

I met Robert 200 feet lower. He wanted to continue. I said I'd wait for him above the Japanese tent. More than an hour later, he finally stumbled out of the clouds. He too had reached the South Summit, nearly lost his way descending, but managed to follow our footprints. He had not seen any sign of Stephen.

We reached the abandoned bivouac tent at dusk. With no sleeping bags, we huddled together at 27,500 feet and worried about Stephen all night.

As we crawled from the tent at 5 a.m., a figure staggered toward us, his face covered with ice. It was Stephen. His voice was very, very weak. "I made it," he said. "I got to the top." Stephen had become the first British climber to reach Everest's summit without oxygen.

We were thrilled, but utterly exhausted. We descended to the South Col and slept. It had been our third full day above 8,000 meters without oxygen. We were as alone as three human beings could be.

The next morning, May 14, we could barely move. We had no food and were clearly weakening. My fingertips were wooden; my left hand appeared the worst. Descending to safety would soon become the fight of our lives.

The two tents were too heavy to carry, so we decided to bivouac in our sleeping bags at Camp II, then continue to Camp I, still stocked with tents and food. I glanced at Robert, listless in his tent. Every so often he would sit up, fiddle with his crampons, then collapse. Stephen lay like a corpse on the ground in front of our tent. I pulled out my camera and he waved halfheartedly to prove that he was still alive.

I left for Camp II at 12:30 p.m. Stepping off the east side of the col, I plunged into waist-deep fresh snow. I waded down the slope, stumbling down through the whiteout, my ears straining for the crack of an avalanche.

I could see Robert silhouetted on the rim of the col, 500 feet higher. I shouted to him not to glissade, but seconds later he was standing right across from me, in the center of the huge snowfield. He had fallen and ridden a small avalanche the entire distance. Luckily, he had stopped.

"What are you doing?" I shouted.

"I glissaded. It looked fine," Robert mumbled. "I guess I got going kind of fast. I dropped both of my ice axes, too," he added. "Can I borrow your extra ski pole?" he now asked. I left it for him.

Stephen saw Robert's toboggan track and glissaded, also losing his ice axe. Now to reach the top of our fixed ropes we had to descend 4,000 feet of crevassed terrain with one ice axe between the three of us. Furthermore, our rope had been mistakenly left on the South Col.

Adrenaline carried me down the next 1,000 feet of deep snow. We reached Camp II at dusk, then heated and drank some hot water before passing out. Unfortunately, we had not left any food at Camp II.

The next day we could not move from our sleeping bags for several hours. I was getting increasingly angry, because I thought we might die. The climb had been so enjoyable, so tremendous, and Stephen had summited. To die now just didn't seem fair.

Except for my frostbitten fingers, Stephen and Robert now appeared in worse shape than I. They hardly stirred. "Stephen," I chided, "you're not going to be famous unless we get down alive."

All day long we tried to descend. First we said we would leave by 11 a.m. Then it was noon, 1, 2, or 3 o'clock. After taking two hours to stuff my sleeping bag, I left at 3:45. The others were still working on their crampons. It would be dark in two hours.

The waist-deep snow was enveloping, somehow comforting. To sit down for a long rest would be so easy. The sky was a light-gray curtain blending with the snow. Visibility diminished to 30 feet. Suddenly I tripped on a short, icy step. A second later, I was sliding down the slope headfirst on my back. Instinctively, I jabbed my ice axe into the snow, then kicked my feet in until I stopped. A hundred feet lower, a gaping crevasse leered up at me, a fathomless blue void waiting with open arms. I swallowed hard. The others were descending toward me, but this was insanity—darkness would come in an hour.

When the others reached me, I argued that we should return to Camp II, brew hot water with our remaining fuel cartridges, sleep, then descend early the next morning. We had wasted the entire day.

Climbing up through the smothering snow took a terrible effort, partly because we had not eaten for two days. Darkness fell as we reached the bivouac site. As we shared a few mouthfuls of hot water, I thought I would probably die if I didn't get to advanced basecamp the next day.

The sun rose golden over Tibet. I left at 10 a.m., abandoning my expedition sleeping bag and down jacket. Robert followed, then Stephen. Moments later, more storm clouds blew in. I used every route-finding skill I had learned in twenty years, breaking trail and navigating through the maze of crevasses. Occasionally I found our orange-blazed wands in the cloud.

Stephen caught up with me late that afternoon; Robert lagged behind, but yelled down that he was OK. I shouted that we were going to advanced basecamp no matter what. When Stephen and I reached the top of the fixed ropes, I thought, "Maybe, just maybe, we're going to live."

We excavated the ropes and rappelled with great difficulty, reaching Camp I by 5:30 p.m. When darkness fell, we discovered that neither of our headlamps worked. Then my right crampon came unclipped and I couldn't fix it with my wooden fingers. I continued on one crampon.

Stephen started down, chopping our ropes free from the ice that had frozen over them. I followed. Rappelling down 2,000 feet of fixed ropes in the pitch-dark was an endless nightmare. We often wrist-rappelled because of the iced-up ropes. We reached the glacier and staggered into camp at 4 a.m. Paul ran out to help me and pleaded, "Why didn't you let us know you were alive?" Earlier that night he and Mimi had drugged themselves with sleeping pills because they thought we were dead. After an emotional reunion, they rewarmed and bandaged our injuries. Robert spent another night on the mountain and descended safely the next morning; Joe Blackburn guided him in.

In all my years of climbing, I had never grown to hate a route or a mountain, but I now hated Everest. I couldn't even bring myself to look up at it.

Two days later, Mimi changed our bandages in the cook tent at basecamp, carefully cutting away the layers of cotton gauze. Until then I never imagined I would lose even part of a finger or toe.

I stared blankly at my fingertips. The ends were black and desiccated, hard to the touch. Images of sunny rock climbing in Eldorado Canyon appeared, then faltered, switching back and forth with the grim reality of my ruined fingertips. Tears flowed uncontrollably down my face.

Would I be able to hold a pen or pencil? Write a letter to a friend? Sign my name? These simple skills flashed through my mind in those first few seconds of disbelief. I was convinced my life was destroyed. Mimi tried to comfort me.

I had known two people who died on Everest, Victor Hugo Trujillo and Roger Marshall. Climbing Everest, particularly by a new route and without oxygen, might demand the ultimate sacrifice. As we started the climb, I had imagined that death—if it did come—would be swift from rock or icefall, an avalanche, or a hidden crevasse. Silently, I had accepted the possibility.

But now as I looked at my black fingertips, I felt my life pivot. I stared at the plain truth: I had made a mistake and I tried to accept the awful, slow agony of severe frostbite and a future irrevocably changed. I had always been incredibly careful with my fingers, for my lifeblood as a climber flowed through them.

In twenty-one years of climbing, I had never once been badly injured. Now this. Over the course of the next three weeks, I learned that I would lose all the fingertips on my left hand, three fingertips on my right hand, and parts of three toes on my left foot.

We had survived the climb by a near miracle, by finding the common will to live. Now Paul, Mimi, Joe, Pasang, and Kasang helped us home. Departing basecamp on May 23, Stephen and I were carried on stretchers for four days to Kharta.

Three weeks after the climb ended, after the interminable journey across Tibet and China, I reached a hospital in Boston. Since then I have undergone seven operations in Denver.

Stephen, Robert, and I each lost part of several toes. Because of my photography, I also lost fingertips. After my operations I am slowly recovering and have even done a few 5.8 toprope climbs. Today I know that my life as a climber will continue.

The *Neverest Buttress* was a spectacular, difficult, and dangerous route. Every day I am reminded of the heavy cost of my all-too-human ambition. But our ascent of Everest's Kangshung Face was the greatest possible adventure, the absolute thrill of our lifetimes. "Everyone," Stephen said, "is entitled to do something completely mad once in their lives."

PART THREE:
THE 1990s

THE 1990s:
SPORT CLIMBING COMES
INTO ITS PRIME

BY RANDY LEAVITT

When getting to the chains replaced reaching the summit, you knew you were squarely in the 1990s. Since the mid-1980s, France had been the Holy Grail of sport climbing, and after many years as a California granite climber making fun of the French for not being able to climb American stone (Yosemite), I suddenly wanted to be like them. I began the 1990s with a trip to the famous *Chouca* (5.13c) in Buoux, France, a route requiring futuristic techniques including a figure-four off a two-finger pocket. There I learned French terms like *a vue* (onsight) and moves like "la Rose," and began to wear brightly patterned Lycra like Patrick Edlinger and the Le Menestrel brothers. This whole sport-climbing thing was cool.

But there was a tension between the era I'd learned to climb in and the era we were entering—between climbing as a distillation of adventure (trad and alpine) and climbing as athletic pursuit (sport). In the fifteen years prior, I'd been a trad and big-wall climber, deeming bolts a last resort. But it had all, to me, been training for the mountains where I aspired to be a badass Himalayan mountaineer like Pete Boardman and Joe Tasker. The problem was those guys—and so many of their peers—had died in the Himalayas, and after a successful expedition in 1986 to Gasherbrum IV (Pakistan), I realized that I, too, would likely meet the same end if I kept at it. When I returned from that expedition, during which our team succeeded on GIV but failed on Nameless Tower, I did some soul-searching. On one hand, I could fulfill my dreams of mountaineering until it killed me or I retired, and on the other, I could fulfill my dreams of real-estate entrepreneurship, which would mean weekend cragging. Selecting the second option, I swore to devote time to improving as a free climber, which had always been my weakness.

More than anything, this decade opened my eyes to what was climbable. With bolts instead of cams, we were no longer limited to following natural features for protection. Rock quality became secondary to the movement. Some cliffs, like the cobble-studded conglomerate of Maple Canyon, Utah, had been rejected as ridiculous choss in the 1980s, but are destination crags today. In 1990, I was projecting 5.13+ and potential 5.14 new routes in Joshua Tree. That same year, I traveled to sport climb with one of my long-term climbing partners, Tony Yaniro, in his new home state of Idaho. Tony was developing hard climbs in the City of Rocks. He also took me to Leslie Gulch, in the eastern desert of Oregon. His visionary lines there were "creative" in a way that would make Michelangelo proud.

During one trip to the City with Tony, we watched with puzzlement as friend after friend split down to American Fork Canyon (AF) in Utah to check out this developing limestone area. We wondered, *Could there even be good limestone in America, like in France?* There were no cell phones, so we had no feedback—other than the exodus from the City. When the top climber of the era, Jim Karn, left the City, where he had been on a rampage, Tony and I followed him to AF. The rock there was not nearly as good as in France, but it was limestone and it was in America! This changed everything.

My close climbing partner, the late Rob Slater, certainly didn't embrace my newfound love of clipping bolts. He was an old-school trad, just like I'd been throughout my years of Yosemite big-wall aid climbing, free climbs in the Needles, Eldorado testpieces, Black Canyon horrorshows, and Joshua Tree sketchfests. I tried to impress upon Rob how cool sport climbing was. "Remember those outrageous places we used to aid on El Capitan?" I asked Rob. "Well, sport climbing will take you up walls like that—except now you're free climbing!" Rob, unimpressed, stuck to bagging desert sandstone towers. Not everyone was on board with the "sport revolution": As one infamous bumper sticker proudly proclaimed, "Sport climbing is neither."

My earliest route development in this decade was in Southern California's Joshua Tree, where I ferreted out the steepest walls I could find, no matter how obscure. One find we dubbed the Snakepit was a hidden, east-facing wall forty-five minutes into the Wonderland of Rocks. Here, my friend Rufy Hofmeister and I got to work on a dozen new difficult lines, including what I hoped would be my first 5.14, *Mamba*. During that period, the formula for success was improving your strength-to-weight ratio, and since we hadn't yet learned how to scientifically get stronger (despite immense training), I found myself working on the weight component instead.

Mamba comprised of a series of brutal gaston deadpoints up an overhanging wall, culminating in some seriously thin, powerful redpoint crux moves. In today's jargon, it would probably be described as a 5.12 to a powerful V10, followed by several sections of thin V7/8 with no rests. Watching every calorie of rice cake that went in my mouth, I began to see tangible improvements in my abilities—perfect. The season at Joshua Tree would inevitably spill over into the warmer months, so to cool off we discovered low-calorie frozen yogurt as a treat on our drive home through Yucca Valley. One day, it was 100-plus degrees Fahrenheit by the time we got to the yogurt shop. We were so skinny that each consuming a large bowl of frozen yogurt lowered our body temperature enough to make us turn on the heat inside the car as we drove through the sweltering desert. The stress of juggling my real-estate start-up business during the worst economic downturn I have ever seen in California also helped with weight loss. My favorite quote of the decade was "You will never find enlightenment on a full stomach."

On each trip to *Mamba*, I made progress, even if just measured in inches. I felt it would go soon. Then, on my thirty-third day (!) of effort, I was ready for the redpoint. I hiked in with my longtime friend Doug Englekirk. However, we were too late. The staunch trad climber/free soloist John Bachar had found my climb and pried off a few key holds I'd discretely reinforced with epoxy. Citing ethics, he later exchanged heated words with me. I had a lot of respect for John as a climber, but since I didn't want to be bound by his ethics I began to consider establishing routes elsewhere.

I needed a new project, and fast! I recalled something Boone Speed had told me two years prior at the annual Outdoor Retailer trade show in Salt Lake City, when he, with boundless psyche, described the soaring limestone walls of Arizona's Virgin River Gorge. Bisected by I-15, this overhanging craggy limestone canyon sits in a slice of Arizona between Utah and Nevada known as the Arizona Strip. Boone and other climbers like Jeff Pedersen, Mike Call, Bill Boyle, and Scott Frye were developing the bullet-hard routes at the Blasphemy Wall there. I took Boone's recommendation and drove the 400 miles from my home in San Diego.

The rock was sexy, bulletproof, multicolored, and sparsely pocketed; the Blasphemy Wall was deceivingly steep. I repeated the established classics like *Fall of Man* (5.13b), *Dark Boy* (5.13b), *Dude* (5.13c), and *Don't Call Me Dude* (5.13c). There was an unbolted wall right of the Blasphemy Wall, where I added projects of my own, with the help of my amigo Jorge Visser. The most memorable was *Planet Earth* (5.14a)—named for the estimated total distance I racked up driving each week (sometimes twice a week) to my "local" crag to bag the redpoint.

The discovery of new climbs and areas—trad or sport—has always been what inspires me the most. Clark Mountain, California, was the most special in this regard. The constant commute up I-15 to the Virgin River Gorge allowed me to observe the desert in all kinds of light. Notably, there was Clark Mountain just west of I-15 and south of the California/Nevada border. From a distance, Clark, with its consistent white-tan hue and curving-grotto shadows, looked worth investigating. As it turned out, this wild mountain contains the closest world-class limestone sport climbing to So Cal. I spent a number of years there, just a few friends and me. The most famous route that I bolted and envisioned, but never climbed, is *Jumbo Love* (the world's first 5.15b), which Chris Sharma redpointed in 2008, sixteen years after I installed the hardware.

My view of the 1990s was from my narrow focus of delayed project gratificationism, but I was also uniquely poised to take the larger view as one of the few Americans driving sport development. During that time, I also visited a number of other new sport areas around the country, such as Rifle, Cave Rock, and the Red River Gorge. And there were still other forms of climbing being done on a very high level—like Lynn Hill's (trad) free climb of the *Nose* of El Capitan, and later her one-day free ascent. The world probably didn't revolve around sport climbing, but it sure felt that way to me.

Toward the end of the 1990s, I traded in my Lycra tights and baggy tank tops for wetsuits and board shorts. I got bit by the surfing bug and started to throw myself into big-wave surfing. Now the only things I had to worry about were two-wave hold-downs and Y2K.

TALES FROM THE GRIPPED

OCTOBER-NOVEMBER 1993, NO. 140

BY JOHN SHERMAN

Tucked above UT-128 E 20 miles east of Moab, Utah, rise the great Fisher Towers— and also their lesser known counterparts directly behind, the Mystery Towers. Both areas comprise pillars made of the notorious Cutler sandstone that shoot skyward like mud-covered rockets. Climbing there is a rotten experience, with rock that crumbles to the touch, here-today-gone-tomorrow features, and a maze of complex trails. The Fishers are challenging to even the most seasoned hardperson. The Mysteries are an even greater challenge. John "The Verm" Sherman, author of Stone Crusade: A Historical Guide to Bouldering in America, Better Bouldering, *and* Sherman Exposed: Slightly Censored Climbing Stories, *takes us there.*

"This is not negotiable."

Tom Cosgriff was on the line, feeding me some bull.

"Listen, we had a deal," I said. "Remember? We were going to climb illegal desert spires until we got caught or you had to go back to Norway."

"No. We gotta climb A5 in the Fisher Towers." Cosgriff was adamant.

"Tom, you aren't getting me anywhere near those petrified turds. Besides, they're legal. What fun will that be?"

"This is *not* negotiable. We're going to the Fishers."

Damn him. How could I say no? He never does. Like the first climb we did together, *Gorilla's Delight*, a classic 5.9 in Boulder Canyon—me with a knee that bent only 60 degrees, Cosgriff with a cast on his wrist. No problem. Now the poor bastard spends most of the year stuck behind a desk in Norway, eyeing some plump blond secretary gobbed in makeup. I relented. Nevertheless, deep down I knew this was his way of getting even for that time I visited him in the Yosemite jail, the time I asked if I could borrow his haulbag, since he wouldn't need it for a while.

He did bend an iota, though, and I got my sentence reduced. We'd climb the 350-foot Gothic Nightmare, hidden far behind the Titan in the Mystery Towers group of the Fishers. Endwise, it looks like one of the Coneheads wearing a jester's cap, dangly bells sprouting out of the top. From the side it resembles a sailfish fin. The Gothic was still unrepeated after two decades, a fact that appealed to Cosgriff. It was rated only A3, a fact that appealed to me.

There was one hitch: We needed gear, lots of it. Hence my descent into the abode of the Evil Doctor, Tom's pal, *Climbing* magazine's gear editor, Duane Raleigh.

Had I not been with Tom, Raleigh would surely have never let an arch-traditionalist like me in his house. As it was, Duane was nervously trying to keep an eye on me, his gear, and his wife, all at the same time. In the gear room, my comments on some nonstandard items were not well taken. When we left, Duane pulled Tom aside and whispered the doctor's orders: "Make him suffer."

At first, the suffering was limited to humping gear up the long approach, dumping it at the base, and hiking out. Then it intensified when we went for beer and pizza at Moab's famous Poplar Place. The jalapeno, garlic, and green pepper combo was, said Tom, "the most evil pizza I've ever had." Tougher to swallow was the wimpy 3.2 stout. The waitress assured us, "A lot of people are really happy to find beer like this in Utah." Yeah, that's like the happiness one feels when he's in jail, and only getting "befriended" by the little guy. The next day we both felt like we'd passed a hibachi's worth of glowing briquettes. We tried a new, uglier approach through several inches of snow. Conditions on the Gothic were wretched. All around, the snow was melting, loosening stones, which hit others, until thunderous rockslides would rip down the walls of the Mystery Towers amphitheater.

We had reached the base, and were now committed to bucking out double loads in defeat. We hadn't climbed an inch. There was no sense in lugging out the beer, so we sat in the saddle between the Citadel and the Gothic Nightmare, and swilled. By the time we had split a six of King Cobra tallboys, tons of debris had worked its way down, and our psyche had worked its way up. Tom started leading.

Only the thought that Tom was suffering more than I was made the shady north-face belay stance bearable. He stepped on a drilled pin and blew the hole apart. He nailed Knifeblades into millimeter-thick calcite seams. With enough pounding they'd go to the hilt and hold body weight. This was Tom's idea of a great vacation.

A few hours later he was at the belay, and I was following. I could've cleaned the pitch with a Fisher-Price hammer. Now it was my lead.

"Damnit. This isn't funny." My yelps only made Cosgriff laugh harder. "Shit shit shit shit shit." My voice was getting higher. "Watch me." It was 20 degrees Fahrenheit, I was in tennis shoes and thin wool gloves, and I was free climbing vertical mud. Not out of my own free will. The perfect number 3 Friend placement I had excavated from the mud, jump tested, and moved up on had just exploded, leaving a depression the size and shape of a chili bowl. The only reason I hadn't fallen was that one foot was stemmed onto a knob. Now I was stuck: one foot on the knob and my shoulder pressed against the opposite wall of the dihedral. All the nearby holds were covered in dirt from my attempts to excavate the next placement. The pump flooded in.

Every piece was a time bomb, and if I fell, it would be onto the anchor. The day before, Tom had stopped me climbing so he could tie off the belay line. He hastily put another bolt in the anchor because the old ones were pulling out under his weight.

"If I get down to that last piece, I will lower off, let Tom finish this, and retire from aid climbing forever." Such were my thoughts, and, "What if I don't?"

I reached down below my feet to the last piece, my balance big-rack, clothes-bundled, tilt-out awkward. My hands and feet were slipping on the dirt. I could grab the stem of the Friend, but knew that it would rotate out if I tried to lower onto it. My only hope was to clip on some aiders and step in.

I had 1 lousy inch of nylon to step through, but it was lying flat against the wall like it was glued there. I tried to flick the aider away from the wall and kick my foot through, usually an easy trick, but not with the top step. The curses spilled out of my mouth in angry tones, plaintive tones, and tearful pleas.

One lousy inch of nylon.

The pump clock was ticking down. Then, like in some *MacGyver* script, when he defuses a nuclear device with a pocketknife, as the timer reads one second left, my foot slid through. I eased my way down, clipped into the piece, and rested my helmet against the wall.

The panic vanished, replaced by a nervousness about the piece I was resting on. Then came a bigger fear. Not the threat of imminent injury, but the fear that if I didn't go back up, I would be a chickenshit forever.

I can't remember how long I hung there, regrouping mentally, forcing the decision, willing courage. Finally, I stood up, grabbed my hammer, and started gouging at the crack through the mud, waiting to hear that scraping sound when I reached real rock, my mind focused on one thing: making that next piece stick.

The summit ridge offered sunshine and snow and no evidence of how Bill Forrest and Don Briggs traversed it to its faraway highpoint. All we found was a hawser-laid rap sling encircling a pile of rubble; twenty years ago it was a sturdy pinnacle. We sat on the ridge, with nothing to do but listen to the intermittent rumble of the towers and walls eroding around us. Four trips in and out, a 200-mile beer run to Grand Junction, and two short, frigid pitches on the north face were all for naught—we bailed.

What possessed me to go back? Or should I say, Who? Not Cosgriff. He was pecking his keyboard, sneaking peeks at chunky hips and painted lips, and suffering through economically induced sobriety (seven bucks a beer in Norway). No, only one other person could drag me back to the fudge-brownie and stale-bread summits of the Mystery Towers.

My partner of countless Eldo epics; the man who sent me on my first heading and hooking lead on El Cap, without telling me that the first ascensionist had decked on the same pitch; the Provider who lent me his portaledge, which ripped, sending me for a headfirst, 4 a.m. wakeup call; Mr. Confidence, Mr. Cockiness, and lover of all that is ovine—Robbie Slater. The Team was back together.

This time it was June. The beauty of the maroon-walled, Roadrunner/Coyote approach canyon was lost in the heat, loose sand, and shoe-sucking quicksand. Our objective was all three Mystery Towers: the Doric Column, the Citadel, and the Gothic Nightmare.

First was the Doric. Say it fast and it sounds like Dork, which is just what it looks like.

Kor was first to try it, but backed off when he saw how much drilling would be required. Forrest and George Hurley then bagged the first ascent in 1969, sneaking onto the summit while their British partner, Rod Chuck, tired of being bombarded at the belays, rested on the ground. The Yanks pulled their ropes on the way down. Chuck was not amused.

Twenty-three years later, in 1992, a fellow Brit, Steve "Crusher" Bartlett, revenged the injustice, making the second with George "Chip" Wilson.

The first pitch was mostly free climbing. A 5.7 dirt mantel gave me brief pause, half an hour or so, for reflection. It wouldn't have taken so long if I didn't keep glancing down to see our half-naked companion sunbathing at the base. Knowing Rob's penchant for flat-chested blonds, I had no worries about him being distracted from his belay duties.

Soon, the anchor was cause for thought. Crusher's bolts, now two months old, were already coming loose in the soft rock. I drilled another, feeling the vibrations through my feet. Later, I could feel Rob clean pins 40 feet below.

The next three pitches climbed a mud-encrusted chimney/groove that resembled the inside of a giant gutted fish. Here, the second-ascent crew had freshly riveted Forrest's bolt and bat hook ladder for us, so progress was quick and easy for the leader. For the belayer, it could never be quick enough.

Mud clods bombarded the belayer's helmet every few minutes, and goggles, bandannas, and long-sleeved shirts couldn't keep the dirt from grinding against the teeth, plugging the ears, and invading every pore. Days after the ascent my nose continued to produce twin strands of red-brown mucus.

On top we basked in the late-afternoon sun, strolling about the spacious summit, clambering up the boulder marking the high point. Forrest and Hurley, not having known they'd bag it the day they did, had not left a register. Crusher had, however, with a note that said, "The Citadel is next."

The Citadel and the Gothic—both unrepeated, both prizes, both tottering piles of choss you could piss a bolt hole into. Crusher might come back any day, so the Citadel was next.

The Citadel looks like an Olympic medal's stand viewed in a funhouse mirror, the kind that stretches you out so you look like Manute Bol. The first pitch appeared to be a casual dirt scramble, so I volunteered for the lead.

Off-route from the start, I had soon paddled across a dirt slab I dared not reverse. I had no gear in, and below was a series of 35-degree dirt shelves with 6-foot drops between them. It would be an ugly fall, like rolling a 165-pound baseball down ten flights of stairs.

As the dirt under my feet continuously gave way, I slowly walked in place. I desperately needed pro, but the only weakness in the rock slab at my chest was a seam thinner than a pencil line. I had no RURPs, so I pounded two Knifeblades in. One actually went in half an inch, before it busted off the side of the seam. I tied off and equalized the pins, then agonized over the flexing 5.5 mantelshelf in front of me for another fifteen minutes.

I figured I'd rather fall going up than going down, and figured I had little choice. What I didn't figure was that the dirt above was dark brown, facing south, and now heated to over 100 degrees. When I got there it was too hot to hang onto. Fortunately, the angle was low enough that I could chop steps with my hammer, like ice climbing in the Sahara.

A hundred feet of zigzag climbing had netted me only 40 feet in elevation. The next anchor was half a rope away so it was decided—I don't remember by whom—that I should lead up to it and get us a full rope off the ground. Had I read Hurley's 1970 article on the Mystery Towers in *Climbing* prior to our ascent, this would surely have been Rob's lead. In it, Forrest recounts the fall he took on this pitch when a ¼-inch bolt broke under his weight. He had removed the bat hooks below, and the only pro left between him and a lengthy fall was a fold he tied off in the mud curtain. Miraculously, the thread held.

I had read about the Mystery Towers in the guidebook, however, and was aware of certain tricks used to ascend them: the curtain tie-offs for one, pins forced in calcite veins for another, and angles driven into the mud tent-stake style. Within 30 feet I had employed techniques two and three, as well as some steps carved in the mud. I reached a bolt and promptly backed it up with the worst bolt I ever placed.

Next came a blank section. The only hint of passage was a couple of millimeter-deep dimples, the remnants of bat hook holes. Given that most of the old bolts were now hanging about an inch out from the rock due to erosion, I figured that Forrest drilled bat hook holes roughly an inch deep. At first I tried to preserve Forrest's pattern: two to three holes, then a bolt. In the last two decades, however, not only had the rock changed, but so had the technology. Bat hooks were no longer in vogue, so as Crusher had done on the Doric, I put rivets in my freshly drilled inch-deep holes. An ethical quandary ensued. Forrest had taken more risk—his hook holes were empty after he passed them. He had nothing to stop a fall except a bolt every 15 feet or so—small consolation in this rock. At least I had eight cents' worth of soft steel carriage bolt plugging every hole, plus thicker bolts backing up his ¼-inch coffin nails. It didn't seem sporting, even if my rivets were the weakest money could buy.

I stopped backing up Forrest's bolts, and began tying off their exposed shanks and using them as rivets—the ones that didn't pull out in my fingers, that is. I nailed whenever possible. Fifty feet above my last bolt, I shuddered, looking down at the string of bent rivets and shaky pins beneath me. A long stretch and I hooked the pick end of my hammer through the rotting slings and gingerly pulled up on the anchor. Slater chuckled up the next pitch, in the process performing the impossible—he fixed a pin in the Fisher Towers. Half an hour of pounding wouldn't get it out. Half a year of erosion probably will.

We were keeping the same pace as the first ascent—100 feet per day. In the guidebook, the Citadel is listed as grade V, even though it is only 400 feet tall. At the rate we were going, it would be a grade VI. Every bit of work done by the first-ascent party had to be redone. The old pin scars and bathook holes had long since eroded away, and only a handful of original bolts still supported body weight.

Day three on the Citadel. We started up the fixed lines early—the thermometer read a mere 95 degrees. The long summit pitch was mine, the endless belay session Rob's. The first 80 feet was mostly putting in rivets, the only fun coming when I plucked out the old bolts—some in only a quarter inch—with my fingers.

I reached a shoulder on the arête and balanced across a doormat-width mud gangplank to the final headwall. Sheer walls dropped away on either side. If the ridge should crumble, I thought, I have to fling myself over the other side, so the rope would catch me. At the base of the headwall, I clipped the old bolt anchor, gratefully. I had plenty of rope left so, after hauling up some water, kept going.

Above, the rock was so decomposed that it was turning into mud in situ. I went to work on the ¾-inch crack. A few taps sent in a 1-inch angle. Fingers pulled it out. Ditto for the 1½-inch. Ditto for the 2-inch. Ditto for the 3-inch bong. Now I had a fist-sized hole in the crack, pouring sand. I might as well have been nailing in a giant sugar cube.

Twenty-five feet up there was a three-bolt ladder to the capstone summit crack. The only way up would be to nail the mud curtain. I grabbed the 3-inch Longware bong, a historic borrowed piece of iron, angled it down slightly, and pounded it until only the sling on the eye poked out through the mud. It went in like a dull knife punched into a jack-o'-lantern.

Pounding in the next bong, I could feel the whole curtain shake. I returned to the ridge to test it, a pattern I would keep up as long as my chain of aiders would reach.

The line went straight up, and a fall would certainly intercept the ridge; I would end up either draped and broken over it, or pound onto it, then fly down the exposed face on the right or ricochet down the steep flute on the left.

The last 12 feet had taken four hours.

I had drained the water bottle at the ridge. We had enough light to make the summit, but I didn't have enough nerves left. In my exhausted and dehydrated state, it would be easy to make a mistake. Day three ended 20 feet shy of the top.

The next day I went back up, shoving a few of the placements back in with my hands. Soon I was grabbing the rappel slings snaking through the crack at the summit. They came free in my hands, rotted through by twenty-three years of sunshine and wind.

As Rob pulled over the lip, he declared it the coolest summit in the desert. Just like he had with the Doric Column. Just like he had on every spire he'd climbed. We sent the temptingest trundle in celebration.

We had run out of time. The Gothic Nightmare would have to wait for another trip.

Eleven months later it was a race. With the exception of the Titan, the Fisher Towers had been virtually ignored for two decades. Now they had become trendy among some of the Boulder crowd. Rob had ticked nearly every Fisher Tower in the guide, and in his outspoken way, had declared his intention to be first to top them all.

Others soon declared their intention to beat Rob, then begged him for Beta and pin lists. "The race will be over when I finish," was all Rob would tell them. "No sooner."

I just wanted to do the three Mystery Towers and in the process settle my score with the Gothic, preferably with the second ascent.

Rob had been in the Fishers every weekend for four months. Loyal to The Team, he had been saving the Gothic to do with me. Our experience on the Citadel convinced us this would be more than a weekend project, and Rob had a Monday-through-Friday job. Hence we extended honorary Team membership to Mike O'Donnell, Rob's *Sea of Dreams* partner, a soft-spoken, red-haired brute from Boulder with a list of wild escapades rivaled by few, including a failed attempt at the Gothic in which an expanding flake both he and I had nailed came loose on its own, fell 25 feet, clocked the retreating Mike in the head, and split his helmet from one end to the other. Mike and I would fix up to the summit ridge, then Rob would meet us and triumphantly lead to the top.

The changes a year makes. The popularity of the Moab area had spread like a cancer, and Onion Creek had been "discovered" by the hoi polloi. Tents and campers filled every turnout. Mountain bikes jammed the road. Little TP prayer flags fluttered in the bushes—signs of the reverence Joe Six-Pack pays the wilderness.

When Cosgriff and I had approached the Mystery Towers two years before, we saw not a single footprint. The canyon was wild, the approach inobvious, the directions in the guidebook poor, the towers hidden from sight until halfway in. It felt as if nobody had walked this wash since Forrest and crew had rolled in the wheelbarrows supporting their ball sacks.

Now Mike and I followed numerous foot and paw prints up the approach. Mike explained that this had become a popular day hike for the Kumbaya-ers, as he refers to the crowd of hippie mountain bikers who now call Moab their own. He started mimicking their behavior, whistling as if calling a dog, and saying, "Dark Star, come here, boy."

We turned the corner where you get the first view of the Doric, and saw a party rapping down—the fifth ascent in less than a year. The Mystery Towers were a mystery no more.

The rock on the Gothic makes the Titan look like granite. Once again I drew the first pitch, which entailed tied-off Knifeblades, expanding blocks, and dirt-dagger free climbing. I hadn't nailed for a year and was pretty spooked. In the South, they'd say I was shaking like a dog shitting peach pits, but this was more like a dog passing sea urchins. Fortunately, it was a short pitch.

Mike methodically worked out the next pitch, knocking off loads of mud and rotten rock. Most fell to the side of me, but one chunk exploded on my belay plate, making me happy I hadn't opted for a hip belay.

After nailing the expanding mud-block traverse the first-ascent party had bat hooked, Mike started chain-smoking. Belaying me on the next lead didn't help matters, though I did my best to help him quit; from 20 feet up I dislodged a chunk of rock that whistled down to knock Mike's "twitch stick" from his lips.

I wriggled into a short chimney between two narrow ridges. It was like chimneying between slightly open scissor blades, and I could easily peer down both the north and south faces. O'Donnell was belaying on the north side. The chimney expanded on the south side. I said, "Listen to this," planted my left foot on the north face and shoved lightly with my right. A portion of the wall the size of my body slowly tipped off like a tree being felled, then traveled 300 feet before creating a thunder that echoed through the valley for minute after satisfying minute. A fine trundle is a rare and beautiful thing. I was reminded of the Kor's words when asked why he climbed the desert towers. "Not so much because they're there, but rather because they may not be there much longer."

Even more of the Gothic disappeared when I groveled on top of the knife-edge ridge the next day. I punched and shoved until the ridge was a foot lower, and the medium I would mantel onto resembled rock. A short stroll along the dirt ridge, similar, but wider than the Citadel's gangplank, got me to the anchor and the end of my leading commitment.

Now Rob had joined us, and went to work. After 60 feet, he stopped at a saddle between two gargoyles, midway along what the first ascent dubbed "The Traverse of the Goblins." The saddle was composed entirely of cobbles, a 3-foot-thick layer, every one of which you could pull out with your fingers. No way to nail it or drill it, and free climbing would be nuts. Luckily for Rob, a storm was moving in, and his partners called for a retreat.

The weekend was over. We sat in a Mexican restaurant discussing our plight. I wasn't about to leave. O'Donnell felt likewise. Outside, the streets of Moab were flooding. This, and a job commitment, convinced Rob to flee. He drove us out to the Onion Creek road, where my van was parked. It was a moonless night and still raining. He dropped us at the first stream crossing, then left us to die.

The first crossing turned out to be an insignificant tributary we had never seen water in. We didn't know this until we reached the real Onion Creek. We stood on the bank—what was left of the road—and listened to boulders rolling down the torrent. I half-expected to see my van float by. We stood in T-shirts, shorts, and flip-flops, me with a bag of provisions, Mike with a borrowed tent, and Rob long gone with the tent poles.

I wrapped myself in the tent, Mike wrapped himself in the fly, and we hiked back to the highway. No cars. Was it flooded now, too? Closed for the night?

The Rob-left-us-to-die jokes turned into serious talk about what to do next. I'm not one to throw away beers, even if they are Utah 3.2 road-pops, but I ditched the sixer, something I would do only in the most-dire circumstances. The nearest ranch house was 7 miles distant. We started hiking.

Finally, a caravan of rafters drove by and took pity on us, two drowned rats wrapped up like nuns with tents over our heads.

"What are you doing out here?" they asked.

"Rock climbing," we replied.

They dropped us off in Moab, where, once again, we knocked on the door of the patron saint of Moab mud-nailers, Kyle Copeland. If it weren't for his hospitality and gear, we would have never gotten into this mess.

Betrayal. The Team ripped asunder by filthy lucre. Rob knew that next Friday was the only day I could go back. O'Donnell was going to be there. I told Rob he must call in sick, especially since he'd already told his competitors that the second ascent was a done deal.

"You've got to wait until Saturday," Rob pleaded, "I'll lose six thousand dollars if I don't go to work on Friday."

"Don't give me this bullshit about chicken feed. This is the second ascent of the Gothic we're talking about."

O'Donnell and I went back alone. Forrest had told Slater that from the summit ridge up it was all drilling. Indeed, the only pins he placed were lost arrows pounded into bolt holes; the rock was so bad in places that 1½-inch-long bolts wouldn't cut it. I finished Slater's lead. Mike led to the glorious summit.

The very top is the size of a park bench, and perfect to sit on. It was time to lift a Mount Everest malt liquor, toast the first ascentionists Forrest and Briggs, toast ourselves, toast Rob who would jug up the next day, and toast all those who have sought adventure in these most stupendous of choss heaps.

"Here's mud in your eye."

A DAY IN THE LIFE OF A MOUNTAINEER

DECEMBER 1994-FEBRUARY 1995, NO. 149

BY PETER CROFT

In summer 1992, the legendary free soloist Peter Croft made the second traverse, onsight, of the Minarets in California's High Sierra, climbing sixteen summits, mostly between 11,000 and 12,000 feet, in a 21½-hour push. The exposed ridge that links them is complicated and involves labyrinthine route-finding on dark, slick volcanic rock of variable quality. Croft has called the experience his hardest day in the mountains. Vern Clevenger and Claude Fiddler made the first ascent of the traverse over three days in 1982.

I'm itchy hot and it's a cool night here at the mountain's roots, here at the beginning. Flat on my back at the end of the road, I'm lying still but my mind swings back and forth, arguing. Geez, I've said it all before and heard it all before.

"Is it dangerous?

"How dangerous?

"Do I want it?

"How much?"

Around and around till I'm dizzy. These conversations used to be about good granite, known ground, home ground. But now, unless I decide against myself, I'm headed for more than a baker's dozen of rotten red-brown spires, the Minarets in

California's High Sierra. Dangerous place, apparently—even the guidebook warns against it.

So here I am with a swirling head and it's getting late and I've gotta sleep. Could go south; there's granite there. Could go north . . . but no, I find that I want this loss of control. I want to feel very small in very deep water. I don't want to know what I'm doing, but to learn it.

I wake up 30 seconds before my alarm—12:30 a.m. Start the coffee pot and sit silently, watching while my mind percolates. Then, too soon, it's time to leave this warm place and go outside where the world hasn't started yet and everything is bigger than I am. The door of my van slamming sounds like a gong. I step into the night and a cold wind washes my head.

I'm light-footed and tripping like a toddler, trying to make my steps longer. My pack, which is bigger than I'd hoped it would be, feels like nothing. It's sort of like a kid on my shoulders, swinging back and forth with each step. Giddyup!

My headlamp is bright, but I don't get a view. The moon's only half and it won't rise till 2 a.m. I'm stuck in a stumbly dusty circle of light, rising up through waves of black forest.

Round a bend a new wave of glacial air hits me. My sweat turns nasty on me and I tense my muscles, but I feel great, like shifting gears or something. No longer a climber. I'm a small boy afraid of the dark but faced with it. The half-moon's up, shedding enough icy light to show me the line of rotting black fangs on the skyline. I'm thrilled to be here because all I can do is my best and if that's not enough I'll still have gone through so many layers of myself that I'll remember it forever. This adventure is like a life and I feel very young.

But I'm still in the dark when the trail bends at the lake and I lose my way and make mistakes that only a child would make. So I backtrack and crisscross and find a gully that heads to a notch between the first two peaks. When I get there a thin strip of pumpkin orange is on the horizon and I get that little rush that the nonnocturnal get when they realize night isn't permanent. Anyway, my headlamp makes my head hurt.

Still too dark for the tricky first tower so I go up the easy second and then back. Now it seems incredible that I can see long distances; but I still get lost, find the climbing hard, and only discover the right way up on the way down. It's fully light now and I take geeky long steps down the gully to look for my gray pack on the gray rocks. From there, up and around on more gullies and terraces to the small ice field, I had hoped would be smaller, that leads to the col. I can't really afford the time and bloody hands it would take to cut steps with a rock, so I hand traverse the upper ice edge to a point where I can get lost on the loose north face of Peak 3. I try to go daintily, but I'm a hunchback with a backpack so the most I can do, it seems, is poke my ostrich head way in the back of corners and, when I can, stuff my hands 2 feet deep to equalize the pressure on the shaky flakes. I reach the ridge crest and my eyes plunge down a waterfall of exposure. From the top, I can see where I'm going, a puzzle just starting to make sense.

Now there's a peak to the south but the main ridge swoops around north and that's where I'm headed. The day and I are too young to be conservative, though, so my pack gets shed like homework and I talus-run to Peak 4 and back in no time. Now the peaks go way up north and I sideswipe more talus to puzzle out Peak 5. I find the wrong way and hurry up it, cursing the guidebooks for undergrading and myself for climbing poorly. At the summit area I look across a heartbreak gap to a slightly higher top, eddies of vertigo swirling between. To backtrack and do it right is a very big detour and the shortcut is so short a cut.

I downclimb to the notch like a cat down a tree and hand traverse on little leaning ledges. The exposure really bugs me and it feels as if my whole spinal cord is curling up like a monkey tail. Have to be careful. At the summit I stop gulping, since I can see the way down isn't nearly as bad.

At Iceberg Lake, I dump my pack, drink all I can hold, and sidetrack a bit to Peak 6, seeing mountain varmints swarming through a boulderfield like it was Swiss cheese.

Back at the lake I fill two water bottles, and consider. The next three peaks are the biggest and I've done a lot to get where I am. I know what I want from life, though, and get on with it. I get to the airy slot between Clyde and Eichorn. I'm on edge because there are so many ways to go and everywhere in these dragon-back peaks the scales are shedding. Clyde is the highest and when I get there, I can see where I've come from, but the future is getting more complex as both the day and I get older. I cross over to Peak 9, toe-shuffling a narrow ledge on this skyscraper, not knowing if my pack will overbalance me.

Now I'm faced with one more sidetrack—Michael Minaret, second highest in the group. I can't ignore it even though it's off the main ridge. I stash my pack with the rope inside—stupid, stupid—and spend way too long scrabbling down and then over fins and into gullies just getting to the spire. I'm miles off route, climbing way harder than I should be. Steep bulges bully me off right until I find an overhanging flaky finger crack. I scratch away with frightened claws at loose pebbles, so I can grab deeper, then, before my hands can sweat, pop a foot way out left and swing into a layback and go. Eventually, I settle into a pace and even peer over and smile at the abyss. At the top I crow like a rooster and it echoes back in a hundred voices.

My pack feels like home when I reach it and again I drink all I can, and eat. It's early afternoon and I haven't stopped for fourteen hours. My momentum is wavering and I enter a midday crisis. Every incident has put little chinks in my armor. I'm a long way from totally shattered, but I can feel the exposure like it is seeping through the cracks. From here I could escape relatively easily. In four hours I could be back at the campground. The way ahead is a crazy crest of spires that just get wilder and wilder, like a mangy set of claws needle-sharp and bending this way and that. Is this what I really want? As a kid swimming in the ocean I was OK as long as I could see the bottom. If not, I got a hollow feeling and my guts would crowd up into my chest till I couldn't breathe properly. As I squint over in the direction my life might take I feel some of that hollowness. Well, what have I come for? I had felt a bit too much in control lately and wanted to get all wide-eyed again. So now I know. It's an amazingly calm powerful thrill to enter water this deep.

I feel more certain of myself. I still make mistakes and get lost, but now I realize that this is part of life. At times, the very best option is a lousy one but is the way to go. I reach a very steep section I have to cross. Better hold on tight because that's a big loose block and I really want to step on it. The block dives out and my body swings sideways, right foot darting into a crack like a swallow.

The smallest spire is the hardest and steepest and the only place I belay myself. I only have a few pieces of gear and nothing is very good. As I climb the summit block against rope drag I realize my silly self-belay is about as much good as an upside-down toprope.

The sun's getting lower and I'm getting older. Have to watch myself now, and use my experience to find a canny way up. So I drop down a long gully and ditch most of my stuff on a great white rock. I go over a couple of summits to reach the main one, zigzagging to avoid difficulties that would have been easy this morning when I was young. Doddering a bit on the way down, I rappel rather than make a five-minute detour. The endurance that I once thought inexhaustible is fading.

I may be too tired. I don't know if I can. . . . I fiddle with the laces of my climbing shoes. The sun is fluttering close to the horizon. One more peak, the last. I just want to rest, though. I can feel the cold of the coming blackness. Cuts and scrapes are all over me. My sunset is very near but the last peak obscures it. I could walk away now but then I would know . . . my love of adventure wasn't strong enough. Promises and decisions I've made in my long, long life this day come surging back. I double-knot my laces and creak to my feet with a lopsided smile, actually sort of surprised at the sudden wave of energy I get, like a sunburst before sunset. With a wondering mind, I climb the face up a wandering route and reach the ridge crest a long way from the top. A bald arête halts me for a minute, then I hand traverse up, feet smearing on ripples, and then it's easy and then it's the top. I raise myself like an old bear on to my tired legs and look north. A deep pass below me and more mountains going away until I can't see them anymore. Now is my sunset and it's beautiful and sad. I still have to get down, but it's over now. I'm happy and satisfied in a way that makes me feel even older.

I stay very watchful on the descent, carefully cleaning the soles of my shoes when they pick up grit. And then I'm down and the tension floods out through my pores. I slip on my walking shoes and they feel like dessert. I begin the long walk out to the end, first on ice, then rocks, then on a faint trail that grows and grows. And then it's night and it's down through those black waves that looked different a lifetime ago. The path that was so well defined looks indistinct now, my rubber legs casting about in the dark for solid ground. My headlamp is still bright as ever, but I'm not and I totter clean off the John Muir Super Highway. I sway south through the forest, then find the path again. I have to be careful. I have to get down, then I can sleep.

Little thought-bits are swirling around when I reach the campground. The bright lights make me stagger a bit on the way to put my load down. In the van, I roll down the road, sipping coffee and making movies in my head, reliving the essence of a long, long day.

I go to bed like an old man, and sleep like a baby . . .

THE SHINING MOUNTAIN

SEPTEMBER 1997, NO. 171

BY ANDY CAVE

Andy Cave and Brendan Murphy's alpine-style ascent of the North Face of Chang-abang (22,520 feet) in India's Garhwal Himalaya was plagued with challenges, including broken equipment, runout terrain, and bitter cold. But the team continued on, finally summiting a peak considered by many as the most beautiful in the world. Then, "so quietly and so softly it took Brendan, sweeping him away to our right," Cave wrote of the moment his partner was hit by an avalanche on the descent.

Momentarily, I stepped outside myself. I watched my exhausted legs trying to move quickly, my feet trying to hold steady on the snow-covered moraine. I slumped against a huge slab of granite to regain a grip on reality, rested my sack against a tall cairn that Brendan had built the previous year, and took a sip of water. Minutes later, when I tried to lift the sack, a pain shot across my chest. Across the peaks and troughs of the glacier I could make out basecamp, normally about an hour away.

I jettisoned the rucksack and, in slow motion using the ski poles to stabilize my jellied limbs, edged up to the first moraine ridge. By the time I reached the top, the chest pain had returned. I was scared. The rotting-fish smell of frostbite forced me on; I had to get some medicine. I had to get there before they abandoned camp. I had to tell them what had happened.

After a full half hour I had traveled only a pitiful 700 feet. I yelled into the approaching mist. There was no reply. The thought of only making it halfway and bivying without a sleeping bag and refreezing my hands and feet frightened me enough to turn back.

After almost twelve hours of much-needed sleep, I crawled out of my snow-covered sleeping bag. I took a short piss, which turned the snow bright orange, then stuffed the sleeping bag into the rucksack with my good hand. I felt refreshed inside, but I still walked like a delirious junky.

In my head I constructed the words I would say to the others. I was convinced they would see me a long way off and would become suspicious at the sight of just one bright-red suit. As I wobbled down the final half mile, I felt intoxicated by the spring air. A small red bird that had arrived with the warm temperatures sang and hopped to the side, guiding me back to basecamp. The overnight ice had not yet melted from the edge of the stream and I staggered straight across, crunching through it in my lead-heavy boots. I was grateful for the ski poles, which let me walk in a dignified straight line. I shouted a small hello, and immediately Narinda and Vikram, our liaison officer and cook, came out of the kitchen shelter. They held out their hands warmly but nervously. It had been eighteen long days. Narinda waited for my words, tears welling in his eyes.

"Mick and Steve are coming," I said. "Brendan is dead."

I appreciated that acclimatizing was a vital part of our preparation, but found it tedious. All the slopes of the neighboring cols and peaks were covered in loose snow topped by a hideous crust that made movement slow and dangerous. Consequently we plodded up to 5,700 meters on a boring but relatively safe slope on the unclimbed Dunagiri Parbat. Although uninspiring in itself, the ascent gave exceptional views of our proposed route on the 5,500-foot North Face of Changabang.

Last year Brendan had joined Roger Payne, Julie-Anne Clyma, and Andy Perkins in an attempt on the same face. On that trip the four climbed an impressive thin line of ice on the right side of the face. Sadly, serious gastric illness floored Perkins, and eventually they were all forced down. This year, however, that route looked almost nonexistent and, besides, there were more logical and direct lines leading to the first ice field. Our group of six would approach the face in teams of two. Of three possible ice lines, Brendan and I chose the central one, as did Mick Fowler and Steve Sustad. Roger and Julie-Anne were also back, and decided on the left-hand line.

Changabang provided a perfect objective for all of us—it wasn't so high (6,864 meters) but promised excellent climbing. Julie-Anne and Roger, who are married, are both seasoned Himalayan alpinists with many trips to steep and remote peaks under their belts. Their amazing organizational skills were something of a novelty to the rest of us. Mick and Steve were blown away when they learned that we were to have a tablecloth for basecamp meals and delicious cakes to accompany our afternoon tea. Back in Britain Mick works as a taxman and is one of the most prolific adventure, new-route activists around. Originally from Seattle but now living in Britain, Steve is an exceptionally gifted mountaineer, although he keeps a low profile. Brendan Murphy had been on several trips to technical but relatively low-altitude objectives in recent years. We got to know each other well on a trip to climb the South Face of Gasherbrum IV in the summer of 1993. I liked his mixture of tenacity and humor.

As well as outstanding climbing there are other reasons that make Changabang special. This mountain has symbolic status. The first ascent by an Anglo-Indian team in 1974 was followed a few years later by the monumental effort of Pete Boardman and Joe Tasker. Boardman's book *The Shining Mountain* is a gripping account of their ascent of the West Face, hailed as one of the most outrageous routes of its time. After this, Alex Mcintyre and John Porter teamed up with the Poles Voytek Kurtyka and Krystof Zurek for the first ascent of the South Buttress. Many of those players have since lost their lives pushing the limits in the Himalaya, but their committing, bold journeys and quest to climb in a lightweight style continue to influence those who perform in this sphere.

I complained about the cold temperatures at such a modest height. After seeing photos and chatting to the team from an expedition the previous spring, I had expected something quite different. They had relatively mild temperatures, good quality névé, and long spells of good weather.

Brendan shook his head and said as he did so many times, "This year it really is a different mountain." How true. Out of thirty days there would be only one when it didn't snow. The long cold mornings froze our feet. I revealed how my girlfriend had threatened to telephone Brendan before the expedition and tell him I wasn't an ideal partner for such a venture—at home, I used a hot water bottle every night and protested strongly when she demanded the bedroom window remain open. He just laughed.

By May 21 we were ready for action. We had good clear weather every morning but storms every afternoon. The plan was that Brendan and I would head up first. Steve and Mick would follow two days behind and Julie-Anne and Roger a day or so behind them. We would climb as independent teams, and didn't want to be too close to each other, both for fear of falling debris and limited bivouac sites.

We would climb alpine-style, whatever that means. In our case the definition seemed simple enough. We had two 60-meter ropes, an alpine rack, eight to nine days' food, and ten days' gas. The only item we had that you probably wouldn't take in the Alps was a small tent. We hoped to pitch it on a series of tiny snow arêtes that dotted the bases of the various ice fields.

One thing alpine-style does not mean is lightweight. Despite close scrutiny of every item we carried, our sacks weighed forty-five pounds. The climbing magazines and picture books often lend an air of romanticism to Himalayan climbing, but the majority of the time it is grunt work. We planned our route meticulously— one hour across the glacier, two hours for the lower slopes up to the base of the first difficulties. How naive we were.

We left at 2 a.m., spent three hours getting to the bergschrund, and, being unroped, almost fell into it. The lower slopes proved anything but a walk. By the time we arrived at what we considered the real climbing, we had broken two out of six ice screws and were about to be baptized by the daily afternoon storm.

Brendan led a meandering mixed pitch between two thundering powder chutes, eventually belaying by the left-hand chute. We searched in vain for a place to spend the night. Reluctantly I set off up the left-hand chute, which was not only extremely steep and rejected ice screws but received regular surges of powder. I finally made it onto easier ground, but by that time both my gloves were full of snow and my fingers numb. Great start, I thought, as we crawled onto a small ledge for the night. Down by the glacier, Fowler and Sustad watched our slow progress with surprise. Two days later they would experience a similar day and bivouac in the same place.

The next two days saw us edge upward, tackling pitches that would have been demanding at sea level. We'd crossed the first icefield, a giant skating rink tilted at 55 degrees with an almost impenetrable steel skin. The constant avalanches had acted like giant polishing rags on the surface of the ice, making it much tougher than we had bargained for. Getting in an ice screw took an eternity, and we now had three out of six functioning normally with one that occasionally bit if persuaded by a violent beating. We had a mixture of 1987 Polish vintage titanium screws and slightly superior 1997 Ukraine jobs. Often we were so wrecked after getting just one of these damn things halfway in we would tie it off and, together with our ice tools, declare a belay.

Dawn on day four saw us at the foot of the second icefield. This point was significant to Brendan, as it was his party's high point of the previous year. The second icefield passed more quickly than anticipated and led to a choice of two steep exits. The right-hand option looked like extremely steep ice with two thin sections yet, despite our serious lack of ice screws, seemed preferable to the steep mixed line on the left.

One pitch higher and the thunderheads were building nicely. Today the ferocity of the storm would intensify to fever pitch. Brendan had just led an impressive pitch and now it was my turn.

The situation looked ugly. Even if I had ten good ice screws I would have been worried, but with just one tied off on Brendan's belay and two more on my harness, I climbed up full of fear. Absurd quantities of powder now thundered from above, pummeling us. The wind increased tenfold and violent thunder boomed from near the summit. I had climbed beyond the point of retreat. Sixty feet above the belay I tried to place a screw. It would not bite. Tiring rapidly, I clipped into one of my tools. It held for a few seconds then ripped. Both crampons popped simultaneously and I fell onto my other tool. Then more spindrift swept upward, numbing my face. I struggled with the weight of the sack, the tip of my right tool staving off disaster. Regaining position, I managed to get the screw turning. At the halfway mark I tied it off and belayed.

We were in the eye of an angry storm. Neck, nostrils, ears, gloves packed with snow. When Brendan arrived he got the hot aches from hell, and retched with pain. Seeing this hard little bastard wince and groan made our predicament seem even worse. Nevertheless, he hacked on, up a brittle ice-filled corner.

I began talking to myself and flapping my arms to stay warm, but I was losing. I seconded the pitch, screaming that I needed something to eat and was on the verge of hypothermia. Brendan held out a food bar and I bit into it, with the wrapper still on. Night was approaching fast as I set off on the next pitch.

The angle eased, and the storm abated. I made it to the edge of the snow arête where we could bivy. At the belay I used all the functioning ice screws, then spent twenty minutes trying to beat in one of the damaged ones. Eventually, I got it partway in and tied off my axes. I yelled a warning that the belay was shit. Normally Brendan was a supermeticulous, steady climber but, within minutes of his starting, I was yanked tight onto the belay and realized all was not well. In the dark I made out a tiny light way below. After taking a swinging, 60-foot fall, Brendan climbed a more direct route up to the belay.

"That was lucky," he said. "I could have lost my headtorch." At 11 p.m. we crawled into our tent, psychologically and physically roasted. In fifteen years in the mountains, I had never experienced such a harrowing few hours. We were both frost-nipped on the fingers and I shivered, cold to the core.

The next day we rested. It was impossible to know what was running through Brendan's mind. He was a private person, and he kept chat to a minimum.

After a day's rest I felt better. Brendan led three hard pitches that left us tantalizingly close to the groove system that cut through the final headwall. We fixed our two ropes and returned to our tent. Mick and Steve, who had set off two days behind, caught up to us at this point. We were happy to see each other and exchange stories. Mick's typical enthusiasm uplifted us, but we were all worried about the danger of being too close. We considered joining forces, thinking it might be safer.

Ultimately, however, we surmised that bivouacking in the steep, upper grooves with a party of four might prove awkward, and we were also reluctant to suddenly change systems. We all agreed that teaming up for the descent might prove beneficial. At that stage, though, we had no idea what surprises lay in store.

Reaching the groove system proper involved some of the most challenging climbing yet, and Mick and Steve, seeing our slow progress, opted for a relaxing day "indoors." But this was not to be. Brendan dislodged a large rock, which beamed in on their tent like a heat-seeking missile. I feared the worst. Eventually Mick appeared and relayed that we had destroyed the back of the tent but that they were OK.

The afternoon snow began falling and filling the tent via this hole at such a rate they considered descending. We felt dreadful. We moved into the grooves, which were comprised of especially hard, brittle ice and succeeded in making two more holes in their tent, events that produced increasingly irate comments from below. I peered up at the next pitch. It looked long and hard. I tensioned off a Knifeblade and stabbed a tool into a blob of ice at the foot of a shallow groove and then followed an intermittent seam of ice over perfect granite. In terms of quality it was one of the best pitches either of us had ever done. I reached the belay knackered but buzzing.

The next morning I woke after a fitful night, and surveyed our surroundings. We were hemmed in by walls of El Cap stature. Huge arching corners, vast blank-looking sheets of icy granite and, here and there, a lonely crack that ran into some mad-looking roof. To be up in this world, to have overcome all that had been thrown at us, now elicited feelings of pride. I began the day with a long, hard mixed pitch in a mind-blowing position.

Each pitch that day had a sting to it. The afternoon weather came in force, but we were close enough to finishing the face that we bore it with extra patience. After negotiating a hideously loose aid section, we could smell the top. But nothing came easily on this mountain. Brendan boldly persevered over granite slabs covered in powder that placed him within striking distance of the cornice. I joined him and then set to work on the final pitch to the ridge. What a pleasure to be hacking through the cornice after eight days' climbing.

The following morning, it was my birthday. To my surprise Brendan pulled out six Snickers bars. He had carried them up and never mentioned them. We couldn't be too extravagant as we had virtually no food left, but we celebrated with a whole bar each. Fortunately, Mick and Steve had overcalculated their food and had agreed to help us out during the descent. The weather that day closed in at 8 a.m. and thwarted any attempts of reaching the summit.

We passed time repitching the tent, as we had discovered that we were sleeping on a fragile snow mushroom, a section of which had disintegrated during the night leaving our feet unsupported. Throughout the day we chatted about all kinds of things. We had grown close during the climb and were like an eccentric couple. We shared one pee bottle, knew what soup or type of tea the other preferred, knew each other's aspirations and fears. Brendan however never talked without a purpose, and there was always a large part of him that seemed unknowable, that he had decided not to share.

I moaned that I was becoming too old for this sport. At 31, I had been at it ten years. But I also loved skiing and bouldering and, after all you couldn't carry on doing this for too long, could you? Brendan didn't say much, but he too loved his rock climbing and spoke about how he had enjoyed last summer just cragging in Britain. Philosophizing high on that twisting corniced ridge seemed like such a luxury after the grinding face. That evening we ate our last meal. We had plenty of gas and enough drinks for another two or three days, but other than two chocolate bars each, eating was officially over until we linked up with the other two.

The first day of June dawned beautifully. I came out of the tent charged with energy. We carried light sacs and conditions underfoot were good. The summit looked close.

"I feel like I am out for a trot in the park. Do you want me to take a bit of your gear?"

Brendan seemed to be moving slower, and handed me the two water bottles to carry. After an hour or so we were forced onto the ridge proper. We roped up, primarily for psychological reasons. But less than a minute later, an enormous section of ridge beside me snapped off and tumbled down the North Face. I teetered there, trying to control the surge of adrenaline racing through my veins. Brendan sat in a bucket seat, a leg either side of the ridge, a rope length away.

Six pitches later the trusty afternoon cloud arrived. Our pace slowed and my earlier enthusiasm waned. A swirling mist enveloped us, robbing us of the magnificent views we had expected. The descent to the col between the horns of Changabang ate up an hour. A layer of soft snow lay over brittle ice and, at the apex of the col itself, we sank almost to our waists. Giant rocks loomed out of the mist. We climbed out from between the horns and began the final, weary 700 feet in appalling visibility. At the summit we congratulated each other, then collapsed.

"I am really chuffed," said Brendan. The lack of food was taking its toll.

As we sat there the clouds dropped below us. Nanda Devi floated in front of us, Dunagiri behind, and in the distance the unmistakable Kamet. We wanted to linger but, with the descent down the twisting ridge still to come, we turned our backs on the summit. In the top of my rucksack I found the remnants of a broken biscuit, which we shared. I was amazed that Brendan still had some of his chocolate bar left.

Voices floated up through the clouds.

"Is that you, Steve?"

A lone figure stood on the ridge far below.

"Yes. How are you?"

"Good. And you?"

"Fine."

Suddenly the mist swept in and he disappeared.

Later there were two figures, this time 200 feet lower and erecting a tent. It looked like a good spot and I chided myself for not having spotted it for ourselves. Once close enough, Mick seemed eager to catch our attention. It seemed they had arrived at this wonderful camp spot by default. Steve had tripped on his crampons and dragged the two of them down. Mick had escaped unhurt, but Steve had been less fortunate. He lay in the tent with intense pain in his ribs and chest. Assured we could do nothing to help, we returned to our tent for the last of the instant soup, if you could call that food.

Despite the fatigue, our minds were in a whirlwind. Exploring every avenue of escape we concluded that everything hinged on the extent of Steve's injuries. Mick and Steve had a rough night: Steve in pain, and Mick perturbed by his partner's irregular breathing and groaning. They were so glad that we were around to help, and we them, as we had now begun to hallucinate about eating some of their mashed-potato powder.

The weather had been so consistently bad that the arrival of another poor day evoked no response. Fortunately Steve could move, albeit with great suffering. We spent a whole day getting ourselves to the Kalanka Col. That evening Mick and Steve invited us for tea. Crammed into the back of their tent, we sat shaking with the excitement of eating. Steve prepared a wonderful dish of mashed potato, a meal that I will never forget. I even got to lick out the cooking pot. Now that was a birthday present!

If the climb had drawn Brendan and me together, now the descent would do the same for the rest of us—more than we could have imagined.

The next morning brought a biting wind. The simplest task took an eternity, as I had to constantly stop and unfreeze my fingers. In near-zero visibility we started our descent, with enough food to last three or four days. For a while the sky cleared and the terrain proved straightforward. But as the weather closed in, it became difficult to find a safe route. All things considered we did extremely well to locate a tiny flat area on the edge of a vast icefield. We were all utterly exhausted, but from here just two or three abseils would see us into an easy gully and then down onto the Changabang Glacier. Mick abseiled first and I followed.

"It's too steep," Mick shouted just as I began. "Too steep for Steve."

Mick was right. Suddenly it became undercut, and a free-hanging abseil with broken ribs would have been dangerous. I climbed back out and Brendan volunteered to set up another anchor out to the right. He spent twenty minutes trying to get a screw in. There was a lot of névé but not much ice.

"I've got a bomber one now," he shouted across to us.

"He reminds me of Dick Renshaw," said Steve.

I didn't know Dick, but from what I had heard there were similarities: quiet, determined, and tough, but always a gentleness and a disturbing modesty and selflessness.

"We used to call him the little angel," Steve continued, "because whenever there was a job to be done, a job that others didn't want to do, he would do it, without any fuss."

Seconds later a muffled noise came from above. Way up, an avalanche released and then another and another. These silent slides joined forces, and headed straight for us. Time stood still. In a panic I began screaming and yelling.

"Brendan! Brendan! Brendan!"

I beat my axe to the hilt into the slope and clipped in. The whiteness took an eternity to reach us. Brendan saw it but had no sling to clip into the ice screw. No rope. No second tool. Absolutely nothing. He tried to grab the screw. Eventually it came. So quietly and so softly it took Brendan, sweeping him away to our right. Stunned, I couldn't move at first and then started rocking my head trying to control my anguish. The avalanche had stopped now, the debris sloughing to a halt just 60 feet away. Darkness was not far off and Mick and Steve led me down to a small, safe spur where we would spend the night. Brendan had no chance of surviving, but still we shouted into the darkness. The next day we searched and shouted, and then saw the giant cliffs over which the avalanche had tracked. I shouted helplessly into the deep, empty basin.

The next two days were going to be the toughest any of us had ever dealt with. During the night, as I replayed the scene of Brendan disappearing, my frozen thumb felt like it was going to burst. The next morning it sported an ugly black blister. As long as the weather stabilized we planned to cross first the Shipton Col and then the Bagini Pass. We estimated that they were both at around 5,700 meters. Our food supply, if we stuck to one meal a day, might just see us through. Although attractive, the alternative descent down through the Rishi Gorge had not been traveled for years and would take too long. We had no choice but to go for it and cross the two cols. We prayed for good snow conditions and a little luck.

We had to get back to basecamp soon. Steve and I needed a doctor, and Roger and Julie-Anne would be desperately worried by now, presuming they made it back to basecamp. In fact, they had spent ten days on the face, reaching the Ice Tongue just above the second icefield and sitting out the terrible storms there before abseiling off. Visions of losing my infected thumb would drive me to leave Mick and Steve below the face, foregoing a night's rest.

We began the long climb to the Shipton Col at 1 a.m. I stared up at an unforgettable night sky. Between Nanda Devi and Changabang were whole carpets of silver galaxies. As we neared the col, the star-studded sky slowly faded and left us instead with Nanda Devi. Morning bathed the sacred mountain in a magical, golden light. I soothed myself by thinking how Brendan would rest in one of the most remote and beautiful mountain valleys on Earth. Soon the tiny spring flowers would be pushing their way through the thinning snow, carpeting the edges of the Changabang Glacier. Before reaching the col, I turned around one last time and said good-bye.

BALANCING ACT

NOVEMBER 1999, NO. 189

BY JEFF ACHEY

In this story, Jeff Achey visits the late Dean Potter (1972–2015) in Yosemite to find out what made this big-wall-speed-climbing, free-soloing, and slacklining master tick. What Achey discovers is a complex man who struggles like the rest of us, but one who also explodes up the rock when it comes time to climb. Achey's visit came before Potter's untethered-highlining and free-BASEing feats, acts that changed his renown from that of a bold rock climber into an aerial pioneer and professional athlete celebrated worldwide.

In a Yosemite meadow, Dean Potter balances barefoot on a strip of webbing stretched 8 feet off the ground. It is snowing. Against the background of frosted pines he is an odd sight, cherubic face and small head perched atop a 6-foot-5 frame. He walks haltingly, eyes fixed forward, then drops a foot off to one side, arcing his body sharply right and left for balance. The 100-foot length of webbing is wet, slack, and unstable. Midway, it finally spits him off.

Dean has walked wilder lines than this: He clinched a place in history when he speed-soloed the Northwest Face of Half Dome, free soloing most of the route. In Moab, the only place other than the Valley the vagabond might call home, he began turning heads with hard bouldering and audacious free soloing including several unroped 5.13 first ascents.

This is my second meeting with Potter. It's April, the beginning of the end of his two-year seasonal residence in Camp Four's Search and Rescue site. He has a cozy tent cabin here, with a wood stove, but The Powers That Be will soon oust him, he's sure—for being a general nonconformist, and for speaking his mind a little too freely in the debrief after the Dan Osman body recovery. Shortly after I visit him he will seal his persona non grata status by mooning a tourist who had objected to Dean's tossing pine cones at a grazing deer. I can imagine this encounter, and the mischievous glee on Potter's face. On the one hand, Dean takes pride in never speaking ill of other climbers—a new resolution, I think, a response to a time when he was more cocky and obnoxious. On the other hand, his irreverent streak is permanent.

But this tourist encounter had not yet taken place when I visited. Not much took place, in fact, making it hard to get to know the guy. He's been popping Altoids and fighting a cold, and we haven't been able to climb. He's cautious around me, "The Media," and sometimes stands me up for our meetings, once to go scout *Widow's Tears*, a 1,500-foot, rarely formed ice route near Bridalveil Falls. Conditions are so wintry this April that Potter and Miles Smart manage to climb the route shortly after I leave. It was 49 degrees Fahrenheit when the pair made their ascent, a nearby 1,000-foot pillar crashed to the ground as they climbed the melting *Tears*, and the effort extended into waist-deep snow well into the night.

Reticent as he is, Potter has agreed to meet me. "In an ideal world I wouldn't want any publicity," he says, but since he's acquired a public image he wants it right. He is sponsored, but dislikes a new Boreal ad that features him "just sitting around looking like a geek." Worse, though, would be to court the media in any way. The weather has relegated us to a circuit of Yosemite Lodge, Degnan's Deli, and this illegal slackline hidden in the woods. We talk about climbing the overhanging West Face of Leaning Tower despite the snow, but Dean's cold has sapped his energy and he isn't into putting on a show. "It wouldn't be me," he says.

I know more of Potter than about him as I watch him mount the snowy slackline a third time. I know he was an early member of the Hueco Tanks crash pad clan of hard boulderers. I know he has done audacious solos in Moab, such as onsighting an overhanging 5-inch layback crack called *Undertow* (5.12+). I know that with José Pereyra in Yosemite last summer he set speed records for the *Salathé*, the Northwest Face of Half Dome, and Lurking Fear—three grade VIs in a single five-day blitz. I remember most the photo in Hot Flashes of his "gladiator-style" solo of Half Dome.

I imagine the details of that ascent. Two square centimeters of aluminum grind against granite as a small Alien flexes under Potter's 180 pounds. He yanks the unit down to his waist, feet smeared, then jams in a higher unit and pops the lower one free. His rope is coiled and lashed across his back. The rock falls away vertically for 2,000 feet.

The dihedrals known as the Zig Zags ease back to 5.10 and Potter finger locks, free solo, to Thank God Ledge. Eyes toward the summit, he hand-traverses across, picks up the pace on some 5.8 free climbing, and yards at top speed through a bolt ladder. On top of Half Dome he glances at his watch: four hours, seventeen minutes. That beats the previous solo record by about sixteen hours.

Later I ask him if this was his best speed ascent. "The team ascent I think was even more," he says, referring to his ascent of the same route with Pereyra last summer. "José and I simulclimbed the whole thing in one pitch without jumars. We each did every move without ever changing gear, in continuous motion in 2:54."

Dean hangs with a handful of young Valley climbers psyched on the new techniques in speed introduced by a group of hardcore Yosemite wall rats that Potter calls the Dream Team—Scott Stowe, Dave Bengston, Steve Gerbeding. "They took the biggest step," says Potter. "They showed that all these walls were possible in the fast style. And of course their times can be whittled down some by guys like me and Miles and José!" In fact, the young guys are fast, and the "whittling" sometimes cuts the old times in half.

The speed techniques range from interesting to frightening. To save time Potter and crew favor a "clean as you go" approach, using Cam Hooks and removing placements as they climb. The team climbs in blocks, with the leader leading multiple pitches in a row. At the end of a pitch the leader ties off, pulls up all the slack on a 60-meter lead line (the team's only rope), and continues rope-solo style. The second cleans to the belay, then the leader quickly drops a rope end and pulls up the cleaned gear. For ultraspeed on "easier" aid sections—sometimes entire routes, as with Dean and José on Half Dome—the team simulclimbs, each climber carrying a locking biner full of Aliens and Cam Hooks on each aider. The leader carries free biners and quickdraws but only a minimal rack, almost never leaving a cam as pro and clipping only the fixed gear.

The simulclimbing method is not safe. Riskier still is the solo technique used by Potter on Half Dome's Northwest Face, which as yet only he is employing. At the time of my visit he intends to use this style to solo the *Nose* and Half Dome in a "day" climbing El Cap in the afternoon and evening, hiking over to Half Dome at night, starting up the *Northwest Face* at first light, and summiting before noon to complete the two walls in under twenty-four hours.

I've learned all this from the photographer Kevin Worrall, also assigned to this story. He too has had to play hide-and-seek with Potter. We talk over the phone about the pressure Dean might feel from sponsors or magazines to push it, and feel a bit like the "Eiger birds" in the Alps, vultures ready to pick at scraps of excitement or tragedy.

Pretty much by chance, Worrall caught Potter below the *Nose*. The route was crowded. Dean waited for an opening to reach Sickle Ledge five pitches up then went for it. He passed several parties and got as far as the swing into the Stoveleg Cracks before bailing in the confusion caused by encountering another speed team.

I didn't get a pretty picture. Dean, too, seemed to get a reality check. Single-cam aid in the A1 cracks of Half Dome is one thing, but on the *Nose*, Potter found himself unbelayed on dicey fixed pins, trying to weave through a tangle of other parties' ropes. When Potter reached the ground, Worrall said he seemed preoccupied, distracted by something, maybe a woman. "I've got to get a better system," Potter said. It was that evening that the deer-tourist incident occurred.

Last thing I heard, Potter had hit the road and left the crowded Valley behind, gone to Estes Park and Red Rocks. He had a good day soloing on Longs Peak—four hours car to car to the summit via the Diamond's *Casual Route*, and just as we went to press he pulled off the El Cap/Half Dome link-up.

Fame first struck Potter in the spring of 1998 when he was living a hermit boulderer's life out of his van in Mill Creek, above Moab, Utah. He was talented on the rock but alienated from the local scene for complex reasons, the simplest being that he had chopped bolts (on routes he had previously free soloed, says Potter, or which had cracks), and because he had a wigged-out girlfriend who liked to accompany him to the crag naked, which made him unpopular with couples.

But life was good. The occasional pang of bitterness only strengthened Potter's resolve on the rock. He avoided the climbing social hours at the Moab Diner and any climbing that required a rope or partner, and hid out in the paradise of Mill Creek, with its secluded yoga rocks and sandstone walls that yielded well to the skills of a lanky white boy honed on New Hampshire face climbing and fresh from four straight seasons in Hueco.

In the sandstone mazes outside Moab, Dean linked the moves on an 80-foot roof-crack boulder problem called *The Crack House* (unrated). The problem is one of the longest and hardest roof-cracks in the country, but it didn't get Potter noticed outside Moab. That happened when he completed another of his projects, a 40-foot free solo he called *King Tut*. Soon after, an eye-catching photograph appeared in a Wild Things ad, captioned in small, subtle letters that read: "Dean Potter, onsight, first ascent, solo of *King Tut*—5.13a."

"Onsight 5.13?" many people wondered. The photo showed Potter way off the deck, on thin climbing that looked like it could be that hard. Potter, however, was quick to set the record straight.

King Tut has a super-highball bouldering crux—V7 or "5.13a," depending on your preference. He worked it out with multiple crashpad jumps, hence his ascent was "onsight" only in the sense that he never weighted a rope. Above the crux, the top-out involved bona fide hard onsight soloing, but the Wild Things photo actually shows a different route, an established 5.11+ sport climb that begins on a ledge 40 feet off the ground, where *King Tut* ends. Potter soloed this route, onsight, to reach the cliff top after completing *King Tut*. In a twisted way, the mix-up is fitting for Potter's public debut.

Before the recent flood of his image onto the magazine pages, Potter had sprayed plentifully about the evils of publicity seekers, and jibing this new fame with his personal philosophy has taken some work. He is thoughtful, frank, and honest, but quick to the defense. "I think there's a humongous difference between someone who seeks publicity and gets it, and someone who doesn't seek publicity and gets it," he says.

"Dean doesn't want to be in the limelight, on the one hand," Worrall muses, "but he knows he has to milk the limelight so he doesn't have to work."

Dean Potter was born in Fort Leavenworth Prison Hospital, Kansas, in April 1972, and grew up behind two older sisters on a dozen different military bases from New Hampshire to Israel. He was the only son of an army colonel father and yoga-practicing mother, and in high school in New Hampshire he was a seemingly normal cross-country and basketball star. Then, at age 17, he and a classmate named John found Joe English—a scruffy 200-foot granite cliff on an off-limits section of the local military base.

On their first day out, Dean and John swarmed up the slippery slabs, ropeless in their Converse All-Stars. Dean says that on a return visit he found their second solo route had been 5.10. Next, John started up another smooth line.

"He did something he couldn't reverse and took this humongous twenty-five-foot ground fall," says Potter, his eyebrows rising with mirth at the memory. "From then on we loved climbing."

The Joe English outings, of course, were "top secret," but Dean's parents caught on as his grades began to slip. Like most teenagers on the fast track toward becoming climbing bums, he missed the maximum allowed number of school days, squeaking through only by merit of his previous honor-roll and track-star status.

His equipment improved—a little. A local shop sold him climbing shoes, some "wacky" chocks that had been gathering dust in the store, and an odd-length rope that constantly had the pair coming up short at belays. On their first lead, at a crag near Pawtuckaway, John led 40 feet, placed a single wobbly nut, climbed 5 feet more, and jumped. Potter tells me this story as a typical "amazing we survived" beginners tale, but I think of his recent antics on Half Dome and wonder if his "expert" days are any safer.

Climbing went by the wayside for a while as Potter entered university in New Hampshire and competed in rowing, soon at the international level.

Dean confides that in rowing he was "driven solely to beat other people." Something about this motivation, or his lifestyle, or the pressure of competing, started to bug him. He missed the purity of climbing. After a year and a half away from the rock, Dean drove back to spend a peaceful day at his old climbing area, Pawtuckaway. Next day he dropped out of rowing and out of school.

To Dean's shock, his teammates didn't care about his strange epiphany. He'd been "stroke" (lead rower) and he'd screwed up the team. "They wanted to fight me," he says. "I had thought of them as friends." But then as now, Dean was on his own program.

Flat broke, Dean hitched up to North Conway and pitched a lonely tent among the black flies in the woods below Cathedral Ledge. Soon he met a small cadre of local climbers his age—Charley and Billy Bentley, Stevie Damboise, "Greeno," and "Little Mattie."

Life improved greatly when Wild Things owners John and Titoune Bouchard took pity on Dean and—as they had other young climbers such as Scott Franklin—gave him a job. They moved him into a cabin they owned near the crags and even lent him a car. He later wrecked the car when he hit a moose on a delivery run through Pinkham Notch, but as Titoune relates the story, she has the fond tone of a mother speaking about a son. "Dean was dependable and did what he said he was going to do," she says.

Potter settled into an idyllic college-drop-out life, bar tacking for Wild Things, clipping bolts at Rumney, and working through the classic climbs at Cathedral Ledge. His favorite thing was cruising solo up and down the 5.9s and 5.10s on Cathedral's Upper Left Side, routes like *Nutcracker*, *Recompense*, and *Book of Solemnity*. Within a year he was climbing 5.13. In summer 1991 most of the young North Conway clan moved to Colorado or Montana, where Little Mattie had actually said, "The streets are paved with gold." It wasn't all gold. Dean liked small towns and Big Granite, and Boulder's traffic jams and sandstone cliffs offered neither. After a few months of couch surfing Potter found himself living "under a coffee table somewhere" in Missoula, Montana, sewing golf bags. That fall he decided to try something new.

On Thanksgiving Day, Dean—sporting dreadlocks in those days—started as cook at "Pete's," the famous climbing hostel just outside the bouldering Mecca of Hueco Tanks, Texas. He stayed all winter and repeated the stint for four years, switching from cook at Pete's, where he felt morally obligated to be responsible, to state park host, where he didn't.

Potter, Ian Glass, and a few others formed a small local elite. Potter confesses to burning off visiting climbers with the same kind of competitive glee that characterized his rowing days. "Dean was real cocky and he wasn't that good," says Scott Leonard, a visiting Coloradan who met him at the time. Then the Euros arrived.

First to show were the Swiss, Elie Chevieux and Fred Nicole. The first evening at camp, Fred and Dean struck up a conversation, and Fred, who had shown up at the boulders sporting flashy dance attire, related that he'd just completed his three-year project, *Bain de Sang*—9a.

"I thought that was kind of unlikely," says Potter. "I mean, who's this guy wearing disco clothes? I was like, '5.15? Yeah right, buddy.'"

The local yahoos (Dean's term) took Chevieux and Nicole on the standard sandbag tour. Both flashed or nearly flashed most of the area's hardest problems. Chevieux had a smooth, uncanny technique, and no one had seen anything like Nicole's raw power. The humbling was good for Dean. In the face of international talent, hubris gave way to more of a team spirit.

In the early 1990s, before park regulations crushed the easy lifestyle, winter in Hueco was the heartbeat of American bouldering. Four seasons there tuned Potter's skills and provided an ever-changing parade of elite climbers to learn from.

Dean tells the story of *The Feather* (V11), one of Hueco's best problems. He and Will Nazarian discovered the beautiful overhanging wall high on West Mountain, sculpted like the imprint of a huge feather. Captivated, they soon found a sequence of holds, but neither could do the moves. Others tried the problem, but no one succeeded. At the time, influenced by Nicole, the locals had latched onto a simple, powerful climbing style. "Fred never kneebars," they'd say. "He doesn't need to." The much-attempted *Feather* remained unclimbed. Then, Nicole arrived for the season and promptly sent the route. With a kneebar.

Another influential visitor was the French climber Marc Le Menestrel. Less interested in pure difficulty than Nicole, Marc sought out the most beautiful lines, often the high ones. He climbed brilliantly, but Potter was most impressed by the energy Marc spent on helping others. He genuinely seemed to care as much about their projects as his own. The camaraderie was contagious, and with concrete benefits. When the group had done well, the evening parties were fueled by the fires of each person's success. This was much more fun than the lone gloating to be enjoyed after burning off one's partners.

According to bouldering ace Hillary Harris (now married to Dean's friend Charlie Bentley), Dean and Ian were "the best spotters in the world," safely catching previously unthinkable falls. Potter and Glass were proud of their "spot technology" and the French photographer and Fontainebleau boulderer Stephan Denys—who met Dean in 1995, Potter's last season in Hueco—says the spotting helped push the hardest problems. Denys also remembers Dean's enthusiasm and fun-loving nature.

"With Dean and Ian, we were joking about climbers like Todd [Skinner] and Scott [Milton]," says Denys, "because they were always training in the house, and got out on the rock for one day after three of rest or training. We were at the opposite—drinking, smoking, 'talking shit' all the days, but always out, with the boulders.

"I can remember how Dean was behind everyone to push you to do the best. He was not so strong as he seems now, but was doing maybe around V8. I was really happy to see his progression. He was always the one who stopped last to climb, always finishing the climbing day in the dark. I really hope he is still the same, simple and full of good energy—even if I've seen he has cut his long hair now!"

Those endless days of "pimping tough in the boulder fields" of sunburned shoulders and shredded fingertips were soon to be only a memory, another bridge to burn. Dean Potter as Official Park Host was a strained concept. "I was supposed to be enforcing the rules," Potter says, "but my site had the most illegal things going on." It was soon time to move on.

One summer between Hueco stints, and on the Diamond in Colorado, Dean met Steph Davis. No one had heard of Potter then, nor had they heard of Davis, soon to become one of the most respected all-around female rock climbers in the country.

"At first she was way standoffish," Potter says, "cuz I looked like a weenie." It was Potter's first trip to the Diamond, which tops out near 14,000 feet, and in typical Potter-style showmanship he sported shorts, slippers, and a pink windshirt. Later, after Dean and his partner blazed up the wall, descended, and watched Davis finish her route, she gave him a second look. The pair spent time in Hueco and Salt Lake City, and Steph introduced Dean to his next "home," Moab. Both climbers' ambition and intensity would make for a tumultuous relationship, and they split after two years. "Dean is one of the most talented rock climbers I've seen," Davis says today.

April 3. It is snowing again in the Valley. The grass is green but the oaks are still without leaves. Yesterday, the sun came out for a few hours, melting huge sheets of ice from the *Shield* headwall, which blew diagonally across the *Nose* and shattered into fragments that landed over by *Sea of Dreams*. You could hear the crash from El Cap Meadow nearly a mile away.

Potter and I have been talking philosophy. I ask him what he sees for the future and he muses about Chamonix granite and Kyrgyzstan, about a job with one of his sponsors or becoming a successful alpinist and entrepreneur like his old boss John Bouchard.

"But I don't really look so much into the future that way," Potter says. "A big part of my lifestyle is the now. I love how I feel when I'm caught up in my climbing and living for that moment. . . . I tend to spend all my money and not care if I'll have any more money. I'm super nice to everybody because I'm not really thinking about the past or what's going to go on."

I've seen this "super nice" side of Potter, this dedication to spreading "positive energy" to not hold grudges, fuel rivalries, or bad-mouth others. Perhaps it is partly an act, a way for Potter to set himself above, but I decide that it doesn't really matter. The action is what matters, and the results.

Another climbing season is beginning in the Valley. In fact, this is merely a pause—just before the recent snows, Dean and Miles climbed *Tangerine Trip* in 11:56, slashing six hours off the record. Yesterday Dean found a buyer for his portaledge, which he'd slept in only once, last fall when he was trying to free climb the *Salathé*, before he injured his finger. In fact, that's how Potter got into speed climbing. Just before he was ready to redpoint the *Salathé* he pulled a tendon bouldering and couldn't climb 5.11. Instead, he went up on the walls and climbed 5.10 AO—which was fast. He was nursing this finger injury, in fact, when he soloed Half Dome. "It was a great feeling of freedom," Potter says, "when I realized I could be injured and still enjoy climbing."

It's strange to an outsider, this lust for speed, this obsession with the stopwatch. Yet there's another side to it, a simple joy in traversing so much rock in a day. If traditional big-wallers are wall rats who live on the stark cliffs, the speed climbers are wall birds who soar and ride and return to comfortable nests in the meadows and forests by the Merced.

This simple joy merges into play. By far the most popular route among the young speed cadre is the *Royal Arches*, one of the Valley's easiest climbs. It is 1,000 feet long, 5.6, plus a fixed line for a pendulum. They run up the route together or alone, in all weather, typically several time a week. It's almost a cult activity. Miles and Cedar Wright even did it yesterday, in the brief window between snow showers that sent the ice crashing down off El Cap. Speed records never mean much unless you know the route, but for those who know *Royal Arches*, and its descent down the notorious North Dome gully, Dean's record will mean something: fifty-seven minutes car to car.

It's my last day in the Valley and all the roads out are "chains only." Four or five of us are bullshitting in the Lodge parking lot. As a visitor to Yosemite over the years, I'm always amazed at the tremendous appetite the locals have for bad-mouthing each other. Worrall blames it on Chief Tenaya's curse on all white men who dwell in the Valley.

And so, I'm not shocked when someone in the parking lot begins a classic Valley discourse on so-and-so's pitiful free-climbing ability and his less-than-record speed on some wall. Dean is standing with his feet wide apart and hands in pockets, gazing up through the massive branches of the oaks, not seeming to listen.

"Look how huge the flakes are," he says. The guy who'd been talking comes up short and everyone stares up at thousands of huge snowflakes that look like squares of cut tissue paper sifting down among the branches. When the conversation begins again it's about the snow, and how wet the slack lines are getting, and whether or not they should do *Royal Arches* again tomorrow.

PART FOUR: THE 2000s

THE 2000s: EL CAPITAN AND THE ROAD LESS TRAVELED

BY BETH RODDEN

Sometimes it's only in retrospect that you realize you're living in a "golden age." For me, looking back now on the 2000s through the lens of history, and seeing how lucky my then-husband, Tommy Caldwell, and I were to push free-climbing standards on El Capitan, I recognize we were living amidst one such era. Sure, it all began in 1988 with Todd Skinner and Paul Piana on the *Salathé Wall* and continued on into the 1990s with Lynn Hill freeing the *Nose* and the Huber Brothers leaving their mark on the Big Stone. But we were able to piggyback on their vision and success in a way that marked another golden age—at least it was for me, with my climbing.

I'd been enchanted by the Big Stone ever since I started climbing, at age 14. Hill freed the *Nose* in 1993, the year I first set foot in a climbing gym, and like most climber girls at that time, I wanted to follow in her footsteps. Each gym I went into had the iconic poster of Hill with her puffed-up hair, cutoff jean shorts, and purple tank top over her bronze skin. In big letters, the poster read, "It goes, boys." I didn't even know where El Cap was; I knew only that I wanted to be like Lynn when I grew up.

I spent my early years as a gym rat competing around the globe, and then slowly transitioned into sport climbing. At Smith Rock, I watched in awe as Jim Karn, Mike Pont, and Lynn floated up the smallest of holds. However, there was something about climbing bigger things, and flowing up long cracks, that grabbed my attention. Even though trad climbing was not in fashion, I wanted to see what it was all about.

In 1999, after lasting one semester in college, I convinced my parents to let me take a year off to pursue climbing. Halfway through that year, I drove into Yosemite Valley in my two-door Honda Civic. I spent the next two months sleeping in the trunk of my little car with the seats down and my feet in the trunk, eating cold canned soup for dinner, and trying to find partners each morning at the Yosemite Lodge cafeteria. I slowly made my way through iconic Valley climbs like the Royal Arches (group free solo), the *Good Book,* and the Rostrum. But for me, those were all steppingstones to El Cap, which I finally climbed via the *Nose* in spring 2000 with the master of the route, Hans Florine, and his then-wife, Jackie. Battling freezing temperatures, wind, and shaken nerves for the entirety of our successful three-day trip, I swore I'd never go back. Still, a few hours after summiting, back on the Valley floor with a hot meal in my stomach, I was plotting my return.

A couple months later, I found myself back up on El Cap, this time with Tommy Caldwell. Tommy and I knew each other from the comp circuit, and he was fresh off a free ascent of the *Salathé.* A master sport climber and also the son of a mountain guide, he had trad climbing deep in his roots. At the time, very few people were free climbing on El Cap. I had heard that *Lurking Fear*, up slabs, splitter cracks, and bullet granite on the left side, was ripe for free climbing—Steve Schneider had freed all but a few feet. After a couple months of effort, Tommy and I pulled it off. We were just kids, climbing on the best playground anyone can imagine. And yet, nearly two decades later, the climb has yet to see an all-free repeat (though many have tried).

After *Lurking Fear,* Tommy and I, now married, would spend every spring and fall in the Valley, living out of a Chevy van and poaching showers at Curry Village. From 2001 to 2006, we focused our attention solely on El Cap. Tommy made his way through nearly every free climb there, establishing roughly half of them. I joined him for team free ascents of the *Nose* and *El Corazon,* but remained the dedicated wall mule for the rest. Over time, we dialed in our systems—stashing food and water, rapping in to work crux pitches, fixing ropes, Mini Traxioning, and so on. These techniques (new at the time) have now become standard.

Freeing the *Nose* was an ultimate dream, if for nothing other than the chance to walk in Hill's footsteps. In 2005, during the two months Tommy and I were working the line, we encountered thirty or forty other teams on the route. Because free climbing on El Cap was still so rare, these parties would sit and watch while we worked the moves. Similarly, we tried to be as respectful of their efforts as possible—after all, some parties were only in the country for six days, four of those on the *Nose.* Who were we to think we had more right to climb than them?

That October, Tommy and I made a successful four-day push, swapping leads and free climbing the most famous route in the world. Tommy went back two days later and freed it in a day, with relative ease.

While Tommy was going through his El Cap rampage, I began to seek out shorter, one-pitch crack climbs by scouring the magazines and asking friends for local beta. It turned out that hard crack climbs were rare, which attracted me to them even more. The singular beauty of the lines inspired me, the way these thin fissures slashed the rock, featured just enough to provide purchase. In 2004, after repeating many of America's hardest thin cracks, I freed *The Optimist*, a 5.14b tips seam/layback up a blank, overhanging wall at the Marsupials area at Smith Rock. The first-ascent bug had bitten me.

After *The Optimist*, Tommy and I settled in Yosemite, building a new home in Yosemite West. I eventually found an old Ron Kauk project in Upper Cascade Creek that became not only the hardest thing I've climbed, but also a route that forced me to reexamine my relationship with climbing. *Meltdown* is a short crack, about 75 feet, next to the waterfall. The polished stone, mega-thin locks, and off-balance laybacking required unending patience and flawless technique. I beat my head against the wall for six months, slowly making progress, even if it was just sorting out a new foot movement or gear placement on any given day. As winter came, the waterfall grew in size, spraying the rock. Moving into spring, a series of heavy, wet snows replenished the falls. I named the route *Meltdown* due to the thawing snow, but more notably because of the fits I threw each day when the spray prevented me from climbing.

I was all consumed, wrapping my entire self-worth up in completing the route. *Meltdown* forced me to climb harder than I ever had, and to be brave in ways I didn't know I was capable of. With first ascents, you must contend with the unknown—I faced so many moments of doubt on this fierce crack: *Is the route even possible? Will my gear hold? Will my feet slip? Will my finger tendons pop? Would the rock ever be dry enough?* After six months of effort, on Valentine's Day 2008, I completed the first ascent. The spray was large that day, but something clicked in me. Right before I started climbing, I said out loud, "Just do this, Beth. You know it; you are strong enough." My body didn't feel as strong as on other attempts, but my mind was focused and determined. I fought my way through the crux finger locks, and placed the gear perfectly. Toward the top, my arms went rubbery with fatigue but I could see the anchor bolts, and wasn't going to stop until I clipped them. A few minutes later, I was balancing on the cold-to-the-touch finishing slab, not really believing I had just done it. I was proud, but mostly relieved—I'd climbed through two finger injuries during the climb and didn't want to sustain another.

After a decade of pushing my body to the limit, it had started to break down, marking the end of my golden age on Yosemite granite and also—perhaps not coincidentally—the end of my marriage. Still, I had no regrets. During a period when bouldering and sport climbing were in fashion, Tommy and I had pursued the road less traveled. I look back now and see how lucky we were to have these routes relatively to ourselves. These days, freeing El Cap is so popular that teams line up to do *Freerider* and other El Cap free walls, routes that took years to even get a repeat.

After *Meltdown*, plagued by injuries, I saw my climbing ability decrease from 5.14 to 5.12 to 5.9 to 5.6. I needed repair and recovery. Settling into a new marriage, and a quieter, less driven life in Yosemite, I started climbing with my neighbors and recreational climbers, on lines I would have scoffed at before—Valley classics I'd overlooked because they were more moderate. As I reconnected with the stone, I realized that climbing is woven into me; it's who I am.

Nowadays I'm the mom of a little boy, Theo, and am raising him in Yosemite Valley. And although I've taken a decade-long hiatus from the Big Stone, the best thing about these great climbs is that they stay virtually the same no matter how many years go by and how many ascents they see. El Cap is still there, just as sheer and majestic as the first day I saw it, rolling down out of the Wawona Tunnel as I traveled into the Valley from my parents' place in Davis. One day I'll venture back up there, but for now, I'm happy staying close to the ground and climbing with my people.

NOW GOING

FEBRUARY 2000, NO. 191

BY CONRAD ANKER

"The best climber is the one having the most fun," the legendary Alex Lowe (1958–1999) famously quipped. And though his ascents on ice, rock, and in the alpine are forever engrained in the annals of climbing literature, it was his infectious attitude—a tireless, optimistic approach to both climbing and life—that left the biggest impression on those close to him. In 1999, an avalanche on the Himalayan giant Shishapangma took him and cameraman David Bridges. Lowe's close friend Conrad Anker was struck by the slide as well, and though injured, made it home. Anker recalls his mentor, Lowe.

Alex, David, and I are walking along a glacier on a clear fall morning at the base of Shishapangma, an 8,000-meter peak in the Tibetan Himalaya. A large ice and snow avalanche takes us by surprise, trapping us in its run-out zone. In 30 seconds, the world as we know it has changed forever. Avalanches are very real, all too real, risks for alpinists, mountaineers, and skiers. We acknowledge them and justify being there by minimizing our exposure to them. Nothing comes for free—the risk of death is something that we accept to play in the mountains. Yet as much as we intellectually accept the risk, consequences can be as unexpected as they are lethal.

Writing a tribute to a lost friend is incredibly painful. And both climbers lost on the 5th of October on the south face of Shishapangma in that avalanche were friends, one a very close companion for nine years and the other a friend for three weeks. With them I'd laughed, climbed, worked, and shared. Both Alex Lowe and

David Bridges were the type of people you seldom meet, but never forget. It's likely each person touched by Alex or David could write several pages of colorful memories. To collect all this is beyond me, so I share with you a few moments I spent with Alex.

Alex was best known to his peers in the climbing and adventure communities as a man of incredible motivation with strength to match. Being able to climb hard and fast is one thing, but the real Alex who affected me was the man who loved his family, and who cared deeply for and offered enthusiasm to everyone he met.

Looking at Alex's résumé speaks volumes for the ability and drive he had for climbing. Seldom can anyone excel at the myriad climbing disciplines. Doing two laps on the summit of Everest from high camp in a week and flashing the standard-setting *Supercrack* in the Gunks are but two examples of Alex's diversity.

The seven expeditions I shared with Alex contained some of the finest moments of my life. Being on an expedition with Alex meant running on "Alex time." We'd wake up earlier, get going sooner, and climb harder, boosted by vast amounts of coffee products. Our favorite saying to each other as we departed camp or left from a rest stop was a Sherpa phrase, emulated with a smile: "Now going." I remember the spring in our step it would bring—and now that Alex has left us it has become a more spiritual meaning.

JUNE 1995

The second week of June, Alex and I were sharing a tent on the southeast fork of the Kahiltna Glacier in Alaska. The season had been uneventful from a climbing standpoint. Alex and Steve Swenson's plans to climb the East Face of Mount Huntington had been thwarted by 9 feet of fresh snow. Alex's and my plans to climb the *Cassin* on Denali sans bivy had been sidetracked by two rescues of Spanish and Taiwanese climbers, who had been trapped by the weather above 19,000 feet. In both rescues Alex was "the man" leading the teams on the sheer volume of his energy. We'd had some fun hanging out on Denali, but now the playtime was over and with a day to spare on the glacier we were thinking of pizza, beer, and the journey home.

Around midnight, I awoke to Alex sitting bolt upright with a wild gleam in his eyes. A gleeful smile broke out on his face. "How about trying the *Moonflower* alpine-style?"

It was classic Alex. The more improbable the outcome, the greater his exuberance and eagerness for the project. We piled out of the tent and began sorting gear, waking a Taiwanese guest we had invited into our spare tent, largely filled with gear and food.

"Going West Buttress?" he asked.

"No—Mount Hunter!" we exclaimed, pointing toward the 4,000-foot *Moon-flower Buttress*. He looked absolutely blank. The last time we had talked, we had discussed flying out together. The incomprehension was with us, too. Feeling like two truants playing hooky from school, we skied up the glacier to Hunter's base. "Is this normal?!" That had been another of our old jokes, rallying cries during an adventure. One pack, two ropes, a stove, a bunch of gear, and smiles . . . who knows? It seemed logical.

We led in blocks of four pitches and joked about this being a frozen El Cap. Same mind-set, different medium. The mixed pitches of each of the rock bands provided the needed dose of focused reality, while the ice aprons lent the perfect alpine feel. We climbed for twenty hours straight, sat on a ledge, brewed hot chocolate, and watched a surreal rescue of a snowboarder from Denali's 14,000-foot medical camp. When we tried to move out in the predawn shade we were exhausted, operating at half capacity. Regardless, we led on to the final two pitches. We were tired, and with Foraker sporting a lenticular cloud, felt it was best to descend. Five hours of continuous rappelling got us back to our skis, with a short jaunt to the tent and then home.

We didn't summit the climb; we didn't even finish the last two technical pitches, but loved the climbing for what it was—one pitch at a time, a good fun time. Alex continually amazed me by making the largest, most ambitious projects seem reasonable. Knowing the way was uncertain brought him a happiness that many people spend a lifetime seeking.

What else do I remember of this climb? On the way home we had an afternoon to kill in Anchorage before our flights. Alex suggested we go to the hospital and visit the four rescued Spanish climbers. Alex brought the injured climbers smiles, laughter, and the same invincible spirit that he had given me on Mount Hunter. Several years later I met one of them on a trail in the Himalaya, as one is likely to do in our family of climbers, and with tears in his eyes he wanted me to thank Alex for his visit to that hospital. This man probably saw twenty people a day in the hospital, and the one encounter that changed his life was when Alex bounded into the room with a smile and a handful of espresso beans.

SEPTEMBER 1996

In 1996 Alex and I ventured to the Annapurna Himal to try the Southeast Ridge of Annapurna III (7,555 meters). We optimistically set out to climb this 2,000-meter route alpine-style and descend an unknown ridge. The season was wetter than normal; the afternoon buildup was depositing several inches of snow daily. We kept our eye on the route, hoping it would get in shape, and decided to "warm up" on the south face of Annapurna IV, a lower-angle face to a moderate ridge. A sucker hole of clear weather lured us to the ridge. To aid our acclimatization process we pitched camp 1,100 feet below the summit. And then the weather changed. The stars turned to snow and our "warm-up" got serious.

Our tent caved in after the first day so we tried to descend in the storm. The conditions had deteriorated to blowing snow, 30-foot visibility, and cold temperatures. Of greater concern was the condition of the slopes we were trying to climb down loaded with tons of snow. We stood on the slope, stalled, waiting for a break in the clouds to see the next bit of ridge. To generate some warmth, I took off my pack and began digging a wind shelter. The wind shelter turned into a small cave as we decided it was best to sit this one out.

By the first evening we had a nice platform, the second evening we built a chess set out of a salmon wrapper, the third we figured out it was warmer to zip our bags together, the fourth we tried melting water without a stove, and on the morning of the fifth day the slope was stable enough for the descent.

The lull allowed us a wet walk to basecamp and then the weather locked down for a week. The route, when it finally reappeared from under the clouds, was coated in snow. It never came into shape and we left early. Again, no success if the yardstick for success is a summit, but we came away closer friends and with a new appreciation for our own limits.

Our plane tickets were the unchangeable type and we had to enjoy a week in Katmandu before flying home. For Alex, the wait in Katmandu was the hardest part of the trip. Alex longed for his family while climbing, but when he was stuck and unable to do anything about it the love and yearning grew. My respect for Alex the climber is great—tales of his feats are shared around campfires throughout the world. My true admiration for Alex, though, was his ability to raise a family and do these amazing climbs. Alex's most important piece of gear on any climb was a recent snapshot of his wife Jenni and three sons, Max, Sam, and Isaac. This photo, always folded and reinforced with duct tape, was his source of motivation and the ultimate card when decisions were to be made. The strength of Alex, I believe, came not from his famous appetite for training, but from home and the intense love in his life.

OCTOBER 1999

On the morning of October 5, David Bridges, the high-altitude cameraman for the expedition, Alex, and I were on a quick hike from our advance basecamp to the base of our intended route on the south face of Shishapangma. We left a few minutes after 8 and decided to take a slightly longer approach than the rest of our crew to the base of the wall, one that involved hiking up a gradual glacier. Andrew McLean chose to hike up the glacier's edge, taking a more direct route through jumbled moraine. This was a rest day, a day without a specific goal. We had set out for a bit of exercise, to get the blood circulating before the afternoon clouds streamed in from the south.

At 9:10 David, Alex, and I crested a small ridge, from which we had a nice vantage to the south. Not far away we spotted Andrew, standing where a small rock promontory met the glacier. We waved at him and decided to hike over and descend the way he had come up. We were hiking along with joy in our step, feeling a simple happiness just because we were in the mountains. And then it happened. A slab of wind-loaded snow cut loose from the col between Shishapangma and Pungpa Ri, 6,000 feet above us. Alex noticed the avalanche, a mass of snow, ice, and wind moving at us faster than we could comprehend.

"Holy shit," he yelled. The avalanche grew as it descended the 6,000 feet toward the low-angle glacier below the south face of Shishapangma. Within 30 seconds, time took on a new dimension. There was something amiss. This was the type of avalanche we had seen many times in the Himalaya, but fortunately had never been caught in, the type we would watch and then comment on how beautiful it was, this force of nature, and how it would not be a good thing to be in its path. This time we were.

Instinct took over. We all ran in different directions. My synapses were firing on a very basic level and I had no time to evaluate the options, no time to confer. We simply acted. David and Alex ran down the slope—I ran across it. The avalanche hit us with a great, sudden intensity. For the few seconds it passed over and tumbled me 70 feet down the slope I thought of nothing. Only that death had finally come. Then the pressure and pounding lessened and it dawned on me that I was alive.

The first thing I thought of was Alex and Dave—where were they? I walked around scanning the slope that scant seconds earlier I had been traversing with my best friends. The worst of my fears started as a silent scream and then hammered into a deafening roar. I was looking for them, holding my watch, which had been torn off, in my hand, watching the seconds tick into minutes, knowing the hope of finding my comrades was waning with each step. I knew they were buried yet it felt to me as if they had vanished into the sky, lifted by a force far greater than humans and carried to a place we can only imagine.

The old questions we ask ourselves about climbing took on new meaning. We knew the risk. Should we have done something different? Are the risks we take worth the rewards they bring? What drives us to climb? The exploration of the unknown has led humanity to where we are today. The quest for knowledge, the willingness to accept risk for an unknown outcome, has allowed people to progress spiritually and intellectually. The thrill of discovering new reaches remains with many of us, in all walks of life. Those of us who find this calling and pursue it in the mountains are fortunate. For Alex this is what climbing was about, the exploration of the soul, the trust and learning gained from attempting something difficult and improbable.

I believe that Alex would not have been the caring person and shining spirit he was if he had not climbed. He found his calling in the wild places. When I ask myself if this tragedy is worth the reward climbing brings, I answer "no." Yet on a larger scale, when I think of the billions of people on our planet and how only a few of them can inspire and motivate others to realize their potential, then the question and answer aren't so black-and-white. It doesn't lessen the pain of loss, yet it brings a small bit of solace to think that so many of us have benefited from knowing and being inspired by someone who was able to use climbing as a vehicle toward human realization.

Thinking back to yesterday, I appreciate why I come to the mountains: not to conquer them but to immerse myself in their incomprehensible immensity—so much bigger than [we are]; to better comprehend humility and patience balanced in harmony, with the desire to push hard; to share what the hills offer and to share it in the long term with good friends, and ultimately with my own sons.

—Alex's last dispatch for the MountainZone.com website

THE *DIHEDRAL WALL*

OCTOBER 2004, NO. 234

BY TOMMY CALDWELL

Before the Dawn Wall, there was its counterpart on El Capitan, the Dihedral Wall (VI 5.14a). To succeed on this mammoth project, Tommy Caldwell trained for and rehearsed the route like a madman, working out the moves until his fingers bled, his body quivered, and his feet throbbed. Then he went down and bouldered until dark, running laps on V10s and harder. During the process, he beat himself down to the point where finishing the route became a question of "if." When all was said and done—and still exhausted after three weeks of rest—he wrote: "I doubt that I will ever do another climb as amazing as the Dihedral Wall. But then again, you never know." In 2015, after seven years of work, he and Kevin Jorgeson established the Dawn Wall, at VI 5.14d the world's most difficult big-wall free climb.

"I don't know if I have this in me anymore."

For the length of my professional climbing career, I shunned these words. I have always taken the theory that I cannot back down even an inch or I will never reach my true potential. But here I was, 1,800 feet up El Cap, feeling like I might finally be at the end of my rope. My arms were seizing every time I lifted them above my head. Blood was seeping from holes in my fingers, knees, elbows, shins, and forehead. I had been abusing my body on this climb for over two months and I was tired. Deeply tired, in both body and mind. Several times over the past two days I had spent more than an hour on a redpoint burn, only to pump out or have a foothold crumble, sending me down to repeat the abuse. I had fallen over a dozen times, having to reclimb pitches each time, and it had taken its toll. Now I was only one pitch from sure success, feeling like I could go no further.

The pain and suffering started in October 2003 when I decided that I needed the experience of soloing a wall. I chose the *Dihedral Wall* of El Capitan because it was one of the most obvious lines on El Cap, the third route accomplished on the wall after the *Nose* and the *Salathé*, and I wanted to recon something that might go free.

I was not the first climber to think of freeing the *Dihedral*. Alan Lester and Pete Takeda free climbed 50 percent of the route in the early 1990s. Todd Skinner and Paul Piana worked on it extensively in 2001 and 2002, pioneering the variations that would eventually allow a complete free ascent.

When I soloed it last fall, it looked nearly impossible. Steep, flaring dihedrals stretched on for hundreds of feet without break. The cracks were thin throughout the bottom half, only occasionally big enough to accept more than a willing fingertip, and up higher they became bottomless and flaring. Often the cracks petered out completely. Face holds seemed to appear, just big enough and close enough together to make me think the moves might go free, but I had serious doubts. If the *Dihedral Wall* could somehow be climbed, it would be one of the most extraordinary free routes I had ever laid eyes on.

I came to Yosemite early this spring—alone, since Beth Rodden, my wife and usual El Cap partner, was still recovering from a broken foot. When I arrived in the Valley, the weather was crisp and clear—perfect for anything my heart desired.

I spent my first days bouldering. Most of my bouldering time in Yosemite had been after big El Cap projects, and my memories were of mosquitoes and greasy fingertips, but this time I had perfect conditions. I had some of my best Valley bouldering days, putting up some new problems—yet something was missing. I wanted an adventure. I wanted to dive into something huge that would take over my time, drive me, and bring me to the next level. So I headed up on the *Dihedral Wall*.

I worked the route solo at first, toproping on my fixing lines. Alone, I was better able to appreciate the beauty and magnitude of the climb. I did not have to worry about anyone else's concerns, and this allowed me to focus more intensely. I got used to the silence. I memorized every gigantic dihedral, fingertip edge, and hairline fracture. I took time to watch the swallows tackle each other in midair and plummet toward the ground, separating just before the treetops. I would say out loud, "That is so cool," even though no one was around to hear me. The view from the route became etched in my mind, as did the thousands of moves I rehearsed. I was alone with my thoughts and motivation.

The *Dihedral Wall* route consumed me. I climbed more intensely and for longer each day than I ever had before. I climbed four or five days a week from sunrise to sunset. On my biggest days I would start at 5 a.m., climb from the ground to the end of the last hard pitch 1,800 feet up the wall, rappel back to the ground by noon, eat lunch, and then go bouldering until dark. I would call Beth at night and fall asleep on the phone. I climbed so much that my fingers wore down to bloody stumps and my toenails fell off. My muscles were so sore so much of the time that I forgot what it was like to feel normal.

Trips home to visit Beth consisted of mainly sleep and food. "What's wrong with you?" she would ask, but deep inside she knew.

Returning to the Valley meant starting up my workhorse schedule again. At the end of each day I would stagger to the car, then try to repair my various wounds. I'd shove food down my throat as quickly as possible, usually cold burritos or sometimes just a PowerBar. I would find a place to sleep and pass out as soon as my head hit the pillow. On a few occasions I fell asleep sitting straight up while cooking dinner, only to be rousted by the rangers telling me I could not sleep there.

The *Dihedral* raised my tolerance for pain and frustration. It also gave me great satisfaction. I was living each day to its absolute fullest. I was working toward a very definite goal and it was bringing me to a new level in my climbing. It may sound weird, but normally Yosemite makes me weak. I usually return home unable to do the most basic power problems or sport climbs. The huge days, endless cracks, and lack of powerful moves turn me into a 5.12 sport climber without fail. But the *Dihedral Wall* kept me strong. On rainy days in the gym I was stronger than I had been before the Valley season. Bouldering in the afternoons left me with a smile on my face because I was able to run laps on hard problems like *Thriller* and *The Force*.

It became obvious that this route would be a huge step above anything I had climbed. It was absurdly sustained. Most of the existing hard free routes on El Cap had only a few 5.13 pitches, but of the first fifteen pitches of the *Dihedral*, one was 5.14, one 5.13d, three 5.13c, three 5.13b, and four 5.12. On top of that, these pitches were sustained. I had to really concentrate from the start to the end of each pitch—none were one-move wonders.

A month into the project, Adam Stack joined me. The scene on the wall completely changed. He was fresh off a free ascent of the *Salathé Wall* and flying higher than ever. We spent hours on our portaledge together, laughing and telling jokes while talking about how lucky we were to be here, the most amazing place on the planet, working on such an incredible climb. With Adam, there was never more than ten minutes without laughter. He would claim that if he "squatted" in one place long enough he could own it, taking the Homestead Act of 1862 to a new level. (I had to break it to him that I doubted the Act applied in national parks or El Cap, and that it had expired in 1976.) Whenever he would free a move or pitch for the first time he would say, "Do you smell something? Oh yeah, I'm the shit!" Adam's energy transformed the effort and helped push me even harder.

After another month, the route started to come together. I could link long sections of pitches, then entire pitches, and soon I had toproped most of the hard climbing. I had originally thought of this as a recon season, since Beth was out of commission. Now, with the perfect weather and the amount of climbing I was doing, I was fitting several seasons into a couple of months.

I developed a plan of attack, and picked a style for my ascent. Climbers spend countless hours debating style in an attempt to establish a social pecking order, and honestly it reminds me of the reasons I did not like high school. I decided to avoid hanging belays and climb from stance to stance, in a continuous ascent from the ground, because it was the best style I thought I could pull off. I believe people should always strive to do climbs in the best style they think possible, but never criticize others for what they choose to do. El Cap is for having fun and having an adventure, not having fights and criticizing others—which does nothing but boost egos and show disrespect for the other people who share your same passion. As long as you are not harming the rock or the route for future ascents, and you are honest about what you have done and your style, you should be able to climb in whatever fashion you want.

Beth's foot was finally out of the cast, and she was now at her parents' house in Davis, only a three-hour drive away. When I told her I thought I could do the route, she offered to come along as belayer. On the wall she wore one normal approach shoe and one big mountain boot to protect her injured foot. It looked like she couldn't decide whether to go running or alpine climbing. Adam also volunteered to help out. I would have been completely astonished by their generosity if I hadn't seen it so many times before. They gave the moral, emotional, and physical support that would be as crucial to my effort on the *Dihedral* as any aspect of my climbing. Beth laughed off the sacrifice by assuring me that she could miss a few episodes of "Trading Spaces," and Adam was up for a few good days of jumaring and jokes. Three days before we were to start, Adam and I hauled five days' worth of supplies to the top of pitch nine. This prep day would allow us to climb without hauling for the first two days.

As everything fell into place I felt an increasing sense of excitement. Something started to grow inside me—my heart rate increased and I spent the nights tossing and turning, rehearsing the climb in my head. When should I start? How fast did I need to climb? How many times could I fall before running out of energy? I visualized the moves and gear placements over and over again: blue, then purple, then baby yellow. I was excited about the prospect of success and frightened of failure. So much was invested.

We began climbing at 5 in the morning on May 18. The weather was unseasonably cool, and perfect for free climbing. The rock was polished and the finger locks far apart—every time I reached I feared that my feet would slip and I would go skidding down the wall—but as the ground receded into the distance I got into the swing of things. I began to find the rhythm I had had up here for the past five weeks.

My conditioning paid off and I climbed the first four pitches in about an hour and a half. Beth said she was jumaring slower than I was climbing 5.12, and I was spurred on by that thought. On the fifth pitch I forgot half the rack and had to do 25-foot run-outs on 5.12 climbing. I took it in stride, and by the time I reached the crux pitch, at about 8 o'clock, I was feeling confident.

The crux pitch was a 120-foot bulge, overhanging for the majority of it, where the route exits the lower, left-facing dihedrals and moves out right onto the steep wall near *Cosmos*. It almost seemed like a bit of Céüse transported to El Cap. When working the route I was never able to link this pitch on toprope, but I was hoping that the psych of the redpoint attempt would help me. I was pretty sure that this would be the hardest free pitch on El Cap, and I knew I would have to climb flaw-lessly to do it. Remembering to breathe, remembering the sequence—and most of all remembering to try hard as hell—were all things I needed to do to get to the belay. I gave Beth a kiss and set off.

I started laybacking up a 1-foot-wide dihedral with no crack in the back. With few footholds on the smooth granite, I was only able to stay on the wall by pinch-ing the outside corner of the dihedral and pressing my feet hard against the wall, testing my shoe rubber to the max. I felt strain in my back, fingers, and neck, and just as the rock got steeper the seam opened up enough for fingers. With no foot-holds in sight I had to continue climbing without pause.

The crack ended and I made a full span right to a sloping ramp, then dynoed for a shallow finger lock. I was pumped now, and my body was visibly shaking. I did not even hear Beth's and Adam's screams of encouragement, which left them hoarse. Already at my limit I entered the next sequence, pressing my thumbs up underneath a small roof and stretching to an undercling far above my head. As I pulled into the undercling I began to feel dizzy. I fumbled for high crimpers, then pulled over into a "5.13 stance" on the slab above. My legs were shaking uncontrol-lably and my mind was racing. "Ten more feet and it will be over," I told myself. I focused, composed myself, and then delicately traversed on micro holds to the stance at the belay.

I felt overwhelming relief, and thanked my ten years of dedicated sport climb-ing for giving me the forearm endurance to get through this one. I had managed to do the crux of the route without falling. But I still had a hell of a lot of hard climbing ahead of me.

Beth and Adam jumared up and we set up the portaledge so I could recompose. Adam started talking about his upcoming trip to Alaska. "Maybe if I buy one of those bear rugs and wrap it around myself," he said, "the grizzly bears will think I'm one of them and will not eat me." With a puzzled look on his face he continued, "I just hope that a male grizzly bear doesn't mistake me for a female." Beth shook her head. My nervousness was quickly evaporating. As I racked for the next pitch I tried to block out the visual that Adam had just put in my head and focus on the climbing ahead.

The next pitch was 5.13b, very slabby and sharp—it reminded me of *Lurking Fear*. Doing it first try would be critical to saving my skin for the rest of the climb. I balanced my way from razor blade to razor blade and concentrated on keeping myself steady. I knew that the slightest shake would cause a foot or hand to slip. Beth and Adam were silent while I climbed; the only noise I heard was my own breathing. I slowly crept from hold to hold and after nearly an hour arrived at the anchor.

I had completed half the hard climbing for the day and it was only 10 in the morning. I was excited, but also knew that I would not be as fresh in the afternoon, not to mention the days to come. I knew that I was going to put my body and mind through incredible stress the next few days.

The next pitch was the Black Arch, a 200-foot arching crack that is one of the most striking features on El Cap. The sun hit the wall just as I started up. Usually for me this means the end of the climbing day, but the cool temps, along with a breeze, kept the conditions good.

I felt a bit hesitant, and slipped off after about 20 feet—my first fall of the route. I rested ten minutes, pulled my rope, and tried again. This time I pumped out after 30 feet. Figuring I had not rested long enough, Adam set up the portaledge and I rested for half an hour. "I can't believe you are still trying to climb. Normally you melt when the sun hits you," Beth said, trying to cheer me up.

Next try I made it about 35 feet, then pumped out again. I started to worry if I had it in me. I rested for forty minutes, pulled the rope again, and went for it, desperately managing to climb to the first rest 40 feet up. My confidence was totally shot. For the next hour and a half, Beth and Adam pumped me with encouragement. "Try hard Tommy, you can do it!" they would yell up at me. But in my head I told myself, "Don't be such a pansy, just suck it up and climb."

I slowly crept up the arch, resting for long periods whenever I could. I made sure my feet were placed perfectly and my movement was exact. I felt like a sloth moving up the wall. Just as Beth and Adam were about to fall asleep, I reached the anchor. Completely exhausted, I fixed the rope and waited for them to arrive.

I only had one more pitch to go before the comfy bivy ledge with all of our stuff, but it was the second-hardest pitch of the climb. I was in pain, my toes were throbbing, and there was blood seeping from underneath three of my fingernails.

I pulled out of the Black Arch into a series of underclings and side pulls separated by gaps I could barely connect with the span of my arms. The pitch defied all free-climbing logic—it is the only slab I have ever climbed that maxed both my finger strength and arm power. I wrestled from feature to feature, pushing the pain to the back of my mind, and arrived at the hardest single move of the climb, a 6-foot gap, blank except for a single shallow divot. Glad for the countless hours I'd spent bouldering in the Valley, I gritted my teeth, pulled hard, and stretched for the divot. Matching one finger at a time in the divot and hopping my feet to higher smears, I began to fade. In a panic I slapped a sloper above. My feet slid out from under me as I matched. I smeared my feet high, sagged back on my arms, and dynoed with my last ounce of energy. My fingertips tagged the edge of the jug above—and I was off.

I shot backward, tumbled down the wall like a pinball, and came to a stop 25 feet below. My last bit of energy was gone. I pulled on gear through the crux and climbed to the ledge 60 feet above. Beth and Adam soon followed.

As I sat on the ledge I could feel my pulse in my fingertips and toes. I had just done more difficult rock climbing in a single day than I ever had before, but it came at a price. I was trembling from the pain and had serious doubts about tomorrow. Beth and Adam noticed my distress and did everything they could to help. Beth gave me a massage and Adam talked about riding grizzly bears into basecamp. By the time the sun went down I was feeling rejuvenated and decided to give the pitch another try. The outcome was almost identical to my first try. I gave it one last try before dark, and fell lower.

As I got back to the bivy, we settled in for the night by headlamp. We had been up at 3 in the morning and gone until 9 at night, but still I wanted more daylight. That is one of the many things I love about El Cap—when you are up there, you get to climb as much as you want, from sunup to sundown if you like, or sometimes longer. Beth was particularly drained—eight months off, then straight to El Cap—but she still managed to give me a massage to help me sleep. "Where's mine?" Adam asked. "I see how it is, I can't climb 5.14 up here, so I get the raw end of the deal."

I woke up the next morning feeling pretty sore but confident. I wolfed down some canned peaches and beef jerky and lowered down 100 feet to warm up. The first few moves felt horrible, but after about ten minutes my fingers and toes numbed a bit.

Adam and I rappelled down to try pitch nine again. I powered quickly through the bottom, determined not to let anything stop me this time. I quickly ran through the moves again in my head. I gritted my teeth as I climbed and made it past the divot without error. I matched on the sloper, got my feet up—and then did something that goes against everything I know about climbing hard: I hesitated. Beth and Adam simultaneously started yelling, "Come on Tommy!" I sagged back and dynoed. This time my fingertips caught the hold. I let out a whoop of excitement and scrambled onto the bivy ledge.

The rest of the day was spent climbing the next three pitches: a 5.13c flaring hand and fist crack in a corner, a 5.13b rounded layback, and a wet 5.12d offwidth. If any one of these pitches were on any other free climb on El Cap they would have individually constituted the cruxes, but on this route, they seemed to fall by the wayside. I fell once on each pitch and managed to summon enough energy to do each on my second try. By the end of the day my toes felt like they might pop right through my climbing shoes. All I could feel was pain, but I was finished with a lot of the hard climbing. Things were going well. I was starting to believe I actually might have a chance to send this monster.

That night Adam headed back to the ground to teach a clinic. It was weird to say good-bye in the middle of a wall. "Don't think that you're allowed to come down, too," Adam said. "If you run out of supplies, I'm coming back up with more." Beth replied with, "Yeah, I'll stay up here even though it is 'Trading Spaces' marathon weekend."

We sent Adam down with a walkie-talkie so he could make us laugh from 1,500 feet below. It was hard to see him go, but I still had Beth, who has been a part of every free route I have done on this big stone with the exception of my first time on the *Salathé*. It amazes me that she is always willing, no matter what the circumstances—even a broken foot—to come and help me up here. "I love being up here with you," she said to me. "It inspires me to watch you climb up here. I'll do it anytime."

That night I barely slept. I lay awake listening to the sounds of the waterfalls and trying to ignore my throbbing fingers and toes. I watched the "half sky" view of the stars and enjoyed the calm of night on El Cap. No noise of cars, motorcycles, or construction. I also thought about the next day's climbing. I only had three hard pitches left. One was a completely wet 5.13b that because of its unpleasant nature I had barely worked on. Then, a 5.13c boulder problem, then another 5.13c pitch that was the scariest pitch of the climb. I tried not to toss and turn too much in the portaledge, so at least Beth could get a good night's sleep.

The next morning I crawled out of my sleeping bag with my eyes half closed. By the time I was racked up and ready to go I was already bleeding from my fingers and knees. I stared at the pitch above, an arching crack, black with water and dripping with mud.

Climbing at this point was no longer fun; it was now just about getting it done. No longer did I think about the joy of the movements or the beauty surrounding me. I focused on the next belay. I finished the wet pitch and lay on the precarious ledge that was my first optional belay. Ideally I wanted to link the wet section into the next pitch, making it another monster, but if I fell on the boulder problem above I was resolved not to reclimb the wet 5.13. I lay on the ledge for a half hour, rehearsing the upcoming moves. Then I committed and cranked through the V9 boulder problem. As I neared the final jug, I pumped out; I caught the jug with my hand, but my feet swung too wildly and propelled me into the air. I lowered back to the ledge, pulled the rope, and sent the pitch next try.

I was now feeling the full effects of three hard days on the wall. Although just one more very hard pitch remained, I thought, "I don't know if I have this in me anymore." Here I was, 1,800 feet up El Cap, near success, but feeling like I might be finished. Would I feel better later today or tomorrow?

Just as I was about to give up and rest until evening, Adam's voice came over the radio. "Nice job dude!" he shouted. "I got a whole crowd of people down here waiting to see you send the last hard pitch."

The solitary nature of the challenge is one of the things that draws me to big-wall free climbing. You never have that group energy you get cragging. But this time, a crowd of people pulling for me 1,800 feet below gave me just the boost I needed.

As I started climbing, my whole body was quivering with pain and fatigue. I had been concentrating for three days straight and my mind was tired. I felt like giving up—but I wanted to give the crowd the show they came for. "It is almost over," I told myself.

I moved from a shallow groove to a small layback crack that marked the last 10 feet of hard climbing. I gritted my teeth a little harder and started pulling. If I fell here, a fixed pin that was at least 20 years old and driven into mud would hopefully catch me—but I did not want to test its integrity. I pressed my bloody, swollen fingertips against a tiny side pull and smeared my feet into a glassy dish. Just as my fingertips reached the next hold, my foot slipped. Panicking, I desperately resmeared my foot and shot my hand into a bomber jam above. The remaining 30 feet of the pitch was the most carefully climbed 5.11 I have ever done.

When I reached the ledge I heard faint screams from below. I turned to face the crowd, threw my hands in the air, and screamed as loud as I could.

Postscript: Almost three weeks after the completion of the climb I am still tired. I tried climbing for the first time the other day and felt horrible. I have felt lethargic ever since, but at the same time deeply satisfied. It was brought to my attention recently that, foot for foot, the *Dihedral Wall* has over twice as much hard 5.13 to 5.14 climbing as any other free route in the world. I have been back on the route twice since the ascent, once to take pictures with my good friend Corey Rich and once to shoot video with Heinz Zak. Both times, the beauty of the climb again struck me. Heinz even called it the "King of El Cap free climbs," and I agree. I truly had to rise to a new level to complete this route. I look forward to many more days up on El Cap, by myself or with friends, but I doubt that I will ever do another climb as amazing as the *Dihedral Wall*. But then again, you never know.

THE LINE OF CONTROL

BOULDERING, BIG-WALLING, AND INTERNATIONAL CONFLICT IN INDIAN KASHMIR

JANUARY 2008, NO. 263

BY MICAH DASH

In 2009, professional climbers Jonny Copp (35) and Micah Dash (32) and filmmaker Wade Johnson (24) were killed by an avalanche on 21,712-foot Mt. Edgar in Western Sichuan Province, China. Here, in an article published the year before he died, Dash describes authoring a 3,500-foot route up a virgin peak in Indian Kashmir with Copp. Soon after the men arrived in basecamp, another team showed up intending to climb their very same line. One team succeeded, while the other barely made it off the ground.

"Hey, Jonny, look over yonder," I said, pointing at distant figures across the Lang Lang Meadow, our little slice of heaven in Indian Kashmir. We—Jonny Copp and I—came here in July 2007 to try a 3,500-foot unclimbed granite wall on an unclimbed peak. Our basecamp, nestled in this grassy meadow, had freshwater springs on two sides and amazing granite bouldering. For a week, we'd lounged in the sun like fat marmots, eating well, "acclimatizing" (camp lay at 13,000 feet), and reading Cormac McCarthy westerns . . . which left us talking like cowboys.

"No way—you reckon that's another climber?" he asked. "It cain't be," I responded, opting to take the optimistic approach for once. "Probably just trekkers. Looks like they got a few ponies with 'em."

Jonny, my friend and climbing partner from Boulder, who has adventure coursing through his veins, had launched us on this trip. We'd begun planning in January 2007, after he'd noticed a photo of a giant, smooth wall—what we would later name Shafat Fortress—in an advertisement for the American Alpine Club's grant programs. The title of the ad was "Unnamed and Unclimbed." I was psyched to be Jonny's partner and had always considered his and Mike Pennings's 2000 send fest of the Trango Valley to be one of the most amazing alpine-rock-climbing accomplishments of all time. In three weeks and climbing alpine-style, they made the first ascent of East Cat's Ears Spire, via the most proud and direct line on the wall (*Freebird*; VI 5.11d A1). They also made the second ascent of Hainabrakk East, with *Tague It to the Top* (VI 5.11 A1), as well as the first alpine-style ascent of Shipton Spire, via the second ascent of *Inshallah* (VII 5.12 A1), up one of the biggest rock faces in the world. When we arrived at Lang Lang Meadow, we were relieved to have escaped the chaos of the Indian cities of Kargil and Srinagar, both only a few miles from the "Line of Control" with Pakistan. Kashmir, a mythical region, has been at the heart of the Indo-Pakistan conflict for six decades, a fact of life that has kept visitors away . . . though it had done little to deter our new arrivals at basecamp (or, as we'd learn, some friends of theirs who'd attempted the wall the year before).

We walked over to the large pack team, which must have crossed the river a few miles south. The ever-friendly Jonny approached a man who seemed to be the group leader, a George Clooney look-alike standing in a bright-yellow jacket. Jonny extended his hand, but the man didn't respond; he just turned his back and started brusquely away.

Then I noticed the bold embroidery on his shell: "Kashmir Expedition 2007." *We're screwed*, I thought. Trying to be as friendly as possible, I asked, "Where are you from?"

"Italia," he responded coldly. "We have permit for this peak, not you."

"Permit? I reckon we don't need a permit for this peak—it's under 6,000 meters," Jonny said evenly.

"We have permit," he said once again, and then walked off for good. I reminded Jonny that he'd told me we wouldn't need a permit; my worst fear was that Clooney would try to shut us down. We'd been dreaming about this expedition for months and traveled thousands of miles over seven days to get here, so damn if we weren't going to climb something.

"We don't—not for anything under 6,000 meters," Jonny reiterated. "If you needed a permit to climb under 6,000 meters in these parts, then every goat herder in the Himalaya would need one." Somehow, these guys didn't look like goat herders.

"Sir, many people coming over the river," our cook, Purtemba Sherpa, said, as, on edge, we arrived back at the tent. Meanwhile, the new arrivals had split into two teams, sending one member, with a team of Kashmiri horsemen, to cross farther downstream while the rest of the team looked for a spot closer to us.

"How many?" I asked.

"Many sir, very many. They have LO from IMF with them . . . his name is Raju." I could hear the stress in his voice. Raju, from the Indian Mountaineering Federation, was the group's liaison officer.

Jonny and I headed over to the long Tyrolean traverse we'd established over the rapidly moving, glacier-fed Suru River a week earlier. Setting it up had been no easy feat: Jonny had to swim across a 150-foot section of unbelievably cold water with a rope tied loosely around his waist. When the shore cut out from under his feet, all I could see was his head and arms moving with wild abandon. To set the traverse, we'd drilled a few bolts, and then using some old ropes we'd scored on the way, pulled them tight. Now the massive Italian onslaught—eleven people total—crossed with ease . . . on our cords.

"You use our spits," one of the Italians said—as if Italy had the sole patent for using and installing bolts.

"No, actually, those are ours," I said, pointing to a half-drilled quarter incher. Jonny again tried to make small talk, but to no avail. The Italians pretended we weren't even there. I went over and introduced myself to Raju, a Hindi man from central India with bright eyes, a big smile, and a missing front tooth. He quickly reassured me that he didn't care what we climbed so long as we asked the Italians first . . . thus sidestepping the conflict altogether.

Classic, I thought later, as I looked up from the door of our two-pole, Boy Scout–style tent, which also doubled as a sleeping tent for Purtemba and our assistant cook, Depess. With square mile after square mile of good camping in the area, the Italians decided to set up their two massive cook tents and nine sleeping tents fewer than 50 feet from us. I asked Jonny what he thought.

"We should head up and avoid any other conflicts," he said soberly. "Let's climb now, and deal with the consequences later." I agreed, so we collapsed the tent, packed our bags, and started up the 3,000-foot talus cone to the glacier and base of the wall. If we went for it and missed, we knew that the Italians, with seven climbers and untold spools of fixing rope, might summit before we did.

"I love Italians," I said cynically, huffing with exertion while I schlepped my thirty-five-pound pack up the talus. "I love Italian food, Italian cars, Italian shoes, and Italian women."

"Me, too, and I'm glad they're here," said Jonny, sincerely enough. "It just spotlights the ol' style debate. Anyway, I think we'll all be friends soon, and I'm sure they've got some good Italian meat and cheese down there. We can share our rum."

Then it hit me: Our new goal was not only to make the first ascent of this walled mountain but to share food and drink with the Italians and resolve our issues. "Now that would be proud," I told Jonny. We laughed at this. The Italians wanted us arrested and taken to some godforsaken Kashmiri jail, to be banished from climbing forever. But Jonny and I kept pouring on the love for all things Italian—in order to face the mountain safely, we needed to rid ourselves of the bad energy that had driven us up the hill. For the rest of the evening, "I love the Italians" became our mantra.

"Tent or sleeping bag?" asked Jonny, as we dangled 1,500 feet above the Lang Lang Glacier.

"Tent's fine," I replied. Careful not to crush the 1-by-2-foot, chiseled ledge of ice that would be his bivy for the night, Jonny reached gingerly into our single forty-liter pack, to hand me the tent shell. I pulled it down to my equally meager stance and wrapped it around me. We were twelve pitches up the Shafat Fortress, our first night on the wall and only twenty hours after leaving the Italian-occupied basecamp. Our route followed a continuous and obvious dihedral system—a line that shot out of the glacier like an arrow. For the most part, it seemed to be the only obvious crack system, though one section—a gaping offwidth three quarters of the way up—concerned us.

Despite our precarious position, we laughed and sipped hot pea soup. An hour before, Jonny had led an impressive pitch of mixed ice on poorly protected ground to reach our tiny camel's back of an ice perch. But, unable to see around the corners and buttresses in the dark, we stopped around 17,700 feet and prepared to shiver until morning. Sitting there, I wondered how we were lucky enough to have ended up on an unclimbed big wall in the Kashmir. I realized, however, that it wasn't by chance.

Kashmir was disputed even before Pakistan won its independence from India in 1947. Since then, the territory has been the flashpoint for two of three Indo-Pakistani wars. (The third came in 1999, when India fought a brief but bitter conflict with Pakistani-backed forces that had infiltrated Indian-controlled territory in the Kargil area, only a few hours west of our first basecamp.) The area was virtually cut off to Westerners until 1980, and since 1989, there has been a growing and often violent separatist movement against Indian rule in Kashmir.

En route to the Lang Lang Glacier, we'd passed through the city of Srinagar, a recent hotbed of violence in which tourists have been prime targets. In the early 1990s, the Al-Farhan, a militant organization, kidnapped a group of Westerners trekking in Pahalgam. They were never seen again. In 2000, only 7 miles east of us, rebels killed three monks. Until as recently as 2003, the valley itself was closed numerous times due to rebel activity. Despite the tumultuous history, the people of Kashmir always greeted us with smiles, kind eyes, and warm tea.

Long before we left Boulder, we knew that to climb the wall in alpine-style, suffering would be mandatory. Our first night proved the point, and the next morning's skies revealed bad weather coming in fast. Fortunately, we spotted a small ledge 100-odd yards to our right. After some wild pendulums, we were there, on a small stance big enough for our tent and protected somewhat from the now-constant rock and icefall. Between snow squalls, we stared up at the corners and cracks that seemed to lead to the summit, many pitches away.

On the morning of our third day on the wall, under a cloudless sky, the sun beamed across the valley, triggering a series of rock avalanches that came within inches of our bivy. We waited out the storm, slurping warm water because we were already running low on food. By 9 a.m., the rock had dried and we were on the move again, leading in blocks for efficiency.

One of the most important aspects of a partnership, especially in alpine climbing, is doing your part. Sometimes that means melting ice for drinking water, sometimes that means cooking dinner, and sometimes that means leading your pitches. Jonny had done an outstanding job on his block, leading both ice and rock, at one point even running it out 15 feet over an equalized beak and micronut on a 5.11 thin-face section. In fact, after a few straightforward pitches off the ground, the climbing had become increasingly complicated and delicate—the rock was chunky, and we had to take great care not to knock down any of the massive blocks. It was, as Jonny would say, "blue-collar climbing." About halfway up the wall (1,700 feet off the deck), we hit the offwidth feature—what we'd later call the Shaft—an ominous, wide, and wet crack. It was my block. I looked up from the belay, hoping to find a way around. There wasn't one.

For me, alpine climbing is a vision quest. It's an artificial war of sorts. It requires my total attention and dedication, and provides opportunities to see who I really am. The offwidth that loomed above was one of those opportunities. The first few pieces were solid, but soon the crack widened. Instinctually, I pressed myself into it, my right foot heel-toeing on the outside while my left side pressed against the icy, crumbly inside wall, which grew wetter by the minute. Soon I was soaked from head to toe. My hands and feet were frozen, and hypothermia slowed my progress. After a miserable hour and a half, I'd probably only gained 100 feet, and except for the first few nut placements, the gear lay slotted between loose blocks in the back of the crack. My brain would tell me to go, but 30 seconds would pass until I moved. I tried to weasel in a few pieces, but they were no good and merely slowed progress. Eventually, I settled for a screw in an aerated ice amoeba.

Not far above, the rock seemed to kick back, so I punched it 25 feet above the screw to a point where the fissure pinched down. On the wall behind me, I spotted solid, though very wet, handholds . . . and maybe even some decent gear. "I need to switch sides!" I yelled to Jonny. But, 150 feet below and under a roof, he couldn't hear. Twenty minutes later, after tinkering in a small wire, I took a deep breath and switched sides, only to watch the piece pop. I screamed—"a scream of true animal terror," as Jonny later recalled. Nothing felt solid except my wooden fingers, but in an instant, everything became crystal clear. Either I calmed down and climbed or I took a 50-footer onto the ice screw, tore it, and likely fell to my death on the ledge below. After a few more feet and at the end of the rope, I found a small stance and concocted an intricate nest of RPs and small TCUs. My hands and feet were completely numb, and my clothes were soaked, but I wanted to go up. I fixed the rope, and within minutes, Jonny was there. He handed me the rack; it was still my block. The next pitch was wetter than the first . . . but easier. A good 130 feet higher, and after a few desperate moves, I stopped at a dry stance.

Again, Jonny reached the belay in a flash. It was nearly 2 p.m., I had spent three-plus hours on two pitches, and the summit lay at least 1,600 feet above. Jonny rummaged through the pack, trying to find some dry clothes for me. Our fate quickly became clear, as my shivering grew uncontrollable. We were not going to summit that day—an open bivy in my condition was out of the question. Like a robot, Jonny fixed our rope, and moments later we'd rapped 400 feet to our bivy ledge. There was no mention of our decision, no second-guessing—the judgment was clear. Going up would have been dangerous—lethal, even.

"Boy, I reckon you got a bit cold up there," Jonny told me in his best cowboy impersonation, pulling out the stove. "Yeah, I feel like I been rode hard and put up wet," I said. "You got a smoke?"

"Roll it yourself, pardner," Jonny replied, handing me the tobacco. "I'm gonna make us a hot brew."

I rolled a smoke and, with it hanging from my lips, set up the tent and got inside. Jonny passed me the single sleeping bag, and then some hot water. After a few hours in the bag, I began to warm. The next morning, we woke at 1 and drank some soup, leaving us with two Clif bars each. We jugged the thin ropes back to our high point. Jonny took the lead, efficiently climbing around ice and loose blocks under clear-blue skies, the Karakoram Range spread out before us.

"I need my boots and crampons," Jonny yelled, halfway through a rock pitch. He pulled them up, and the rope began to move again, but this time more slowly. I knew it had to be hard and held the rope saying nothing, just as Jonny had done for me the day before. The pitch looked intricate and loose, forcing him to climb difficult stretches of rock between large ice smears in the steep corner.

We had spent nearly four days on the wall. As I started up from the belay on the twenty-first pitch, a microwave-sized block of ice and snow plummeted from the summit, hitting Jonny on the head. *"Are you OK?!"* I screamed. There was no reply. I yelled again.

"Yeah, I think I'm OK," Jonny at long last replied.

The massive chunk had brought the indestructible Jonny to his knees, knocking him out for a second, but he shook it off. I continued leading, reaching the summit ridge moments later. Jonny jugged up. His face was pale and sweaty as he pointed to his cracked helmet. We said little else about it. I reracked and led the final chimney pitch, to the summit. It was the first time I'd summited an unclimbed peak. I stood atop Shafat Fortress with my hands stretched out in front of me, taking in the landscape as the thin air and cold wind surrounded me. Jonny joined me moments later, hollering like a cowboy. He took a few pictures, and we began the descent.

We didn't want to rap directly down the corner system, to avoid rock and ice fall, opting instead to gun 15 feet to its side . . . which required us to be crafty. At one point, Jonny equalized a RURP and a half-beaten-in, ¾-inch angle backed up loosely to a blue TCU. When it was my turn to rap, I pulled the TCU and descended—damn if we were leaving any booty.

A day and a half later, we were back on the glacier, tired to our cores. In an almost hypnotic fog, we staggered back to our initial basecamp, Campo Italiano. There were no congratulations or traditional celebration. Rather, Purtemba told us that the police had come and that we needed to visit the local station, 7 miles away. The Italians, it seemed, still wanted us arrested. After a few days rest in camp and some more bouldering (and no trip to the police), we decided to confront them.

"I love the Italians," Jonny said, as we headed toward their cook tent. "All we can do is be friendly."

My heart pounded. We unzipped the tent door and stepped inside. We all stood face to face, and Jonny and I, elated by our first ascent, had yet to wipe the grins off our mugs. The Italians picked up on this and instantly changed their tune—one minute cold and unfriendly, the next slapping us high fives and sharing their food. *Did I just miss something?* I wondered. We sat, our hands still cracked and bleeding, as they cut a slice of ham for each of us. I glanced across the small camp table at Jonny and smiled bigger. We had fulfilled our first goal. A few nights later, like old friends, our egos drowned by rum, we all drank and danced under the Himalayan sky.

Micah Dash and Jonny Copp, recipients of the 2007 American Alpine Club Lyman Spitzer Cutting-Edge Award and WL Gore's Shipton/Tilman Grant for the trip, spent the following three weeks in basecamp bouldering. The Italian team, meanwhile, reached a high point 650 feet up the wall.

THE BLACK DOG

FIVE FIRST-PERSON RIFFS ON THE DARK SIDE OF THE CLIMBER MIND

APRIL 2008, NO. 265

In the world of climbing, there are peaks and valleys, hardship, death, and love. The very same thing can be said about climbers' minds—or anyone's mind, for that matter. In the essays that follow, five climbers divulge their struggles with interior darkness and how they learned to live with it. Some are guides, some are filmmakers, some work in rescue. But what they all share is their love of the sport and how it's been there for them in times of need, as both solace and escape.

Last year, when I pitched the idea of a depression/obsession-themed issue to our publisher, he balked. "We need to give people something to read," he said. "Not a reason to jump out the window." He had a point. I climb, you climb—we climb—to escape pain, loss, illness, and stress. Climbing is an out, and it's a great one at that. But you have to return home at the end of the day, and home is where the head is. And even on the best days, pushing doubt, fear, and anxiety from your skull can be cruxier than any lead.

Here, we've gathered five essays linked by a common thread: dark manifestations of the climber mind. Why? The reason is twofold. First, it's because I think many climbers face these issues, but cowed by the cacophony of the dirtbag-chic, free-wheelin' climbing community, silence themselves. (This seems to be status quo especially with depression, a condition carrying the stigma of malingering and contagion.) Second, I think darkness and climbing can be flip sides of a coin. I won't try to explain, and maybe this is one of those truths that blurs when stared at head-on. In any case, five writers—Kenneth Long, Fitz Cahall, Majka Burhardt, myself, and Chad Shepard—have given it a go. As you'll see, three of these stories also feature free soloing. It seems when things grow black, the rope, for better or worse, is often left behind. Draw your own conclusions.

—*Matt Samet*

RAGGED EDGES

A Private Suicide

by Kenneth Long

When I was 12, I climbed *Ragged Edges*, a 190-foot 5.8 in Willow Springs Canyon, at Red Rock, Nevada. I didn't know how to climb very well then—my brothers and I used borrowed equipment and a "creative" belay solution—but the late Randall Grandstaff saw our blundering and taught us how to climb correctly. Hence, I would live to be old. Now, at 37, I resent Grandstaff's altruism. I suffer from depression.

I fight it—I have for years and I will for years to come. I hope someday to find happiness, to write a book about how I became "cured." Yet for now, I cannot see writing that book. I wake up with a crushing weight on my chest and a cruel fog painting the world black, turning it distant and muted. I lie down at night, fearing I won't awake. The Black Dog first came when I was 21. I had a college scholarship in Utah and found myself happy, getting good grades and climbing. Then, out of nowhere, came a feeling of darkness—of anxiety, uncertainty, and self-doubt so strong I knew I'd never be the same. I ran to a hospital, thinking that I was dying. The doctors could not help. I ran away—I ended all relationships and dropped out of school, riding my bicycle from Provo to Las Vegas, where I hoped old friends and familiar rock would ease my pain. I lost my scholarship and my fiancée. Eventually, I returned to school, disappearing to the rocks when the darkness came.

In February 2007, after I lost my job as a prosecutor, the Black Dog returned. This time, he stayed. Last March, I couldn't get out of bed; I couldn't breathe. I could barely move for the pain. I decided to make it end at Red Rock, where I'd climbed all my life. A "climbing accident" would be easier on my mother, wife, and daughters than a suicide.

On March 17, 2007, I drove west into the canyons. I parked my car in Willow Springs and shoed up. Ten feet up *Ragged Edges*, I paused at the imaginary line where a boulderer would stop, the crux still 60 feet above. Would I have the courage to let go? I wondered. I kept climbing, my forearms burning and the desert floor growing distant. Then, suddenly, 60 feet up, I felt something I'd not felt in months: elation. I breathed deeply, soaking in the beauty of the canyon, the exhilaration of climbing. And I started to think of ways to retreat. Perhaps I could downclimb or traverse way left. Or I could, as planned, just release the rock.

Yet I didn't. I clung tightly to *Ragged Edges'* buckets, and then breezed through the wide fists crux. Fifteen minutes after starting up, I scrambled to the top and lay down, the ice-laden sandstone sucking away what body heat remained. Twenty-five years ago, I'd lain near this exact spot, so full of life.

I have survived cancer, high-altitude cerebral edema, decompression sickness, and the deaths of my grandparents, father, and nineteen friends and relatives—and depression is still worse. Never did I imagine this terrible reality. When I had cancer, no one said, "Snap out of it, stupid ass—cancer is a choice!" Yet the few people in whom I've confided about my depression seem to think that "toughening up" is the answer. If only it were so easy.

Atop *Ragged Edges*, I turned to the right, walked off, and then swapped out my Ninjas for tennis shoes. Back home, I told my wife I'd been hiking. She served me cold fajitas on a paper plate; she knew I'd lied, but neither of us had much to say about it.

As night fell, I retreated to bed. I found two Xanax tablets amidst my cluttered bathroom and dissolved them under my tongue. The tranquilizer numbed my brain, and I drifted into sleep. Some minutes later, I started out of bed to the sound of a barking dog. There in the driveway stood a black boxer, baying toward my upstairs window. I looked at the dog—I looked at it squarely—but it didn't avert its gaze. Soon it turned and disappeared into the night.

THE SLENDER CORD

Free Soloing and the Road to Perdition

by Fitz Cahall

Functional as it is strong, the figure 8 is the first and most important knot a climber learns—it attaches him to rope, gear, and partner. Between two climbers, a figure 8 makes the vital and magnificent promise, "If you go, I go, too."

Sometime around my twenty-second birthday, I quit tying in. It wasn't a death wish or an adrenaline craving that pushed me into the mountains. It was frustration. I'd already soloed for two years, but those ropeless ascents were spur of the moment. Partners proved too cumbersome—they showed up late or not at all. They made excuses or got scared. Climbing alone, I could speed through a full day's pitches in a few hours; I could pack a month's worth into a single day.

By eliminating clutter, I made the system exponentially more efficient. If I could streamline climbing this way, I reasoned, why not my entire life? It was a dangerous direction, one that complemented my strengths—a genetically encoded work ethic and confidence in my ability—and pandered to my weakness—a lifelong shyness.

I stacked training sessions atop classes at the University of Washington and part-time writing jobs; then, leaving only a cryptic note on the refrigerator door describing my whereabouts to my roommates, I'd disappear. I would return two or three days later limping and sunburned. My nonclimbing friends dubbed them "freak-outs."

True, it was getting harder to tell the difference. It wasn't that my solo projects became riskier—it was that climbing solo had become the norm. Whether it was long enchainments on Washington's wilderness peaks or a single, demanding pitch that I had rehearsed mentally a hundred times, these solos began as sudden, impetuous flare-ups that absorbed my thoughts until I finally rushed toward the mountains. When I arrived, chest heaving from running the approach, the anxiety eased and my breath settled into a calm rhythm. Once I laced up and twisted my swollen knuckles into finger cracks, I was never afraid. It almost always felt like I was in the perfect place and moment.

Climbing was no longer about having fun—it was about fulfilling potential. I was getting stronger, but my ability to connect to anything other than my own small world had withered. I had trouble sleeping. That razor-edged clarity I felt soloing eluded me in daily life. When friends tried to fix me up with a work acquaintance, I sat swirling my beer and let the conversation flow past like water around a cold river stone. I expected to find happiness on summits, but instead discovered the obvious—by nature, mountaintops are lonely. I had fallen in love with something that could not love me back.

One evening while sorting climbing gear, I pulled out a slender cord, still wet from alpine snowmelt. My hands worked it into various knots until they came to the figure 8. I twisted the rope into its first "8," and then followed it back through. In my hands sat an empty circle backed up by a powerful knot. I tossed the noose over the rafters, letting it sway until it went still in the stagnant air of the garage. I let it hang there like an open-ended question: What was I doing?

Becca and I were two people headed in different directions, or at least that was what we told ourselves after a chance run-in. It had started years earlier as a simple summer fling. She was older and, after graduating, left Seattle to chase snow and a career in science. Neither of us remember ending our relationship. There were no muttered apologies or worn-out excuses. One day we were together; the next, thousands of miles separated us.

It went on like this for a few years. Becca left Colorado, took a job in Alaska, and moved in with a boyfriend in Oregon. Meanwhile, I spent six months in Australia, graduated, and moved to Arizona.

That fall, Becca called. "I've left Oregon," she said. "Can I come see you?" I stammered my approval. Three days later, Becca walked in with a winter wind licking at her heels and smelling like the promise of snow. A week later, she asked to stay.

With 2x4s and plywood, we converted a 1993 Toyota pickup into an extremely low-ceilinged mobile home. Together, we bumbled through our first big walls in Zion. We dropped cams, wrestled haulbags, and tangled the ropes. At night, we sat cross-legged with our backs to the wall and washed down premade pasta meals with warm beer, until the stars appeared and the conversation and laughter reached a relaxed conclusion. Our ancient, hand-me-down portaledge swayed ever so slightly in the desert breeze like a canoe adrift on an unseen lake.

Becca's fieldwork often meant she was away for weeks at a time. Left alone again, I'd feel that manic energy creep in. I would rifle through topo maps, guide-books, and handwritten notes. I'd think in the cold, scientific terms of efficiency and probability. Then I'd pack a bag with water and food, and slink into snowy ranges. Mentally nourished by my and Becca's happy relationship, I picked away at goals that had been nothing more than daydreams—5.11 circuits at the local crag, link-ups of moderate alpine classics, and my first 5.12 solo—for me, huge accomplishments that I instinctively omitted from our evening phone conversations.

A year after Becca appeared back on my doorstep, we found ourselves on the road. Becca and a close friend tiptoed their way up a 300-foot route at Lover's Leap while I sat in the forest below, writing. I jotted down disconnected ideas until my mind dried up. There was a pair of climbing shoes and time to kill. Above me, Becca neared the top of the cliff. I curled my toes and slipped them into the tight climbing shoes. Lathered my hands in a thick layer of chalk and started up. Without the weight of a rope, I flowed, sinking my fingers around granite curves and latching onto flawless edges until the angle eased and I stood on solid ground at the clifftop.

I followed the trail down until I caught up to the women, on the descent. When Becca turned to see me, we both stopped. I smiled nervously. She turned and kept walking. Beneath her thin, green T-shirt, I could see her slender shoulder blades heave and sag. When I placed a hand on her shoulder, she spun and slapped my hand away. I stood there mutely, a red welt forming on my left wrist. I coiled my arms around her, entwined my fingers until they fastened like a knot.

"Don't ever do that again," she said, her voice quivering with fear. "You're climbing for both of us up there."

I froze. I had avoided making that connection as long as possible. Every time a climber ties that knot, it's a reiteration of a promise: I will catch you if you fall. I had untied from our shared existence. As much as I didn't want to believe it, happiness came with its own weight—responsibility. It was clear I'd have to make a choice.

These days we exist in the cityscape of Seattle and pick our way through our respective careers. The weekends are tiny handholds that keep us attached to the mountains. After hours glued to the computer screen, ordering ill-behaved words into sentences, I grow a little frantic. I begin to scheme, like a wily adulterer consumed by aimless lust.

Then I remember Becca's face, broken and tear streaked. I remember my unspoken promise—you go, I go. My mind goes quiet, much as it did when I used to disappear amongst glaciers and rock. I smile, think back to all the shared routes, and forward toward upcoming adventures. I can shut my eyes and smell the sage in the desert air, feel the portaledge trembling with the rise and fall of Becca's breathing. I feel the strength of the unseen knots that bind us.

TRUE TO SELF

Life and Delusions on the Mountains

by Majka Burhardt

I'm a mountain guide—which might mean I'm a control-obsessed thinly veiled masochist or that I'm a climber who likes teaching people how to stay safe in the mountains. It definitely means taking risks. I've guided thousands of pitches from 5.0 to 5.11, ice, big mountains, and long hikes. Although I'm not a full-time guide anymore, I've worked, loved, and lost in the guiding world for a dozen years.

As a young guide, I refused to admit fear or apprehension. Part of this was being a 21-year-old female guiding 50-year-old men around the glaciated peaks of the North Cascades. But guiding didn't give itself easily to me. Injuries, academia, and life always intervened so that I was constantly forced to question my choice.

Being an overly analytical person, I decided to tackle my apprehension from a logical angle: I would write an article on female guides. And so I interviewed nine top female guides and alpinists. In the end, I wrote a neat, tidy story that no one wanted to publish. Now it's four years later, and four of those nine women are dead. Sue Nott, Karen McNeill, Laura Kellog, and Christine Boskoff all died in the mountains within a year of each other, in 2006–'07. None were guiding. You can say they were all pushing big routes, that all were taking chances, but when is climbing not taking a chance?

These women are not statistics. I have pages of notes from each. Quotes like, "Guiding? Me and guiding? Every time I think about it I realize I have a hard enough time taking care of myself" (Karen McNeill). And, "My philosophy about climbing and guiding? You need to carry your weight, be a good psychiatrist, and learn how to let things go" (Christine Boskoff).

When I think of dying while climbing—about holds breaking and my body slamming into rock—my heart pounds, my palms sweat, and I can't catch my breath. When I'm climbing and these thoughts enter, I can barely hold onto the biggest jug. So what happens when my job is altogether to remove death from the equation, but the thoughts come anyway?

It's early September 2002 at Lumpy Ridge. After a long summer guiding, I'm out with my friend Jeff. We warm up on a 5.8, Sorcerer. On the second pitch, the crack disappears and a sticky face takes its place. Out on the sharp end, I cannot move—I cannot picture going up but only falling down and cheese-grating. I make a move, I come down; I make it again, I come down again. I regularly climb several grades harder than this; I regularly guide several grades harder than this. Today, I cannot make it. I lower off and hand Jeff the rack.

"Too much guiding?" he asks.

"How'd you guess?" I reply.

Jeff, once a guide himself, has climbed with enough other guides to know the glazed look when you finally let down and let it in. Maybe there is a limit to how many pitches you can do on which you're putting yourself out there, on which your belayer understands gravity in theory but still lets go of the rope to scratch her ear. I'd had more than forty clients that summer and I wasn't even guiding full-time. The numbers had taken their toll.

Five years later: July 2007 in Eldorado Canyon. I'm on the sharp end, guiding the perfect client. "5.10 all day," he'd said on the phone. When he told me he led 5.9, I asked if he wanted to swing a few leads. "I'm on vacation," he said. "No responsibility."

What he didn't say but we both know is true is that I am the one being paid to be responsible—to take and manage the risks. That is my job. I am supposed to do this even though three weeks before, for the first time in my life, my foot slipped and I took a 25-foot sideways fall on the Diamond. That same weekend, another friend fell headfirst on the same wall, shattering a quarter of his teeth. And another friend helped carry a buddy with a shattered femur from a crag in Aspen. But none of this matters to my client. He signed a waiver. Nothing bad is supposed to happen.

This works . . . for two pitches. But soon I'm shaking on 5.10a. I'm placing a piece every 3 feet, climbing past it, reaching below to clean and place it again, sweating off edges as big as truck stops. I know my client sees this. I wait for him at the next belay, and then ask if he minds taking a break. I tell him about my fall, Pete's fall, Jonny's rescue. I admit to being scared. My client pats my shoulder and tells me it will be alright. And then, miraculously, it is . . . for that day.

Admitting we are scared in the mountains is never easy. It's bad juju to talk about dying when you're on a climb on which you really might die. But what about finally letting in the dark realization you can always die climbing (or anywhere)? Most of us don't—it opens up the door of darkest possibility. Instead, we talk about it after the fact, after the danger has passed.

Part of the reason for my fear is that this community—in particular, the guiding circle—diminishes with every month. Twelve years ago, I'd tell my mother climbing was no more dangerous than driving. That was before I'd been to a half-dozen climber funerals in the same picnic area in Eldorado Canyon. That was before I'd spent one of those ceremonies watching the pregnant belly of a new widow, waiting to see her baby kick, as if that sign of life might make things OK again.

We fool ourselves that what we are doing makes sense. We go to funerals and tell each other our friend died doing what she loved. We surround ourselves with climbers, call them "our people," because they understand us. But in the process of writing this essay, I've thought so much about death and responsibility and consequences that sometimes I cannot go more than 8 feet above gear without hyperventilating.

I think daily about the climbers I know who've died. I see their smiles fading as they come to realize a snow-cave bivy has become a tomb. I feel their excitement at flying over their perfect alpine-ice objective, moments before their plane smashes into the side of the mountain. I see them confidently kicking steps up blue-white snow that, without their knowing, hangs moments from catastrophic slide. I see them plugging a cam into a crack that is actually a rope-slicer block.

I see these things and I try my best not to see them. I see them and I make a choice. I see them and I decide to climb.

CALLING ALL THE HEROES
A Black Day in the Texas Desert

by Matt Samet

Know this: Doctors, girlfriends, climbing partners have diagnosed me with every condition they could pronounce short of schizophrenia. I've been labeled Type II bipolar, major depressive, generalized anxiety disorder, panic disorder, obsessive-compulsive disorder, seasonal affective disorder, mood-cycling disorder, misanthropic altruist disorder, disorder-disorder, and orderly disordered disorder. Whatever.

It's been like this for twenty-five years. I've tried to burn clean the pain in ways too wicked to list, yet climbing always proved the most effective. The rocks have broken my bones, popped tendons, seared sinew, and blown out shoulders and knees. I climb anyway. The meaning is the message. On the lighter side, we're all good at deluding ourselves: "Hey, climbing is good for you!" and "Climbing is my religion!" Pleasant thoughts all, and probably true. But I climb because I have to. I climb to kill the darkness. If I shut my eyes and trace the contours of my life past the boulder problems, ridgelines, ill-begotten sport piles, and razor-edged splitters, I arrive at a specific day, marked like an X on a topo map. It was the day my love for climbing turned to lust, a black day bathed in chemical self-loathing.

1989: Hueco Tanks, Texas. Mesquite and cat's claw tore at my legs as I hiked across the desert with my friend Dave. In my hand, I held a bear-shaped cookie, chocolate sandwiching a lardy crème: my fifth Fudge Family Bear. Dave and I noodled along Hueco Tanks' East Spur, our minds not right because—for one of a very few, regrettable times in my life—we'd taken a hallucinogen.

Aside from the half-devoured packet of cookies, we carried water and a chalk bag. I remember tearing the Fudge Family Bears limb from limb, provoking a murderer's guilt and downward emotional spiral. Still, they were our only food: The massacre continued apace. We walked until we reached the Sandmaster Boulder, a lonely prow of iron rock at the Spur's southern tip.

I slumped onto a shelf beneath the overhanging wall. Within that cave, my gob lousy with Bear entrails, I beheld an intimidating line of scalloped huecos—*Sandmaster*, 5.12b—defined by a couple of funky star-drive bolts. I looked beyond those, parsing a fixed nut, and then above that, another bolt or two: *Calling All the Heroes*, a Todd Skinner 5.13d, then one of the hardest routes in the country. In the harsh, drug-fed light, it looked evil—a forest of razor blades on a shimmering plaque. 5.13d—who, exactly, climbed 5.13d? Me . . . ever? Never? Did it matter? Somehow, I knew in that instant that I'd never complete this route. I would never measure up to Five-Thirteen-D.

My stomach grew heavy and hot, dismembered Bears clawing back up my craw. Dave, meanwhile, sat on a rock killing more Bears. I wanted to leave, I told him.

We exited, looping around West Mountain and leaning into a wind that skimmed the dam's gravel lip. At the End Boulder, I surged into a V0, feeling the rough crystals along the crest of some lips but also the smoother bevel of the older holes. Then a car emerged from the chaos.

The car's windows descended power-smooth, and then an elderly couple—tourists—unfurled their bones, to stand on the tarmac and watch me climb. I gripped a hueco and looked their way, at their flickering and crenellated pieholes agape with unwarranted awe. I climbed because there was nothing left to do.

They clapped when I topped out, and then snapped photographs. What I had done was not so very special, but they clapped nonetheless. They couldn't see that this climb lay beneath me, an aspiring "radboy." They had no way to peer behind my Wayfarers to see I'd been psychically commandeered and that their applause only twisted in my gut the daggers of self-hatred sown by *Calling All the Heroes*.

As the late-winter afternoon sun paled, I saw myself in that aging couple. In some distant year, I, too, would be 80. I, too, would age, wither, and die. No rock or mountain could change that. Climbing itself would prove meaningless—I could have free soloed *Wyoming Cowgirl*, a 5.12 just 20 feet left, and garnered the same applause.

Still, after all these years, climbing is the only thing I really care to do. I know I'll never complete all the climbs I want, carrying the sickening surety that even if I onsight an entire crag in a flurry of Legrand-esque dropknees and Sharma-like kips, the minute I drive away, some mad developer will add one more line and I'll have to return. But I climb anyway; there is no choice. I climb because I have to. How about you, friendo?

Matt Samet is the editor-in-chief of Climbing. *He began climbing twenty-one years ago near Albuquerque, New Mexico.*

THE BLACK HOLE

Night Soloing in the Tuolumne High Country

by Chad Shepard

I turn off my headlamp, and as my eyes adjust, the abyss beneath crashes open. From my small ledge halfway up the *Southeast Buttress* (III 5.6) of Cathedral Peak, I can scarcely make out the pine trees several hundred feet below. The peak, rising ominously above, is defined in silhouette by brilliant stars.

Two hours earlier, I'd set out from my cabin in jeans and a long-sleeve T-shirt; it's late summer 2007, and the days are still long. Tuolumne Meadows has been my home from open-to-close for the past eight years. I come to climb, but I've taken various jobs to legitimize my long-term presence in the eyes of the government. My current position with the concession service has earned a cozy canvas cabin just behind the Tuolumne store. On the occasional evenings when my mind is restless, a short walk, a few deep breaths, and a glance up at the Cathedral Range are often enough to quiet my thoughts. Tonight, I need stronger medicine. Tonight, I am depressed.

I've been cyclically depressed for as long as I can remember, but the highs and lows seem to become more pronounced as I age (I'm 32 now). I remember being high-strung at a young age. I first contemplated taking my life when I was 7, growing up in a small town in Oregon's Willamette Valley. It was autumn, and the fields were ablaze, smoke plumes rising like mushroom clouds. (Burning fields was a common practice, to revitalize the soil between crop cycles.) The sun filtered weakly through the curtains of my bedroom window, and I sat with a dull hunting knife poised at my stomach, a red welt developing where the point pressed skin. I was crying, scared about how painful it was going to be but angry for hesitating.

Back on Cathedral Peak, I sit and tuck my fingers into my armpits. The occasional gusts cut through me; they carry up the faint butterscotch fragrance of the Jeffery Pines. The pale light of the waning moon just begins to touch the summit above, rolling the jagged shadow of the adjacent ridge back from the peak, as if exposing the mountain for some private unveiling.

Events have compounded over the past couple weeks, leading to this impasse. Each problem, be it financial, work, relationship, or health-related, is manageable, but taken together, they overwhelm. This cascade is not entirely random—it is more of a pattern. Something triggers the cycle, and then the pattern unfolds. It's taken all my energy to keep up appearances; on the phone with family or friends, I feign false optimism, possibly to avoid fumbling attempts to explain the unexplainable. I begin to loathe questions like "How are you?"

Several hundred feet up, my problems have followed. The past: I see mistakes and regret. The future: hopelessness and fear. I look further forward for meaning. In some sort of metaphysical twist, I begin to see the world in geologic time: the Cockscomb splinters and topples. The nine Echo Peaks slough into the abyss. Unicorn Peak crumbles into a nameless heap.

I lie back and roll to my side. The position of my body on this ledge—it's darkly familiar. I responded to a climbing accident here four years ago, on this route I've probably done 200 times. The guy had fallen 80 feet and lay in a cascade of blood, looking out dead-eyed.

I roll my head into that same position, to complete my tribute. A half-hour later, a glimmer catches my eye: Moonlight has overtaken the face. The rock is reborn in the delicate light. I climb again, tracing intimately over familiar stone, granite known as well as a lover's form. Hundreds of feet up, I allow an indulgence in the moment, a pure right-now instant ropeless on perfect glacial patina.

I do not look to climbing to cure who I am, but seek rather to make it a sustainable part of a depressed life cycle. Tonight, I am here for clarity of mind. In my darkest moments, I will find no happiness, but I can find peace in the mountains. Near 3 a.m., I stand on the summit.

FANTASYLAND

JULY 2008, NO. 267

BY KELLY CORDES

Take two cutting-edge alpinists—a youthful and exuberant Colin Haley and the elder statesman (with some bro-brah flare) Kelly Cordes—add a massive Patagonian objective, and you've got the fixings for an epic tale. Below, just as the action is taking place, Cordes spirits the reader away to a different land, one rife with devil sticks and dreadlocks in moonlight—at the old camp on the outskirts of El Chaltén, a scene he loathes—then back to the business. What's real, what's fantasy?

The kid wouldn't let up. First, an e-mail. Then phone calls.

"C'mon, duder, you've got nothing better to do," Colin Haley said into the phone. I took a swig off my margarita, looked out the window at another splitter October day in Estes Park, and then threatened to call his parents.

Colin's always psyched. Only 23, he has the skills and alpine résumé to humble most crusty old veterans. When Colin was 10, his father took him mountaineering in the Cascades. In high school, to harden himself for bivies, Colin slept on plywood—until he started getting laid, anyway. He recently had one of the finest yearlong (ten months, actually) alpine sending sprees ever, starting with his and Jed Brown's tremendous new route on the 7,600-vertical-foot north face of Mount Moffit (13,020 feet), in Alaska's remote Hayes Range. I'm 16 years older than Colin and I envy his enthusiasm in a wistful, longing way. It makes me smile. I also knew it could only help me if we partnered up.

"Yeah, Colin, good point," I said, sighing and scanning my list of excuses: piano lessons, not quite done with this bag of chips, forgot my crampons.

"You keep *talking* about Patagonia," Colin said. *Ouch.*

I was broke, just returned from Pakistan, and didn't feel like getting serious about climbing. Once I commit, my pride gets in the way—I'd have to train. Hard. Now. Another swig off the marg. "I have a life, man," I lied. The Ultimate Fighting match between Tito Ortiz and Chuck Liddell was December 30, and Hooters always shows the pay-per-view fights free. I didn't think they had Hooters in El Chaltén (at least, not ones with TVs). Besides, I'd never been to Patagonia and I hate to break with tradition. And I have a "hippie" problem.

Now don't get me wrong—I'm a peace-loving guy. But bongo drums and slacklines make me want to break things. And Patagonia, I'd heard, had the worst kind of hippies: the faux-hippie-football-jock-frat-boy-combo hippies, those über-annoying bro-brah-braus. Rumor had it they infest El Chaltén, where the notorious weather means they can just smoke weed and spray. After festering for seven weeks in Pakistan a couple months earlier—complete with retreat heartbreakingly short of Shingu Charpa's summit after three days and forty-five pitches—maybe my brah-chi was off. Festering with a caravan of twirling gold-brickers sounded about as fun as a gutful of pinworms.

I thought for a moment, developing my defense. "You shouldn't be going either!" I replied. *Touché.* Colin kept taking months off the University of Washington to climb. But this time, he insisted, he'd only miss a week—the maximum allowed before the U automatically dropped him. (When you're on the ten-year plan, apparently you know these things.) That, along with his winter break, meant Patagonia, four weeks door-to-door.

"We'll be going early, while it's still cold," Colin said. *Hmmmm.* Good point. Hippies hate cold, even in their llama-wool ponchos and putumayo toques. "You're building this up in your head—it's not that bad," Colin continued. "C'mon, man, I know you've been wanting to go."

"Yeah, well, but—"

"—So you can keep talking about it, or you can step up and make it happen." *Bastard.*

El Chaltén, mid-December: We plopped down in the yard of Albergue del Lago, our launching point for the mountains. The mass of clouds known as the "Wall of Hate" so obscured the peaks I started to wonder if Cerro Torre even existed. It was starting to look like another expensive camping trip.

Patagonia seems like the ideal place if you want to talk the talk. With conditions not even a Slovenian would climb in, you can leave empty-handed and no one will fault you for dragging out that time-honored chestnut: "Aw, yeah, we got shut down by the weather, dude. We really wanted it, ya' know [make steely-eyed "hardman" look], really wanted it, but what can you do? Live to climb another day, bro."

Maybe my biggest fear of Patagonia was to come home with nothing to show but that damned excuse and some webbing-shaped calluses on my feet. I'm the king of goofing off, so I can handle some weather. Still, even if I fail—and I fail a lot—I don't want to be like *that*. There's a difference between being smart and making excuses, and it has nothing to do with the level you climb at, what your best send is, or any of that bullshit. If you love it, at a certain point the cartwheels stop and you go up.

If fantasies garnish any peak, they make Cerro Torre. It attracts not only the obsessed, but also the crazies. Maybe its beauty and inhospitable nature simply clash with a hubristic inability to accept that there are some things we just can't have.

Nothing so illustrates the need to "possess" Cerro Torre as the Italian climber Cesare Maestri's legendary 1970 siege up the Southeast Ridge, now known as the *Compressor Route*, absurdly done to "prove" his bizarre 1959 Cerro Torre first-ascent claim. (Despite absolutely zero proof against overwhelmingly contradictory evidence, Maestri claimed a futuristic alpine-style ascent of the daunting north face in 1959, with Toni Egger. On the attempt, Egger fell to his death with the team's only camera.) In 1970, the obsessed Maestri commandeered a large team for two seasons, fixing thousands of feet of rope and drilling more than 400 bolts with a gas-powered compressor. He placed bolts near perfectly good cracks and used them deliberately to avoid natural features. It wasn't a case of "different standards in a different era," for the assault was then globally decried (Maestri's climb was largely the impetus behind Messner's classic diatribe "The Murder of the Impossible"). But for all his efforts on that 1970 route, Maestri retreated just below the top.

Not that this is unusual on Cerro Torre. Before our trip, we studied the peak's history: Of eleven "routes," six didn't summit, and three of them simply ended in the middle of nowhere. No summit, no somewhat-accepted modern definition of intersecting an existing route or stopping at a distinctly defined landmark. Maybe it's just a dumbing-down to fit us into a challenge we can't meet on its own terms.

Most impressively, consider this: exclude routes that rely on Maestri's manmade path, and only two routes had summited Cerro Torre. I love that. *El Arca de los Vientos* (Beltrami-Garibotti-Salvaterra; 2005) climbs spectacular and historically significant terrain up the north and northwest faces, covering much of the ground Maestri claimed in his 1959 charade. And then you have the 1974 *Ragni di Lecco* route up the West Face, rightfully known to all but true believers as the FA route on the world's most beautiful alpine spire. (Maestri's fairy tale would make for good fun, but it's not "all good," because he robbed his rival countrymen of their rightful place in history.)

Perhaps Cerro Torre—along with the bro-brah-brau—best represents the fantasy of Patagonia. And in some sordid sense, perhaps Maestri does, too. Then again, maybe the wind just drove him crazy.

Like our hula-hooping brethren, we had an ambitious plan: a new link-up on Cerro Torre. It had shut down better climbers, but conditions and timing are everything. According to our big talk, we'd pack ridiculously light—daypacks plus a stove—and punch it.

The lower "route" has a French name I can't pronounce, but back in 1994 François Marsigny and Andy Parkin started from the southeast side and climbed a serac-threatened, ephemeral ice-and-mixed couloir for 2,600 vertical feet to the Col of Hope, intersecting the 1974 West Face route (which starts on the remote icecap side) where it wraps around. The plan and the prize had been obvious: continue up the remaining 2,000 feet to the Torre's summit. Hit the summit and you can go over, zip down the *Compressor Route*, and stroll on back to your bivy, *sin problema*. Right. Marsigny and Parkin got battered back by storms some 1,000 feet below the summit and retreated to the icecap, their to-hell-and-back epic lasting nine long days.

We wanted to climb Cerro Torre, and the *Compressor Route* didn't inspire. Rappel it, though? Sure. Everyone draws his line in the sand, and we didn't care if we rappelled over ours. If we could *climb* Cerro Torre by fair means, that would be enough. That was our fantasy, anyway.

Wind shook buildings in El Chaltén. At Campo de Agostini, several times I scurried out of my tent, terrified that a tree might blow over and squash me. The Wall of Hate dominated, swallowing the peaks despite usually decent weather (wind notwithstanding) in town and even at basecamp. Perfect for hanging out talking about climbing. Inside the black clouds of the Wall, hurricane-force winds made even walking up-glacier nearly impossible. But my *idée fixe* about climbers in Patagonia proved most baffling: I liked everyone, damnit. No brahs, slacklines, or hula-hoops in sight—just friendly locals and a handful of normal climber folks. We must've been too early.

Day after day we slept late, walked to town for pizza and beer, raced back to stay fit, and ruined ourselves on nine-peso ($3) fifths of Doble V whiskey near our friend Freddie's tent. The Doble V sessions always started innocently enough, but then progressed with spot-on predictability into barely comprehensible rant-offs.

Then, no shit, it finally happened: Freddie bludgeoned the mouse that had been raiding his food box and hung it from a tree, an offering to the weather gods. And in early January, just before our flights home, the skies cleared from Patagonia to Siberia.

We walk up the glacier. I take my time, inspired by the dirty old parable about the young bull and the old bull. When I join Colin, he's sitting on a glacial erratic, staring through binoculars. I think the lower route, the *Marsigny-Parkin*, looks like snow-plastered rock. Discontinuous white streaks angle from left to right beneath a serac big enough to take out half a neighborhood. Debris from other seracs litters the approach. Our line appears reasonable, though, and after 1,500 feet in the serac's barrel, a rightward traverse leads to a nonthreatened couloir for another 1,000 feet to the Col of Hope. From there, we'll join the outrageous rime formations of the upper West Face. It all seems reasonable—not "safe" like tennis or the couch, but reasonable—if only the route looked good.

Grinning, Colin hands me the binocs. Still looks like snow-plastered rock to me.

He grabs the glasses again, studies, and says, "I don't think we'll ever have another chance like now." I contemplate my laziness. It'd only be about a three-hour approach from our bivy, predawn when everything's frozen. If it were no good, we could head back to basecamp and learn to play the didgeridoo.

"Well?" Colin asks.

Surrounded by a circle of bros, I'm swaying back and forth, playing a bongo while squinting into the sun. A brau throws me a pair of devil sticks; I bongo with my feet and say, "I'm soooo ready to send the sickness once the weather clears."

"Whoa, like, how do you do it, AlphaBrah?" one chick asks. She's so furry I think she has Buckwheat in a headlock, but it's all good. Maybe we can hook it up later. I flip my hair and reply, "Look, when I get up in the afternoon, I put my pants on one leg at a time, just like anybody."

"That's what I'm talkin' about," another bro says.

"Namaste, brau," squeals another, trying to hold his bong hit.

"It's just that when I do," I continue, "I blast the Enormodome in 1 hour, 23 minutes, and 17.2 seconds. That's just how I roll." I strip down.

"Ohhh, it's on! It's on!" they cheer, tweaking with bromantic adulation.

"It's on like Donkey Kong," I say.

"Let's do this!" another yells.

"Here, hold my shirt," I say coolly, looking away and tossing it into the circle. "I'm gonna go slack some line."

My eyes snap open in horror and I sit bolt upright. Suddenly, I realize I'm not inside a comfy drum circle, but languishing in a bivy tent on the Torre Glacier. Morning sun beats down. Through bleary eyes, I look at Colin, 3 feet away. Cuts lace his swollen face; he looks horrible. I mumble a few words and try to shake the cobwebs.

"Dude, I'm a dirty hippie, so smelly people don't usually bother me," Colin says. *"But you stink." Is this any way to talk to an AlphaBrah?* I feel like asking, but my gummy mouth hangs open uselessly.

My body throbs with exhaustion. My hands won't close. Freaky nerve zingers zap down my arms. I think I'm following Colin's words, but I need confirmation, because I can't believe I'm so damned lucky. Colin tells me he's wanted to climb Cerro Torre since he was 12. Huh? We climbed Cerro-F—king-Torre? Come again?

I blink hard, shake my head, and stare into my sleeping bag. Dreamlike images flash before me, visions of fantastic ice sheets, falling debris, and the unforgettable grandeur of the icecap. Of rime-ice towers and snow mushrooms rising in gravity-defying, fairytale-like shapes. Of treasure hunts, seeking wind-carved tunnels that yield passage into the desperate mushrooms, and a landscape so surreal I expect goblins and hobbits to streak past. Exhaustion, hallucination, staggering in the dark on the rubble-strewn Torre Glacier.

I've been here before, strung-out worlds from my couch between dreams and reality, and still I can't understand it. Closing my eyes, I envision Cerro Torre's beauty and inhospitable nature, and I can't believe it's something I could know, even for a moment. Maybe someone mickeyed my water bottle with peyote.

I poke my head outside and look for bro-brah-braus, but see only a disheveled heap of climbing gear and a handful of real-deal climbers. I shake my head again, and then crane my neck upward at Cerro Torre. Incomprehensible. No way. Silently, I thank Colin and laugh at my laziness, old-guy crustiness, and hesitation. When have I ever regretted going? Funny how that works, but they say the wind does things to people.

PART FIVE:
THE 2010s

THE 2010s: A LIFETIME OF CLIMBING

BY CHRIS SHARMA

I was one of the first climbing gym–generation kids. Up to that point, usually it was an uncle or a friend—a mentor—who introduced the next generation to climbing. My dad was a surfer and grew up in a different world. I always had a natural inclination for scrambling up trees, but I started climbing in gyms in the early 1990s because there was one close to my home in Santa Cruz, California.

There, at the Pacific Edge Climbing Gym, I met climbers who took me under their wing. To this day, I feel super grateful to them for showing me around Castle Rock, Pinnacles National Park, Yosemite, and beyond.

Out with friends at the boulders and crags, it felt good to be surrounded by nature. But back on plastic, it was often a different story. Here, the adults were taking themselves way too seriously. They dressed in Lycra and threw embarrassing wobblers at comps when they blew a sequence and fell. At first, I thought sport climbing and competitions were dorky.

But I loved getting out there and doing my best, like in 1994 when I competed in nationals at City Rock, going against heavy hitters like Scott Franklin and Doug Engelkirk. Before I knew it I was winning, and it felt good to know I had finally found something I was good at. Tommy Caldwell, Beth Rodden, Katie Brown, and I made up this youth movement, bringing new blood to the sport. In 1995, all of us came onto the scene, and that changed things—we were kids out there just having fun and not thinking too much about the importance of clipping the chains, taking first place, or being top dog.

Around that same time, a small crew of dedicated boulderers including Fred Nicole, Boone Speed, and I visited places like Hueco Tanks, Texas, and Ibex and Joe's Valley in Utah, where we put up V12s and V13s—cutting-edge problems at the time. Meanwhile, bouldering had taken off in Yosemite, with problems like Jerry Moffatt's *Dominator* (V12/V13; 1993)—and that influenced me a lot. The hard-pushing, supportive vibe reminded me of when I was 13 or 14 and bouldering with Ron Kauk in Camp 4. Soon, finding bouldering FAs became my main focus. Unlike all the hard work of bolting and cleaning a new sport climb, with bouldering first ascents you need little more than vision, some crashpads, and a toothbrush.

I traveled to Europe when I was 16, and that opened my eyes to the world of hard sport climbing, there at the great, sweeping, legendary limestone walls of Buoux and Céüse, France. Before heading to Europe, I made the first ascent of Boone Speed's longtime project *Necessary Evil* (5.14c) at the Virgin River Gorge in Arizona, the hardest climb in the country at the time—1997. I completed that and Jibé Tribout's *Just Do It* in the same month.

During those early years, I loved sport climbing and bouldering equally—and some trad, especially in Yosemite. But I wouldn't take sport climbing seriously until I got much older. Climbing is a lifetime thing, and as we grow and change, so do our interests. Over the years, I've followed a trajectory that's taken me from bouldering to sport to competitions, and back again.

FROM BLOCS TO WALLS TO SEA

I lived in Bishop, California, from 1998 to 2000, bouldering avidly and putting up new problems like *The Mandala* (V12) in the Buttermilks. I didn't want to just follow the lines that were set, but to embrace the creative process and author my own first ascents.

That process brought me to Jean-Christophe Lafaille's (1965–2006) ultimate project, the most perfect route out there, *Biographie/Realization* in Céüse, which I redpointed in 2001, establishing the world's first 5.15a. (Alex Huber's *Open Air* (1996) at Austria's Schleierwasserfall could also be the world's first 5.15; it's debatable. It was certainly the most difficult line in the world at the time.)

After *Biographie*, I felt complete as a climber and considered moving on to something different. But then I traveled to Mallorca and got my second wind for climbing with deep-water soloing (DWS): climbing ropeless above the sea. This emerging activity combined sport climbing, bouldering, and a dash of adventure. Soon I was pushing myself in a way that was once again unique and different.

DWS created a new form of climbing that felt so free. Growing up by the ocean as a kid, I felt comfortable in those surroundings, so the sport came naturally to me. After my first DWS experiences, where I repeated or established routes up to

5.13, I thought about my transformation on *Biographie* and began seeking out that next perfect, futuristic line. When I found *Es Pontàs* (5.15a), a natural sea arch off the coast of Mallorca in 2006, I sank everything I had into it. That 65-foot project took me three years to complete.

Driven by my love for DWS, I started organizing the Psicobloc comps—DWS competitions held on an artificial wall in Utah—in 2013. That's the same year Adam Ondra redpointed my project from 2009, *La Dura Dura*, authoring the world's first 5.15c. When the 20-year-old Czech phenom ticked it, I knew it was time to pass the torch. Now Adam has flashed 5.15a and redpointed 5.15d. Incredible.

Of the many talented climbers out there, Ondra, with his singular focus; quick, dynamic style; and heroic training sessions, perhaps best defines performance rock climbing in the 2010s. It's a decade that's seen the first redpoints of 5.15 by women (Margo Hayes and Angy Eiter, respectively, with *La Rambla* [5.15a] and *La Planta de Shiva* [5.15b], both in 2017), the world's first V17 (Nalle Hukkataival's *Burden of Dreams*, 2017), the world's first VI 5.14d big wall (the *Dawn Wall*, freed in 2015 by Tommy Caldwell and Kevin Jorgeson, then rapidly repeated the next year by Ondra), the first free solo of a VI wall on El Capitan (Alex Honnold's ropeless 2017 ascent of *Freerider*, 5.13a), insane mixed-climbing standards up to D16, and an explosion of light-and-fast solo or two-person-team alpine blitzes like Honnold and Colin Haley's *one-day* repeat of the Torres Traverse in Patagonia in 2016.

Through it all, I've felt grateful to still be immersed in the sport I love. Over the years I've grown and changed, becoming a husband, father, and business owner, but climbing, as ever, is still about reinventing myself, being passionate, and finding the next life chapter. Today I embrace the spontaneity of climbing without pressure and am careful to follow the playful side of the sport.

It's important to see climbing as a personal journey and to realize how it can be about reaching for something beyond your grasp. As the level gets higher and we get more young crushers, it's crucial to understand why we climb and also to share that journey with the next generation. Today, I share climbing with my daughter.

Now my main focus is finding out how hard I can push myself with pure sport climbing. As I dictate this, I'm in Oliana, Spain, looking up at *La Dura Dura*. It feels great to be out here surrounded by friends. In the distance, I can hear people cheering on someone as they complete their project. Their voices remind me how much has changed but also how much has stayed the same since I began climbing back in the 1990s. Ten years ago there were no routes here, and today there are 10 climbs rated 5.15. I'm happy to know I still feel that same stoke for climbing I've had since I was a teenager back in Santa Cruz.

In 2013 I helped open Sender One in Orange County, California, and in 2015 I opened Sharma Climbing BCN in Barcelona, Spain.

HALF LIFE

FEBRUARY 2011, NO. 292

BY JEFF ACHEY

For fifteen years, the headlines and ads read (and continue to read): "Climbing is now spelled Sharma"; "The Impossible Climb"; "Chris Sharma: World's First 5.15." You couldn't pick up a climbing magazine without seeing Sharma. And he was always the star in the videos, too—he was the best at bouldering, sport climbing, and deep-water soloing, and not too shabby on trad either. As the sport grew, he grew with it. All the while we watched with awe as he powered and dyno'ed his way up the wildest routes in the world. Jeff Achey caught up with the climbing phenom when he turned 30 to talk about where he was in life and climbing, as well as his future goals.

You could define an old-school climber as one who remembers a time "before Sharma." From his boy-wonder teenage days to his meditative 20s, Chris Sharma has captured our imaginations, inspiring us not only with his routes—*Necessary Evil, The Mandala, Realization, Witness the Fitness, Dreamcatcher, Es Pontas, Jumbo Love*—but also with his humility. Sharma was so soft-spoken, so mellow, that when he showed up at a national championship or the X Games, he seemed almost out of place. And when he'd win, it was as if the victory belonged to climbing itself, a triumph over the competitive and narcissistic hang-ups tainting our art-slash-sport. Besides, his free-swinging style was great to watch.

Sharma has delivered everything that "the next generation" is supposed to in rock climbing. He has been setting new standards for fifeen years—half his life. And now, on April 23, he turns 30.

We caught up with Sharma in October, outside a bagel shop in Boulder, where he had come to do a benefit slideshow. In a three-hour interview, it became very clear that he's still just as psyched as when he was a scrawny 15-year-old, campusing to the top of the climbing world. He firmly believes his hardest climbs are still to come. But now he has a house, a girlfriend of three years, and a dog. His soul patch has grayed a bit, and he has wisdom to share about climbing that all of us can relate to. Which shouldn't be surprising. An athletic gift is given by nature, but for the gift to keep on giving, your guiding philosophy must stand the test of time. Sharma's has.

THE INTERVIEW

You have this public image as the "spiritual climber." Is that an accurate description?
I feel like I have been portrayed like that. People, interviewers, whatever, they try to put you in a box, you know? Not that it's not true, but at the same time I feel like that's not telling the whole story. I think it's really just trying to be true to yourself and as authentic as possible. Not trying to strategically create some image.

So, as a professional climber, how do you keep it real?
I think for me, whenever I've gone climbing, it's because I really wanted to go climbing, not because I wanted to try to outdo someone or prove something to the world. There is this side of my climbing that's professional—it's like my job. But I feel like I've found a good way of separating those things. If I go to a trade show, or a competition, or a slide show, that's when I'm on the clock, being a professional climber.

Don't you feel like on some climbs, though that you're trying to just get the job done? Does that still happen to you?
Oh, yeah. It totally happens. It's a constant process. It's like relearning the same things over and over again—kind of like every route. It's hard to have that pure attitude. You know, you wanna send it, but that's almost inhibiting you from just being yourself and climbing it like you know you can. When I climbed *Realization*, I was kind of feeling tired that day, and was like, well, whatever, I'll give it a burn,

just to remember the moves. And then you kind of trick yourself into not really caring about it, and then you're free to just do it, I guess.

I feel like that goes for competitions, too. More often than not, when I'm successful in competitions, I'm pretty pessimistic going into the whole thing. Everyone always says you have to have a lot of belief in yourself, and I think it's true, but for me, it's more about taking the pressure off. If I'm already set that I'm not going to win, then I just let go and have fun, and I'm able to really climb well because I'm not worried about winning anymore. I haven't found a formula for that except for trying to trick myself, you know? Basically trick myself and talk to myself in that way.

When you come to a competition, everybody expects you to win. It's got to be hard—it's a lose-lose situation in a way.
Yeah, I definitely have mixed feelings about competitions, because more often than not, I don't prepare for them. But I try to have the mindset that I just go to participate in the climbing community and share my climbing or share myself with other people.

Personally, that's not ever really been my deal. I mean, competitions are fun, but fifteen minutes after the competition they take the holds off. It's way more important for me to put up new routes and develop my vision in rock climbing. Create a legacy, create something lasting. No one remembers who won the freakin' World Cup in 1997, but people know who put up *Action Directe*.

Talk a little bit about your upbringing. Didn't you grow up in an ashram?
My parents were both students of Baba Hari Dass. When they got married, they took the name Sharma. It means "good fortune," or something like that. It's actually a pretty common last name in India. I went to school at the Mount Madonna Center, in the Santa Cruz Mountains. I lived in Santa Cruz, and we would go up to the school every day, but we didn't live on the center.

Did this background affect your early climbing?
For me, it never was just blindly like, OK, I'm a climber, I'm just gonna climb. I definitely relate that to my background and to my friends, Andy [Puhvel] and Sterling [Keene] and other close friends from Santa Cruz. It wasn't like we were in a climbing scene. Being a famous climber was never really something that I tried to make happen.

What set you on that path?
I won the national championship when I was 14. I had amazing opportunities like that. But when I was 17, I had a really bad knee injury. That was a pretty powerful experience for me because all of a sudden, I couldn't climb. And I'd kind of put all my eggs in that basket. I'd gotten my GED through an alternative high school that basically just accepted my life experience as my schooling. When I was 16, I was hitchhiking around France with Tommy Caldwell, climbing, and that really has been my education. Traveling and meeting people and just life experiences. I guess I didn't learn so much math.

A lot of us who sat through school can say the same thing.
Yeah, but I did really commit to climbing—that was all I wanted to do. And not too long after that, I blew out my knee, and I couldn't climb for a year. That was a really rough moment for me. It was really depressing.

What was your comeback after all that?
I was probably 18 or 19, and at the trade show I met Christian Griffith. I'd already gone once to try that route *Realization*, and he encouraged me to go try it again. He told me that it's something I'll look back and be psyched on. At that point, I wasn't sure what I wanted to do, whether I wanted to maybe go back to school. I felt like I had a really good run, I did a lot of stuff I wanted to do, but I thought, before I do something else, this is definitely one thing that I have cliff hanging, you know, this *Realization*.

Between trips there I spent a lot time in Asia. In Japan, I went on this crazy trip, walked about 1,000 miles around this island [Shikoku, a 1,500-year-old Buddhist pilgrimage], totally by myself, just sleeping in the forest in Japan. I went to meditation centers in Thailand and Burma and India. That was a big part of my life for a while. And climbing, as a comparison, was just so external. I worked on *Realization*, and that was kind of the exception. I was really miserable when I hurt my knee, and it made me realize that climbing is pretty ephemeral.

So . . . I got back, I got a girlfriend, and I went to Majorca and totally fell in love with deep-water soloing. Perfect rock over the ocean, and climbing onsight, ground-up. Just super pure.

Did you have any sponsorship issues around your knee injury?
I've been really lucky in that way. Beaver [Theodosakis] from prAna has known me since I was a little kid, and he's always had a lot of faith in me and respected my need to grow as a person. I feel really grateful for that, and in the end I think

it actually enhanced my image for them. That I've just been able to be myself and have my image not be that of a typical athlete.

I guess I got lucky that I wasn't ever playing that game. I wasn't grading my climbs. I was able to climb how I wanted to climb, and I was really fortunate to meet people like Josh and Brett Lowell and shoot videos with them.

So about your label as a spiritual climber . . .
What I don't like about the idea of being a "spiritual person," is it's like, OK, I'm a spiritual person, so I'm going to act all peaceful and try to be all saintly or something. But if you're feeling pissed off in the moment, it's much more true to be pissed off than try to act all peaceful.

I've been living in Spain for a long time now, and people are very expressive there, very fiery, but very authentic. It's like you have to express yourself, even if that's frustration or something. From what I've studied in Buddhism, that's the goal, right? To not be caught up in your own personal image, but actually be authentic, whatever expression that takes.

So my sound bite can be, "At age 30, Chris Sharma is outgrowing the stereotype of the spiritual climber"?
To be stereotyped like that definitely detracts from me personally. Like I said, I'm totally happy talking about this stuff. I just don't want to make some image for myself like I'm some sort of saint or something. I get frustrated, and I get bummed out.

Do you kick and scream on climbs?
Eh, not so much, but once in a while. It can be frustrating as hell to fall off fifty times at the last move, you know? And to act like it's OK, it's all good—that's kind of like bullshit. [Laughs.] I feel like I've learned a lot from Daila [Ojeda]. She's very much true to her emotions and, like, a typical fiery Latin woman, you know? But very true to her feelings.

Is it serious with Daila?
Yeah, we've been together for three years or something.

Thinking about getting married?
We'll see . . . I'm not ruling that out, that's for sure.

Like to have kids some day? Do you think about that?
Yeah, yeah, for sure. I think so. But, uh, first things first. We've got a dog now. A black Lab, Chaxi. That's a good start.

Talk a little bit about Catalunya and the house there you two have been fixing up. How does it feel to have a real home base?
It's pretty much the first time I've ever had that in my life. Since I was 3 years old, I was going week on, week off, at my mom's and my dad's houses. And I've basically been on the road for ten years, not really knowing where to call home. I'd been spending a lot of time in Spain, and Daila and I just said, "Where are we going to live?" And we decided to live in Lleida. Now I've got a place where people come and visit me, and we've ended up creating a community where we are.

Describe the landscape where you live.
There's a lot of agriculture, orchards, and stuff like that. Olive trees and almond trees and peach trees. We live in a little village of about a hundred people. It's almost like if you're coming to the Valley [Yosemite] through Mariposa or something like that. Similar kind of climate, maybe 2,000-foot elevation, and the closest crag is a ten-minute walk.

What's a typical week at home?
Well, it depends. When it's climbing season, we're basically like, "No more home projects." We're climbing five days a week, always going to the crag, driving a lot. In the wintertime, it gets dark pretty early, so even if it's an hour and a half drive back home, it's OK.

Any really exceptional projects in the works?
I've got two projects in mind right now that are in Margalef. One is *First Round, First Minute*, and another is one that I bolted last fall [*Perfecto Mondo*]. So, just trying to focus, you know, on a couple things right now, not get too spread out.

How many projects do you have that you've bolted but haven't sent?
Probably ten.

Have you given up on some of those? Left them for the next generation?
There's one in Oliana that I have kind of given up on, but I did all the moves. Each individual move is really, really hard, and I think it'd be no doubt 15c or d—really gnarly. But it also has really small holds, and that's not really my strong point.

In the past, I would always just focus all my energy on one route. Like OK, I'm going to go to Clark Mountain and just camp out in the desert and stay till I do it. And that was a cool experience, but it's really hard to have an everyday life, and you always have these time constraints. Being in Spain, I have these projects, these amazing futuristic lines that I'm working on, but I'm able to mix that with everyday life and develop a little bit of a home base.

And that's a first for you.
I'm ready to settle down a little bit, you know? I can be at my house and not be sleeping on the floor of someone's house or camping out in some random foreign place that I have no connection to whatsoever. So it feels a little more holistic. And I feel like I can work on harder routes because I don't have to plan out my time so much.

Do you think your current projects will be your hardest yet?
Yeah, for sure. Some of the stuff I'm working on will be harder than anything I've ever done. But everything kind of loses its significance there, in a way, because there's so much hard climbing that one route doesn't really stand out from the next.

I feel like, as soon as you do one new level, other people are like, "So when are you going to do the next hardest thing?" That's not really how it works. It took me, like, seven years to go from 15a to 15b. It's not like, oh, so I did some 15b—when's the 15c gonna come? It's not as simple as that. And it shouldn't be. Every time the scale goes up, it seems like it should be a significant difference.

And I'm super-stoked on a lot of different kinds of routes. It's cool to do a long route like *Jumbo Love*, and it's also really cool to do a short bouldering route.

Are some of these projects shorter?
Like 40 feet. I've always loved bouldering. Where we live, there's not that much bouldering, but some of these shorter routes maybe have V14 boulder problems in them. It's really cool to get in that zone where you're just like—[sound effect]—really going for it hard in that bouldering style.

I'm just kind of mixing it up, always trying to reinvent something, I guess. Taking bouldering and route climbing and kind of fusing those styles together. I think that helps me stay psyched.

Speaking of mixing it up, you've ventured out a little into other disciplines, like doing Moonlight Buttress *and* The Rostrum. *There was a rumor that you once showed up in Yosemite Valley with the idea of trying to onsight the* Nose. *Is that true?*
[Laughs.] Well, my buddy and me were gonna try it. And on any route I try, if it's my first time on it, I try to flash it, you know? That's what I always try. We went up the first seven pitches, and I fell on, like, a 12c move . . .

Seven pitches up those traverses into the Stoveleg Cracks?
Yeah, right there. So that's something I would love to go back on. I don't know if we really did it so strategically—like we were hauling and stuff, and ended up fixing line to go back to the ground. And the next day we woke up and were just both so tired. We were like, uh, I think we're just gonna go bouldering.

I would love to do more high-off-the-ground stuff like that. Bring what I've done in sport climbing and apply that to longer routes. I'd love to find some rad, overhanging 600- to 1,000-foot wall and find a 5.15 on it. But I feel like there's some work for me in single-pitch sport climbing still, some improvements I'd like to make, and some harder routes I'd like to do before I move on.

But 30 years old, the clock's ticking . . .
I might be ready, you know . . .

Settling down. You've got a house now, and a dog . . .
I might be ready, actually, but there are a few projects that hopefully this fall I can climb. And I love putting up routes, much more than to repeat another route. It's such a complete process—to see something, dream it might be possible, and then you have to really work your ass off to make it even possible to attempt it.

So, back to an earlier point. Your new home base—this is the next step for you in order to climb harder?
Yeah, for sure. Some of the strongest climbers now are from Spain, and where we're living is really what southern France was in the mid- or early 1990s, you know? Right now, there's literally 15 5.15s within an hour and a half of each other. So it's really kind of a special moment in Spain.

And you're saying that you can't reach a new level if you're always globetrotting.
I went to China last year, to Yangshuo, and I bolted four amazing routes, really great projects. But we were there for three weeks, and there's just no time to do any of them. Like I was saying, to put your life on hold and go camp out in the Mojave Desert is stressful for your relationships. It's pretty amazing that Daila

went with me, like, five times to Clark Mountain. She looks around, and she's like, "I don't get it, there's a million crags in Spain . . ."

It's totally worth it to find a route like that, but in the game of finding harder climbs, it's not like you can just whip 'em out every week. Or every year. It takes consolidation—that's the dirty work.

So you're kind of pushing the numbers now.
Yeah, yeah, it's interesting. People asked why I started grading things again. I felt like, yeah, look, this is not the most important thing, but at the same time, to just not pay any attention to that is a little blind, too, you know? But for me, it's always going to be mostly about finding cool routes—that's the motivation to try something hard.

How do you see yourself staying involved when you're no longer a professional athlete?
Well, outside of climbing, seeing how professional athletes evolve through life, you have guys like Tony Hawk that stayed very relevant, stayed very in tune with everything. Then you have guys like Mike Tyson, who kind of crashed and burned . . .

Which direction do you see yourself going?
[Laughs.] Hopefully not toward crash and burn. I was just talking about this with Boone [Speed] this morning. Boone is a great example—he's staying connected to the industry through design and photography.

So how would you work it?
Well, I'm actually really motivated on shoe design right now. I'm going to Evolv tomorrow. I've also worked with a kid's climbing camp called Yo Base Camp— one of my best friends, Andy Puhvel, and his wife, Lisa, just a mom-and-pop company—doing a scholarship fund for them called the Sharma Fund.

I had a lot of support from my local climbing community, and without that kind of support, I know I wouldn't be here today.

But for now, still an athlete . . .
I'm super-psyched to keep pushing it as long as I can, but I think I've tried to be aware that there's gonna be a time when I'm not the best climber. What I felt, just traveling all the time—you're having these great experiences, meeting great people, having these connections, but you never really go anywhere with those connections. My family is the friends that I have, because I don't have any brothers or sisters. My mom passed away, and I've never been super-close with my other relatives.

I wanted to start to build something so that in ten years, when I'm really washed up and over the hill, and . . .

No more slide shows . . .

That's just kind of a sad image. So being in Spain is really trying to find a balance. Continuing my climbing, but also trying to develop something more that's, like, a life.

I mean, even now I feel like a lot of the pressure's off. There's a new, younger generation to push new standards. More of the pressure is on them now. I'm still enjoying it, so why not? I'm still good, I'm still psyched, but I don't want to approach things from the perspective of trying to hang on to something. I feel really happy that I have a house and a girl to go back to.

VAMPIRE DIARY

DECEMBER 2012-JANUARY 2013, NO. 311

BY JEFF ACHEY

Pat Goodman can't get enough of the Vampire Spires in Canada's Northwest Terri-
tories. He's gone six times (and counting), recruiting new partners for free routes on
the sweeping walls in Nahanni National Park. Artist Jeremy Collins, photographer
James Q Martin, and writer/editor Jeff Achey were his partners for this trip, during
which the team utilized a raft to approach their objective. Goodman promised them
the climb of a lifetime—the 2,500-foot northeast prow of the Phoenix—and he did
not disappoint.

Soaking wet but still upright, we were spit out of a smooth, yet fast rapid into a wave train trucking headlong into yet another blind bend. I spun us into an upstream ferry and called a hard "Forward!", hoping to buy another second or two to pick a line through the next drop, but the fast-approaching rapid was so steep that all I could see were occasional splashes cresting the horizon line. I chose a random notch between boulders and spun us downstream.

We shot through the rocks below, busted through a wave at the bottom of a trough, and when I wiped the spray from my eyes, I saw that we were bearing down fast on a big boat-flipper of a wave coming off the right wall. The Little Nahanni seemed determined to be the most exciting part of our trip.

Pat Goodman, James Q Martin, and I were plunging headlong down this remote northern river not because we were expert boaters—we were not—but because we were climbers, and the river was snaking to the base of the Vampire Peaks, a group of granite spires in the vast, rugged wilderness along Canada's Northwest Territories/Yukon border. This loaded down 10-foot raft was taking us climbing.

I had vaguely recalled reading about "the Vamps" years ago in an issue of this very magazine. They were somewhere near the famed Lotus Flower Tower, right? Details were fuzzy, but if I recalled correctly, the climbing scenario there was somewhat less than ideal, involving mosquito clouds, grizzly bears, and ascending long, moss-filled cracks in the rain. Only about a dozen climbing parties had ever visited. That's about all I could conjure up when Pat invited me on an expedition to claim a first ascent on the area's most prominent tower.

For Goodman, the Vampires were practically home (this would be his sixth trip), and the difficulties of climbing there were part of the area's charm. He sent me enticing photos of our main objective—all taken in sunny weather—noting that it was probably the greatest free-climbing prize in the area. I'd met Pat about five years back in the New River Gorge, West Virginia, where he now resides. He was a North Carolina climber at the time, and before that, hailed from Farmington, New Mexico. This background plus his brawling Irish temperament had made him a strong and scrappy climber drawn to a variety of masochistic disciplines: soft-rock hoodoo soloing, offwidth roofs, 5.13 X headpointing, and gnarly alpine big walls. He was the expedition leader, and had secured an American Alpine Club grant that would pay for much of the trip. It didn't take much to convince me to join the team.

The Vampires are part of a large granite intrusion in the middle of the Mackenzie Mountains, a vast, mostly sedimentary-rock range that forms the divide between the west-flowing Yukon and east- and north-flowing Mackenzie, two of the North's largest rivers. The Cirque of the Unclimbables, a much better-known area that includes Lotus Flower Tower and Proboscis, is nearby, about 15 air miles to the southeast.

The expedition's main objective was to establish a free route on the 2,500-foot northeast prow of the Phoenix, probably the most striking climbing feature in all the sub-valleys that make up the Vamps. Goodman had already made the first free ascents of both Vampire Spire and the Fortress; he considered these and the Phoenix to be the "top three" in the area, and the Phoenix was the biggest. The only previous party to top out the buttress had not attempted the icy and steep scramble up the final ridge, so the true summit of the peak had never been reached. It was hard to imagine a more enticing target.

WATER

The river component actually makes sense. Approaching the Cirque or the Vampires requires air support from a floatplane, a helicopter, or both. Planes carry more and airtime is less expensive, but they are limited in where they can land: You need a lake or a wide, straight stretch of slow-moving river. Choppers can pick you up and drop you off almost anywhere, but they are more expensive. Our solution? Raft the river to get that much closer to the climbing, and save on costs. But we would get an airlift from the water to our high basecamp, sparing us an epic load-ferrying effort up the steep, wild Vampires valley.

Nahanni National Park—where the Vampires lay—is much better known for its rivers than its climbing anyway. Lower down, closer to where it empties into the huge Laird River just above Fort Simpson on the Mackenzie, the South Nahanni surges through several limestone gorges, eventually plunging 300 vertical feet over the stunning, Niagara-like Virginia Falls, one of the most impressive waterfalls in North America. The whole Nahanni valley was an area of some mystique during Gold Rush times. Several grisly, unsolved murders befell some early prospectors, and local place names bear witness: The Broken Skull River, Deadmen Valley, Hell's Gate, Headless Creek, the Funeral Range, Vampire Peaks. The Nahanni was referred to as "The Valley of No Return."

The Vampires and Cirque of the Unclimbables were high up in the river basin, so we'd be stopping well above the main gorges and falls, in the rugged heart of the mountains. We started on the river's southernmost tributary, the Little Nahanni, which we accessed by floatplane at its source, a remote place called Flat Lakes.

Getting to Flat Lakes, however, took some doing in itself. It's possible to fly to Whitehorse, the only place in the Yukon with an international airport, but like the majority of climbers who visit the area, Goodman and I made a marathon drive to a point where we could be picked up by bush plane. We all-nighted from Colorado across Wyoming and Montana, then continued up through Alberta. Past the rolling fields of Edmonton we crossed into British Columbia, soon reaching Dawson Creek, the official start of the Alaska Highway, or the Al-Can, as the locals call it. Beyond there, the country became distinctly wilder. Towns disappeared, the highway twisted through spectacular river canyons and over high passes, and the few-and-far-between gas stops came to look more like logging camps. After fifty driving hours we reached the last settlement we'd see on our journey, Watson Lake.

Watson Lake is populated by a hardy mix of about 1,000 Sourdoughs and Kaska Dene "First Nation" natives; it is a rough-around-the-edges way station for tungsten miners, loggers, and Al-Can tourists. Its best-known attraction is the "Sign Post Forest," a small park just off main street featuring thousands of street signs from all over the world. Go figure. Just behind the Forest we found the community center, with its one-room Greyhound station, where we picked up "Q"—photographer James Q Martin—thus assembling the complete river team (our fourth climber, Jeremy Collins, would meet us in the mountains).

From Watson Lake, we had another four-hour drive, to Finlayson Lake where Warren LaFave would pick us up by plane. This last stretch of driving followed the Robert Campbell "Highway" a gravel spur off the Al-Can that had us bottoming out violently on a regular basis, but paid us back with caribou, moose, bear, and wolf sightings.

Finlayson Lake is the main fuel-depot and passenger pick-up point for Warren LaFave's Kluane Airways. Its rustic quarters hardly prepared us for the poshness on the other end of the flight, the Inconnu Lodge, a high-end fishing resort run by Warren and his wife Anita. Inconnu is the jumping-off place for most climbing trips into the Vampires or the Cirque. Late the next morning, Warren picked us up in his vintage Havilland Beaver and flew us in. The Inconnu is a self-sufficient timber-framed lodge, and the only habitation on McEvoy Lake, a seven mile-long fisherman's dream packed with grayling and 50-pound lake trout. Anglers pay $1,000 a night, but Warren seems to like climbers and never begrudges a few free nights in the guide cabins pre- and postclimb as part of the deal. From the Inconnu we flew about 50 miles over tundra-covered peaks and vast expanses of scraggly-treed flats to a velvety landing on Flat Lake to wade our loads ashore. When the Beaver disappeared we suddenly found ourselves all alone, in total silence. We blinked at each other, then got to work inflating and rigging the raft to begin our 100-mile paddle to the Vampires.

Our raft bore down broadside on this ominous lateral wave, and there was nothing to do but paddle like hell. The boat was heavy with gear and slow to change direction—good for punching through waves but in this case, our possible undoing. As impact seemed imminent, I could imagine two possible scenarios: We'd be flipped immediately by the curling wave and sent upside down into the rapid below, or else pulled into the seething eddy on the upstream side of the wave and thrashed against sharp rocks until the raft ripped. My teammates, however, dug in with previously unseen vigor, and we just barely got enough momentum to bump the wave and spin off.

When we finally reached a stretch of relative calm, I reflected on how different climbing is from boating. When you reach a crux spot on the rock, you can stop the action, step back to a stance, hang on gear if you have to, and take your time to make a decision. If you pause in a rapid, the action keeps going. Hesitate, and the river decides for you—and there's no such thing as rapping off.

It's also true that in climbing, you never get anywhere except by your own exertions, while on the river, barring disaster, the current will bring you where you want to go. You can sit back and float. Despite a few adrenaline high-water marks along the way, most of the Nahanni was significantly mellower.

Which is not to say boring—our four days on the Nahanni alone would have been worth the journey. The river had started out small, with bony rock gardens and places where we had to wade the gravel bars and drag our raft.

Small tributaries flowed in from both sides and the river quickly gained power, with waves that splashed over our dry bags. There was not a sign of human presence anywhere: no footprints or fire rings on the gravel bars, no trails, no camps. There were a few cabins marked on the map, but we didn't see them. We drank the clear water directly from the river. The nights were starry and short.

On the next-to-last river day, the Little Nahanni joined the main ("South") Nahanni, and the water changed character, becoming much bigger and lazier, cloudy blue green instead of clear, with widely braided channels and only the occasional run of straightforward standing waves. The river was placid, and we paddled hard to cover the miles.

As we got closer to the Vampires, a squall moved through with rain and thunder, the first weather we'd seen since arriving, and the mountains above took on an ominous look. Goodman watched the shoreline on river-right, consulting the map, waiting for a flash of recognition from his last time here. It was big country, and when viewed from the river, the broad valleys all looked quite similar. I was glad he was in charge of figuring out where we were.

Suddenly, we drifted into an alignment with a side valley that triggered a six-year-old memory, and Goodman announced that we had arrived at our pickup point. At just that moment we heard the faint thwack-thwack-thwack of the chopper descending from Phoenix basecamp after dropping off our final team member, Jeremy Collins. We beached on a gravel bar and scrambled to get ready, derigging and deflating the raft and quickly separating gear. The helicopter landed on the gravel bar, we loaded up, and, just like that, we were flying into the face of a gray and gusty rainstorm, into the Vampires.

ROCK

We came in low, under the clouds, up a steep, rugged valley, and when we suddenly crested a rise we got our first view into the upper cirque. There was Vampires Lake, site of an incident where a grizzly had once trashed a team's camp while they were on the wall, rendering them without food for over a week. And there, looming beyond the lake, was a massive rock peak that I recognized immediately—the Phoenix—looking significantly bigger than in the pictures Goodman had shown me.

Rain pelted the helicopter's windshield, and beyond the buttress, partly obscured by mist, was a hanging glacier with a monstrous hole like a gaping mouth. I'd never seen anything like it, in person or in pictures, and I thought about the Nahanni region's spooky history, wondering if perhaps there wasn't a legitimate supernatural force at work here that had generated the plethora of sinister occurrences and myths.

We were above 60 degrees north latitude, at an altitude just over 5,000 feet now, and on all sides lay cirques and subcirques filled with small glaciers and tall granite walls, many untouched. The 2,500-foot Phoenix prow was the most impressive. It had one completed mixed free and aid line, *Freebird*, done in 1998, which went to the top of the peak's "big-wall" section, and another route, *After School Special*, done a few years later, whose complete ascent had been thwarted by ice just a few pitches from the top. Two other visiting parties had also been stopped short.

Few of the prow's key features matched the hand-scrawled topo we had, but it was pretty obvious that the discontinuous cracks in the vicinity of *After School Special* promised the most feasible start for a free climb. Every possible route up the lower wall, however, was crossed by long, black water streaks and involved significant blank sections that looked improbable even through binoculars. We had only a handful of pins and bolts for protecting any sketchy face climbing.

Goodman seemed unconcerned with the terrain; his doubts revolved solely around the weather. We'd already had five near-perfect days in a row, and he surely felt like we'd used up our share. We all felt an urgency to get started, while at the same time an uncertainty about where the route would go. The sound of our high camp was a river sound, a soft roar coming from a glacial cascade a half-mile above, and when I closed my eyes as I lay in the tent on that first night, I saw water: sparkling water tumbling over dark rocks, glassy tongues ending in V waves that crashed over on themselves, turquoise eddies running upstream against undercut banks. Riverside images floated past at river speed: a grizzly among the willows standing up to sniff the air, a grayling tinning in the shallows, an osprey wheeling above the water, moose tracks on the sand bars. Swirling water.

But now it was time to rock, and the next morning, we went up on the wall for a recon. We scampered up two easy pitches on low-angled slabs to the base of the main prow, where a series of overhanging cracks offered several options. The first steep pitch fell into place as I led up. Many sections of crack were filled with grass, but the rock was generously featured with knobs, ideal for free climbing. After 150 feet, I pulled a final overhang and arrived at a weathered rappel anchor, our first concrete evidence of *After School Special.*

Despite the steepness, the pitch had gone onsight at mid-5.10, and the black water streaks had been dry—an auspicious start, but the real business was yet to come. Collins headed up into thinner terrain, jamming in a couple of small cams, then fingered the opening moves of a steep and committing-looking seam. Feeling the flash pump and seeing nothing to go for, he hung on his top piece—which immediately ripped, along with the one below it, sending him for an alarmingly long fall that left him wide-eyed and level with me. Hanging from his sole piece of pro remaining in the rock, he looked over and chortled. I smiled back, saying nothing, but I couldn't help thinking to myself, "Dude, we are a long way from anywhere."

Knowing I'd done my lead for the day, and seeing that this might take a while, I handed off the belay to Goodman and began descending to camp. When Collins headed back up he chose an easier line, up an angling dihedral. Then he busted across a line of edges that drifted back left, pioneering the first strategic traverse, across one of the route's biggest blank sections. The effort took several hours, which used up most of the daylight, and at 8 p.m. Collins and Goodman rapped from the high point, leaving four ropes fixed.

And so it went, for four days, Collins and me teaming up, then Goodman and Q, ferreting out pitches that gradually found a way up and left across the first thousand feet of the wall, occasionally finding and sometimes using the belay/rappel anchors of *After School Special.* Usually, two of us would work on the route while the other two hiked, bouldered, or rested in camp. The leader would almost always need a few points of aid to clean grass from the cracks, which would then go free the next day at some kind of 5.10. We placed one bolt and a couple of knife blades, but otherwise found adequate pro from cams and nuts. The cracks ran from fingers to offwidth, connected by sections of face climbing, plus the occasional scary flake or moss-hummock mantel. It was stellar alpine rock climbing, and we became increasingly psyched about our line.

Any ethical concerns I had about our siege style were outweighed by the obvious benefit: precious time to wander and explore the pristine Vampires wilderness. On one of my off-wall days I took a long hike up onto the glaciers above camp. There was no sign of human passage.

On the way up I had a face-off with a smallish caribou, who snorted and advanced with head lowered until I made a good threat display with my trekking poles. Higher, I found canid tracks in the snow leading up and over the col that led into the next valley: a lone wolf.

I eventually summited a peak that was one of the highest in our cirque, earning a stunning 360-degree view. To the south were gigantic ice fields and the backsides of Cirque of the Unclimbables. Somewhere in that same general direction was the high point of Northwest Territories, a rugged granite peak known to climbers as "Nirvana" but officially unnamed.

It was just a few hundred feet higher than where I stood. To the north, I had a sweeping view of the Phoenix and the other arm of our valley that contained Vampire Spire and the Fortress. To the northeast were the deep canyons of the Nahanni and the Broken Skull rivers, with countless peaks on the horizon beyond. So much country. So much water and rock. So many possibilities.

Finally we had fixed all our ropes and it was time to make a decision, so back in camp, talk turned to tactics. All of us would have preferred a light-and-fast ascent, but with ropes already strung, four climbers, and a single lead rack, a "disaster-style" assault made little sense. When no one proposed a specific plan, and a chilly evening drizzle put a damper on the next day's free-climbing prospects, I started loading up a haulbag to add to the one already stashed at the base of the wall, and announced that I would spend the next day hauling two modest bags to the top of the lines.

The weather cleared, the hauling went smoothly, and I returned to camp with daylight to spare. The following morning we committed to a summit push. It took us a good part of the day to pack the remaining essentials, get out of camp, and establish the four of us at the top of the fixed lines, but by late afternoon, Goodman finally began racking up for a free attempt on pitch eight. Everything had gone free at 5.10 to this point, and the weather was holding.

Thirty feet up lay a highly questionable crack switch, the last blank spot on the lower wall. The *After School Special* team had aided through here by penduluming from a bolt, and the rock between cracks was steep and smooth. True to the route, however, a perfectly positioned cluster of knobs appeared, and Goodman lurched across the blankness at 5.10+. He then fired up a steep hand crack, which widened to fist and then offwidth, but never slowed him down.

The pitch ended at the base of a striking, 150-foot dihedral that our topo called the Dixie Crystal Corner, a "fourstar" pitch we'd been admiring since we first glassed the wall. Beautiful as it was from afar, up close the Dixie was a beast—the first 100 feet of crack tapered gradually from 7 inches to 5, one of the most strenuous possible sizes to contend with. The left wall was smooth and dead vertical and the right only a degree or two less. It looked like it would be a fight, and it was my lead. Life was suddenly very simple. My job was to lead this pitch, quickly, free, and onsight. Nothing else mattered.

I swung the rack onto my left side, rigged our two biggest cams on full-length runners clipped to the lead rope, shoved one into the crack, and began chugging. Bingo! Protruding crystals on the right wall allowed me to stand with one foot out of the crack, shaving full number grades off the difficulty. It was strenuous offwidth climbing, and went on forever, but never got really hard.

The crack finally thinned to hands, leading into a series of small ledges. By now it was almost dusk, and the most pressing task was to find a bivy spot. Forty feet higher I could see what appeared to be a ledge, but I was out of rope. We had a set of small two-way radios, and I called down for Collins to follow the pitch. He did, then put me back on belay, and I scrambled up onto the grassy, sloping terraces that would be our camp for the night.

Stretching my lead beyond a rope length created a small hassle for hauling, so while the team sorted it out, I worked on our night's quarters. The grassy shelf sloped badly, but by peeling back the grass, leveling the dirt and gravel beneath, and then replacing the turf on the flattened terrace, I fashioned what I thought was a pretty fair sitting bivy.

A gentle rain settled in as the team arrived, and we huddled under our hardware-store tarp, hobo style, and cooked up a warming stew. A few remarks circulated about my choice of bivy ledge, but everyone made the best of it—except Collins, who dealt the ultimate insult by rapping down 50 feet to a lower ledge, where he found an even more miserable perch to pass the brief but rainy Northwest Territories night.

The next morning dawned clear, and we went for the top. The climbing was the stuff of dreams, with steep and continuous cracks, challenging but never desperate. Everyone onsighted his pitches. Very near the top, an intimidating squeeze chimney cast some serious doubt on our success, but Collins dispatched it with aplomb. As the pitches went by, one by one, we became ever more hopeful and elated. This thing was going down, today!

We hit the summit ridge, and the vista opened up into a world of swirling clouds, with glimpses of ice-clad peaks. Only the *Freebird* party had reached this point before us. They had called it good here, and we might have too, but finding dry, late-season conditions, we were able to continue. Climbing alone, occasionally waiting for each other, we scrambled unroped and in approach shoes, up the last 2,000 feet of knife-edge. Pat, in the lead, waited before the final rise, and we scrambled together onto to the untouched, tabletop summit slab of the Phoenix.

In thirty-five years of rock climbing, I've been privileged to participate in many fine first ascents, from New Hampshire and Maine to Canyonlands and the Black Canyon, but our route on the Phoenix was one of the very best—sort of the *Naked Edge* of the Northwest Territories, if you will. More classics await future parties on the flanks of the Phoenix itself, and on nearby formations—but if the Vamps ever get more popular, this one will surely get repeated, due to its Half Dome stature, superb and textured rock, elegance of line. Not to mention climbing that is so much more reasonable in difficulty than it had any right to be.

Yet at least for me, Pat, and Q, the route will always be entwined with the river. I will think back to this Vampires adventure as a time when we moved through the unknown as good adventurers should: solid on the water, and fluid on the rock.

EXPADDICTION

MARCH 2014, NO. 323

BY MIKE LIBECKI

In 2013, National Geographic named the Utah climber Mike Libecki Adventurer of the Year for his out-there expeditions. Both alone and with a team, Libecki's gone everywhere and done it all when it comes to big-wall climbing, whether it's trips to the jungle, Greenland, or Antarctica. He's made fifty expeditions—and has one hundred stamps on his passport—and aims to double that number before he dies. Perhaps he's addicted to far-off places; only Libecki knows.

I was definitely in denial. Sixty feet up a shattered wall of basalt in the Arctic, I just hoped to find a place to set up my portaledge, out of the reach of polar bears. The rock—for lack of a better term—was shitty. But I was still headed up. A couple of soccer ball–size rocks crashed onto the talus to my left, exploding like small bombs. As I hammered in a Knifeblade piton, a huge flake shattered like a plate of glass. The fragments sounded like ceramic tiles as they hit the talus below. I needed to find a way up this wall, but this line was death.

I downclimbed and peered through the fog and rain for any sign of bears. Back on the ground, I dragged all of my gear out of the rockfall zone toward the nearby beach and broke out my stove to make coffee. A huge pile of polar bear feces mixed with bird feathers sat between me and the ocean. I had no rifle. I needed to have a little talk with myself about my next move. For the past eight years, I'd been dreaming of climbing a rock wall in Franz Josef Land, a Russian archipelago 1,000 miles north of the Arctic Circle—farther north than Alaska, Baffin Island, and all but the northern tip of Greenland. If I succeeded, it would be the northernmost rock climb ever done. Now I had bailed less than one pitch up.

I'd only been permitted to climb on this section of the wall because no seabirds nested here, and suddenly I realized why: The birds knew it was too dangerous. It was time to wake up. I would not be safe in a portaledge on this eroding-in-real-time rock. On the ground, a polar bear encounter was almost guaranteed, and without a gun I was just a fool. With hopes that a bear could not follow, I climbed up a nearby ice couloir and called for a pick-up on my satellite phone, and the next morning the Russian sailboat I had hired returned. The boat's horn blared twice—their signal that they had looked for polar bears and it was safe to load my rafts. I paddled out through the rain and wind. But as I climbed into the boat's sanctuary, I felt a hollow feeling. I'd made the right call, but it felt like I was walking away with my tail between my legs. Now I had unfinished business. I would need to go back.

It used to be something I joked about, sort of laughed off to my friends and family. But now, at age 40, it's time to just come out and say it: I'm obsessed with expeditions. Maybe even addicted. Each year I plan multiple exploratory trips to unclimbed rock formations in remote and harsh environments. At some point, there's always a personal choice: go or don't go. And I always go. Knowing there will be suffering. Knowing I could die. Even knowing I have to leave my 10-year-old angel of a daughter, Lilliana, for months at a time. I believe anything worth doing in life takes compromise and sacrifice. So far this obsession has led to more than fifty expeditions in more than thirty countries. My goal is to complete one hundred expeditions before I die. And it all dates back to a day when I was just 6 years old. It was 1979, in the foothills of the Sierra Nevada, less than an hour's drive from Yosemite National Park. My first "expedition" began on a normal Saturday morning after hot chocolate, Honeycomb cereal, and Bugs Bunny cartoons. I had seen mountain lions sneak into the woods more than once on my 2-mile walk to the school bus stop, and now I grabbed my Red Bear bow and arrow and pump pellet gun, and went to find one of these wild cats—I was going mountain lion hunting. I headed off into the forest without telling anyone where I was going.

Amazingly, I did see a mountain lion that day, with two cubs. She stared me in the eyes before following her babies into the woods. That day I also had a run-in with a 5-foot rattlesnake and shot it with my pellet gun. Where the pellets punched holes in the snake, eel-like baby snakes slithered out. These moments of connecting with wild nature started it all. I could not have predicted what would happen that day, and this is what still drives me to go on expeditions. Not knowing what I will see, touch, smell, taste, and hear, and what or who I will meet. I need to find what I don't know is waiting.

Inside my home at the foot of Little Cottonwood Canyon in Utah's Wasatch Range is a stack of metal USGS map drawers filled with hundreds of maps collected over almost twenty years. They cover all of the planet. I pore over these maps like Sherlock Holmes, looking for clues that will lead me to large, unclimbed rocks. Fifteen years ago I started acquiring maps of the northern Arctic: Canada, Scandinavia, Russia, Greenland. I called, faxed, and emailed every polar institute or society I could reach, requesting maps and information. This is how I came across one of the most remote places on the planet, Franz Josef Land, a 192-island archipelago in far-northern Russia.

After exhaustive research, I found no clues about any climbing-specific exploration in Franz Josef Land, nor any evidence of big, steep rock formations. Which is actually how I prefer it. That meant I would have to find a way to get there and have a look for myself.

In 2004, after receiving information from famed Russian polar explorer Victor Boyarsky about a ship heading north, I found myself standing on the bow of a huge icebreaker, the *Capitan Dranitsyn*, on its way to Franz Josef Land. My nose hairs frosted from the Arctic wind as I watched the half-meter-thick steel bow of the impressive ship split the sea ice. I spent two weeks in the Franz Josef archipelago, getting to know the Russian crew and peering through the fog for rock spires or walls that would be tempting to climb. I knew some of the islands rose to over 2,000 feet, so it seemed possible that large cliffs existed. I glimpsed one island with appealing rock walls, but only from a distance—too far away to know if they were worthy of climbing. The icebreaker stayed on its planned course, and all I got was a tease. But the magic, power, and beauty of the area had entranced me.

Geographically and politically, Franz Josef Land is one of the toughest places to reach on the planet. This is where famed Norwegian explorers Fridtjof Nansen and Hjalmar Johansen spent the winter of 1895–1896 after retreating from an attempt to reach the North Pole. There are rumors of abandoned military bases and hidden submarines among the islands. Travel for reasons other than military or research purposes is highly restricted. And even if I did get permission from the Russian government, how would I find an island with good climbing and safely get to the cliffs? For seven years I contacted anyone and everyone who could possibly have information about permission to explore and climb in Franz Josef Land. Every clue eventually led to a dead-end. But I am not one to give up easily.

Year after year I contacted Arctic veteran Victor Boyarsky for any new information, and in 2011 he finally told me about a couple of captains in Spitzbergen who might be willing to make the trip. They both were interested—for a hefty price—but were unable to get permission. However, one of these sailors told me about the young Russian captain of a 50-foot sailboat that was supposedly heading to Franz Josef Land. I contacted the captain, and he responded the same day, saying, "I can take you to Franz Josef Land, no problem, and I can get the permissions." (The captain has requested anonymity.) Just like that, a new expedition was in the works. Now began the usual planning, gear buying and packing, budgeting, grant applications, and proposals to sponsors. With a visa in hand and a verbal nod from the Russian captain that everything was a go, I boarded a flight in July 2012 to Arkhangelsk, Russia, about 800 miles north of Moscow by the Barents Sea, with the same sense of excitement and curiosity I'd had going mountain lion hunting at 6 years old.

Once the sailboat was stocked with vodka, porridge, pickled herring, beer, drinkable water, and optimism, we sailed north from the Russian mainland. It took us seven days and nights of nonstop sailing, with everyone aboard manning the helm in six-hour shifts, to sail more than 1,100 nautical miles to the first of the islands. From my research and what I'd seen eight years earlier, I believed two islands might have beautiful rock walls to climb. But I'd never seen them close enough to be sure.

In 2004 we had needed an icebreaker to pass through these islands, constantly crushing through the sea ice to make our path. So, I had prepared to be dropped off at the edge of the sea ice, and then travel with a combination of skis, small rafts, and sleds to reach an island and climb. As we sailed through the islands, however, we encountered very little ice. Reaching shore would be easier and faster than I'd expected.

I also hoped the lack of sea ice might mean I'd be less likely to run into bears. During my previous visit to Franz Josef Land, we'd seen many polar bears among the islands. With no indigenous people living here, the bears may look at humans the same way they view seals: as a tasty meal. Two Russian scientists working at a research base in Franz Josef Land had been killed by bears the previous year. The thought of being hunted and devoured by this half-ton apex predator was just as frightening as avoiding the Taliban during a solo expedition to Afghanistan the previous year. I had had several polar bear encounters in Baffin Island and Greenland, and firing a rifle into the air had always scared them away. But in Russia, getting access to a rifle proved to be very difficult. The captain had assured me he would supply one, but once we neared the islands I was informed that the government's rules were too strict: I could not take a rifle with me. I had only flares. The Russian crew laughed and said my flares would be like birthday candles on a cake as the bear ate me. I laughed, too, but then felt that surge of emotion you get just before crying. I was really fucking scared about the polar bears.

Surrounded by fog, we motored around icebergs as we neared the cliffs I hoped to explore. Only by radar could we see the island in front of us. After eight years of believing, of dedication, I was elated. After four hours the fog finally lifted, and I could see the walls: beautiful seaside cliffs, perhaps 1,000 feet high. But as I prepared to board my little raft train (one for me and one to tow my gear) and head to the island, I wondered about the real nature of those beautiful rock walls. They appeared to be columns of basalt, capped by an obvious band of rotten rock.

Unfortunately I knew all too well the dangers of rockfall. In Antarctica I pulled off a few loose flakes that unleashed a landslide that crashed by as I trembled in the fetal position. In Afghanistan I had to climb past a hanging flake the size of a 1-foot-thick garage door. I carefully moved across the wall beneath the huge loose flake, and less than 10 minutes later, as I was making an anchor about 10 feet to the left, the flake let go and exploded against the wall, cutting into the cores of my ropes in three places.

I zipped up my dry suit and PFD, loaded my haulbags into the second raft, and said good-bye to the Russian crew. Less than an hour later, I started shuttling loads to the base of the wall. I watched the boat disappear as fog encased the island and rain started to fall. Polar bear tracks crossed the snow, but they were not fresh. I carried two flares in my front pockets, hoping to scare off a bear if it arrived. The plan was to call for a pickup by satellite phone once I was done climbing. If they didn't hear from me at all, they'd be back in one week.

The thin basalt columns of the buttress were packed together like pieces of uncooked spaghetti in a package. I chose a line and started climbing, but when I was 60 feet up, the loose stone and rocks falling around me forced a decision: I had to bail. I've only backed off a few other routes because they were too dangerous. Making a decision like that can be difficult and emotional. This time, though, I felt proud of myself. I felt like I had absorbed all my experiences and learned from them. I recognized death before it found me.

I have been on my own since I was 16 years old, when I first had my own place. Independence and responsibility not only came fast as an adolescent—they were all I knew. Still in high school, I was forced into early adulthood, with obligations and bills to pay, and to this day I've never missed a payment on a utility bill or credit card or loan. Even in the years when I racked up $45,000 or more on three credit cards or took a second mortgage to pay for expeditions, I always came home and worked nonstop to pay my bills.

Now, after the second expedition to Franz Josef Land, I felt I had a new kind of debt to repay. I felt an emotional obligation to somehow get back to those walls and climb a good route. No one else on Earth would care whether I returned to Franz Josef Land, and no one would blame me if I didn't. What debt should be easier to forgive than a self-imposed obligation? But I felt I owed it to myself to finish what I'd started. Returning to Russia would offer little mystery—the main element that drives me to plan expeditions. I knew exactly where I was going. I knew the rock was some of the worst I have ever climbed on. I was terrified of the bears. I always say it's the unknown that drives me. This time it was something else. Did I need to prove something to myself? As I neared 40, was this some kind of midlife crisis? The expedition lifestyle is what I have known for so long—really all I know, aside from being a father. It's how I define myself, who I am. I wondered if I could ever give it up. When my daughter's mother and I split up eight years ago, we tried to work it out again and again, until finally we had done everything we could, exhausted every angle, and realized it was over. There was some consolation in the fact that we did everything we could. And to this day we are great friends. Maybe it was the same thing with this third expedition to Franz Josef Land: I had to try everything I could before I could actually walk away.

I landed in Arkhangelsk for my third trip to Franz Josef Land in early July. It was like one big déja vu. As we sailed north, I caught myself feeling like a fool. These cliffs were only about 1,000 feet high—much smaller and less technically difficult than walls I had soloed throughout the world. My only goal this time was to choose a different line and top out. As I steered the sailboat, dolphins jumped out of the ocean and two huge whales blew gusts of breath, seeming to welcome us as the first of the islands of Franz Josef Land came into view.

We sailed straight to the island I had visited before, spotting only two bears along the way. The sea was mostly calm as we dodged mazes of icebergs. The plan was the same as before: The Russians would return in a week unless I called earlier, sounding their horn twice if there were no bears and it was safe to head for the boat. Of course the promise of a rifle had not worked out. There was nothing that could be done. I had the option of going or not going. I always go.

I pulled my pack rafts ashore, and the sailboat disappeared. I had stashed flares in my front pockets again as bear defense. All alone—why do I love this so much? The frozen air filled my lungs with a feeling of freedom and vulnerability, and despite the wind and gloomy mist, a smile as wide as the Joker's stretched across my face as I shuttled gear to the wall.

A couple of hours later, I started up a line about 200 meters to the left of the route I had attempted the year before. Once again, my plan was to set a portaledge camp far enough off the ground to be safe from bears. The climbing was wet, mossy, and muddy. It was steep, but there were great holds here and there. Soon after starting, I sent a big block crashing to the ground. Just like last year. Huge sigh, but no surprise. Rocks fell from above up and down the cliff line. Fuck. I slowly downclimbed.

I had been up for at least twenty hours since my last shift on the sailboat, and all I wanted was to get some sleep in a safe place. I switched to crampons and axes, stuffed a pack full of bivy gear, and quickly climbed up a nearby ice couloir to a small rock perch about a hundred feet up. It seemed unlikely a bear could reach me here. I cooked some freeze-dried pad Thai, had a couple Builder's bars, drank cold water, and curled into my sleeping bag and bivy sack. I stared up the couloir behind me, sandwiched between two big rock walls that disappeared into the fog, wondering if rock or ice would funnel down the gully and onto my ledge. I felt like a prehistoric man.

About eight hours later, I woke to wind and high clouds, and got a boil going for some instant coffee and oatmeal. I was only a couple of hundred meters from the ocean, and waves crashed heavy and loud on the shore. I downclimbed the steep couloir to my gear. I had one more idea for a route: an arête leading into a chimney that split the wall and seemed like it might be more straightforward. This climb would have nothing to do with ratings, movement, or a beautiful line. I just wanted to climb up safely, stand on the top with my Year of the Snake mask, dance, sing, and rejoice. Why? It's like asking me why I prefer chocolate over vanilla. I just do. I can't explain it.

My plan was to climb the route in a push and then descend the back side of the wall, cross a big dry glacier, hike back to my bivy, and wait for my pickup. The descent would put me in a position to encounter polar bears, which scared the hell out of me. First things first, though: I had to get to the top.

The previous year the weather had been mostly blue skies with warming sun. Now the sky was gray and misty. But once I started climbing, my psych exploded and I was back in the moment of tunnel-vision focus. Aside from the loose rock, upward progress was pretty straightforward. This was probably the easiest route on this entire section of steep wall, but I still self-belayed each pitch, and then rappelled to clean the gear on jumars. I moved slowly and meticulously. I couldn't seem to lose myself in the moment like I usually did while climbing. I was spooked.

I found a good anchor with several solid cams, quickly equalized them, rapped down my trail line, grabbed my pack, and jugged and cleaned the pitch. Just getting a pitch done gave me some confidence. Finally, I had some momentum. Joy started to creep back in and clean out the haunting webs in my brain. Organically, naturally, I was acclimatizing, figuring out this rock. I started to make peace with these old mounds of stone. Hammer-tapping here and there and getting a good read on solid columns of rock or detached blocks, I could start to feel it and hear it. I had found some of the keys to this castle.

It was just above freezing, and everything was wet, but the climbing continued to be easy, and moving meant warmth. Lichen and choss. Deep, spongy pockets of yellow and green moss. Good gear here and there. My feet got soaked as I shoved toes into dripping cracks. After three pitches, the wind picked up, and I could feel the wet cold setting in. My soloing philosophy has always been "slow is fast." Keep moving and before you know it, you are there. Four pitches. Rap, jug, clean, stack, go. I had to tighten up my harness as the sodden gear and ropes dragged on my waist.

The chimney turned into a big gully filled with moss and loose rocks, and I cut right on a big ramp. Just an easy slab and scramble to the top. I cleaned the gear and jugged, realizing I was laughing out loud. The Joker face was back. No more shitty rock. It was windy and raining lightly, but I was too fired up to care. I took my Go-Pro from my pocket, put on my Year of the Snake mask, and captured pictures and video of my celebration on the summit.

The top looked like another planet, a plateau of rock and lichen and small bits of vegetation that disappeared into fog and snow and glacier. The feeling of being only halfway set in, as it usually does on a new summit—the true summit was waiting back on the sailboat. I put both flares in my front pockets again, stuffed my pack, coiled ropes, and started down. As I walked toward the center of the island and then down a dry glacier, I never stopped looking for bears. A snaking stream of water had cut a runnel in the ice; I scooped it up in my water bottle and sipped to avoid an ice-cream headache. From the top, it took less than an hour to return to the foot of the wall. I held a flare ready in one hand as I traversed the base of the wall. An hour later, I had climbed back up the couloir and onto my rock perch. Into my bivy sack, down jacket on, stove firing hot water. I was safe. It was over. Or so it seemed.

My satellite phone had full bars as I dialed the Russian sailboat. No answer. I ate, rehydrated, and tried the sat phone again. The captain answered and said he would be able to pick me up in about twelve to fourteen hours. Sweet! A few hours later, as I lay curled up on the small ledge, the rain started to pitter-patter like a drum. Then turned to snow. Then rain. Then freezing rain. The wind gusted. I already had on everything I'd carried up to the ledge except my plastic boots. I stuffed my phone and a few Clif bars into the inside pocket of my down jacket. Everything else was in my pack behind me on a small ledge. Huge gust of wind! *Whoosh!* I fell asleep, in and out of dreams of polar bears and of the sailboat picking me up.

When I woke up, a layer of ice glazed the bivy sack and the rock around me. It had been more than fifteen hours since I talked to the captain. Wind, *WHOOSH!* I sat up. My pack had blown off and fallen down the couloir with all my food, water, and stove. The boat should be here anytime, I thought, so I settled back into half-sleep and semi-comfort. Twenty hours. I called the captain again. Another sailboat in the area had engine trouble and needed help. It would be another twenty-four hours.

That's when I started to experience something I'd first heard described by the Inuit: iktsuarpok. It's an immense feeling of anticipation, leading you to keep looking outside to see if anyone, or anything, is coming. Whenever I opened the lid of my bivy sack, I peered down to the talus and the ocean below, and I kept expecting to see a bear. I couldn't get it out of my mind. Could a bear climb up the ice to reach me? Back in my bivy sack. Instantly back to looking around. In and out of sleep. *Iktsuarpok*, again and again. I was soaked from rain and perspiration; my hands were wrinkled and numb. I was hungry and out of water, but I didn't want to move until the sailboat arrived.

I called the captain. No answer. Called again. He said the weather was very bad, and he hoped to be able to pick me up by the next day, but not to worry. Hoped? Another twenty-four hours? Bear paranoia had possessed me, and I didn't want to move. I imagined a bear pouncing on my bivy sack and tearing my flesh apart as I screamed in agony. I shrank into my bivy sack and ate my last Clif bar. Toes numb. Sleep. Awake. No bears. Wait, what is that? Just ice. *Iktsuarpok*. Another call to the captain. No answer. Again. No answer. Cold, wet, cramping. I kept looking at my watch. I pictured getting on the boat, going home, and seeing my daughter. Twenty more hours passed. Waves crashed on the shoreline. Then . . . *Rrrrrt! Rrrrrt!* Two high-pitched blasts from a horn. I sat up. Was it real? I couldn't see anything through the fog and rain. Two more short bursts . . . *Rrrrt! Rrrrt!* It had been almost seventy hours since I climbed onto the perch.

My muscles felt stiff and atrophied, and I could barely move, but as quickly as I could, I rolled my wet sleeping bag and bivy sack into a ball and crammed my feet into my plastic boots, put on crampons, and grabbed my axes. I downclimbed to the talus and began dragging and trundling my haulbags toward the shoreline. Half an hour after I reached the ship, we were sailing away from the island. The crew had baked a cake to celebrate the fact that I didn't become a polar bear meal. When I told them I'd made it to the top, they pressed vodka shots on me. But my body was devastated. I felt something like heart palpitations and couldn't breathe right. Scared, I drank more tea and told the Russians I had to sleep. Thirty hours passed before I rose from my bunk.

My toes and feet throbbed in horrific pain as we sailed back toward the mainland. One of my big toes turned black, and the nail eventually fell off. I had lost fifteen pounds. I'd gotten schooled. The expedition that I had obsessed over for years, sacrificed for, compromised for, was over. Now it had become a training trip for the next. And then that next trip would eventually lead into the one after. When would it end?

I turned my mind away from such thoughts and began to focus on logistics. I was due to meet my partners in less than ten days for an unclimbed wall in China.

A BELIEF

APRIL 2015, NO. 334

BY TOMMY CALDWELL

Nineteen days on the wall. Seven years of grueling work. That's what it took Tommy Caldwell and his partner (for the final years), Kevin Jorgeson, to complete the "Hardest Climb in the World," El Capitan's Dawn Wall (VI 5.14d). "I don't know what's wrong with me, but I love this shit," Caldwell famously said in one video while jugging up to his portaledge under falling snow. And the world took notice too—big time. During the final push, news vans showed up to El Cap Meadow in droves, pushing out 13 billion media impressions.

The *Dawn Wall* became so much bigger than Kevin and me. That was definitely not by design—it just sort of happened—but I can't imagine a more positive outcome. I've been totally obsessed by this project for years—in fact, "El Cap" was one of my little boy Fitz's first words, which is pretty funny. He spends time in the Valley with me and my wife, and he could sense the excitement around our climb. It's such a beautiful line, just an amazing thing. I totally reformatted my life for the past seven years to do everything I could to reach this dream.

It took a couple years of swinging around on ropes studying the wall with a microscopic lens just to find the line of holds that could get us to the top. Then we spent years and years figuring out all the logistics and strategies for where basecamp would go and just how we would work the route. I've climbed a lot of routes on El Cap at this point, and I've used various styles of big wall climbing. With the

Dawn Wall, I tried not to make hard and fast rules in terms of ground-up or top-down or using fixed ropes. I've done them all. I've gone ground-up in a day with just a small backpack, but this was going to be something more at the other end of the spectrum.

I see style as something you can play with to construct the greatest possible experience. We knew that in order to finish this climb we'd need both ample time and to focus on the climbing, so we decided it had to be done in a single push. But we also knew we needed to give ourselves basically every other possible advantage we could find, in terms of pre-stashing a basecamp right in the middle of the wall and having supplies brought up to us. That really worked out. I knew I wasn't a good enough climber not to have fixed ropes or to do it in a day or something crazy like that. Plus, if we had stuck to a ground-up ethic, we never would have found the route to begin with. It just couldn't have been done ground-up, and if you tried to do it that way, you would have had to drill literally thousands of holes to aid climb your way up the wall in all these different directions to find out if a free climb was even possible. In the end, the single-push style is just what made sense.

This year, we spent two months working on the *Dawn Wall* before we even went for the final push. We'd jumar up every day and work on the route from 4 p.m. when the route goes into the shade until 10 p.m. or midnight. Then we'd come down and take a shower and kind of live our lives on the ground. We did it like that so we'd gain strength throughout the season. I even left Yosemite a couple times to train in the climbing gym. Part of that was to refresh skin, and part of that was to keep strong in ways that you lose when you're only on El Cap. I also read *The Rock Climber's Training Manual* [written by Michael L. Anderson, Ph.D., and Mark L. Anderson, this manual covers a training program that's become known as the Rock Prodigy method] and did a lot of fingerboard training over the years, which is especially important for me since I'm missing a finger. I need to compensate for that in terms of finger strength. Building strength, working on technique, and practicing patience were key.

I knew my biggest challenge would be the dyno on pitch 16, so I rebuilt it on my shed and tried it literally thousands of times. Ironically, I didn't even end up doing the dyno on the final push. After failing at it over and over again, beating my body up, and getting really depressed, somehow I saw this ramp going down the wall 30 feet back across the previous pitch. I guess I just never looked at that exact part of the wall. I never thought the way forward would be to climb 30 feet back across the pitch I'd just climbed, climb down 100 feet, across and back up, and then essentially end up only five feet from where I started. It seemed too absurd to look for something like that, but that's what ended up happening! The dyno was super-cool, and I wish I could have gone that way. But this was a creative solution that I definitely needed.

Pitch 16 was the biggest battle of any on the final push for me. It took me five or six tries, mainly because I hadn't practiced it that much. But every other pitch I did within two or three. I felt really confident up there, but every single one of those hard pitches was a fight to the death. There were probably twelve pitches on the route where I was completely maxed out—absolute battles, which was really cool.

It's weird, in retrospect, how you can look at things several times, even with that microscopic lens, and not know for sure whether it's going to be possible to free climb. Usually I'm really optimistic, but when Kevin first came onboard, I showed him the crux traverse pitches, and he said, "Uh, these don't look free climbable to me!" We tried toproping the moves because I was like, "Yeah, I think it's possible!" It ended up going that way, but it took a combination of analyzing every inch of rock and building a belief that it was possible. Luckily, on this push, things came together, and it was a really positive experience for me for those nineteen days.

The fact that we were able to share our experience so effectively in real time through social media gave people a glimpse into it. Other people were able to see what makes it so cool in a way that you don't generally get with this type of climbing. I think the fact that we were up there for so darn long created this really cool format where people could check in each day to see our progress, which had the snowball effect of getting more people interested. And then it went viral—people were excited just because other people were excited. A good percentage of the interviews we've done, especially early on, were with people who really didn't even know what we were doing up there. They were just excited because there was a lot of hype building.

Climbing becomes more and more mainstream every year, and there are climbing gyms now in every major city. So more people knew about climbing prior to this, but this climb was cool even outside of that world; people who haven't been to climbing gyms or ever climbed seemed to understand it suddenly. This project articulated climbing in a way that helped people recognize that this isn't some sport for adrenaline junkies and thrill seekers. That there's actually a depth to it, that it can be life-changing and amazing in so many ways. The reasons that we, as climbers, love climbing are now apparent to more people.

It makes me feel like I need to be a good ambassador for what we do, for the outdoors, for Yosemite National Park, and just to be a really good person all around. With the *Dawn Wall* and other things, like Jimmy Chin's *Meru* film making it into the Sundance Film Festival, I feel this energy, like we're on the verge of something new in climbing, which is exciting. Climbing is an incredibly healthy and awesome way to live. It's this life-driving force for me—how awesome if that can be shared!

I came down from the wall feeling completely blessed and lucky to have such a great family and friends, and to have stumbled across this thing that drove me for so long.

I'm still on a high from that, and I'm not sure I'll ever come down.

THE *FREERIDER*

AUGUST 2017, NO. 355

BY JAMES LUCAS

~~~~~~

A grade VI El Cap free route ropeless. That is, climbing 5.13—and tons of 5.11 and 5.12—waaay off the deck on monolithic granite, with only a chalk bag around your waist and sticky shoes on your feet to help you stay in contact with the rock. It was Alex Honnold, often called "the greatest climber of our generation," who did it. Unbelievable. Some see it as one of the most impressive athletic performances of all time (even beyond the world of rock climbing), requiring the perfect blend of skill, power, endurance, and nerves; others see it as sheer lunacy. Honnold banged out the Freerider (VI 5.13a) without hesitation in 3 hours 56 minutes. His friend James Lucas followed his story, roping up with him along the way, as Honnold prepared for the solo of soloes.

~~~~~~

"So stoked. I just sent the proj!" Alex Honnold said in a voicemail from El Capitan on June 3. "Hiking down the East Ledges. Thanks for the support up here this season and, you know, just in general. I'm feeling pretty stoked out of my gourd."

That day, Honnold, 31, made the first free solo of a VI on El Capitan. At 5:32 a.m., Honnold pulled on a pair of TC Pros and began up *Freerider*, a 2,900-foot 5.13a on the southwest face. Honnold navigated ten pitches of slab on *Freeblast* to Mammoth Terraces, where he downclimbed 190 feet to Heart Ledges. From Heart, he deviated onto an unbolted 5.10 face to avoid a 5.11c slab move. Higher, he stepped away from the standard line and entered the 200-foot 5.10d *Monster* off-width lower than normal to avoid an exposed 5.11d downclimb traverse. Honnold continued on *Freerider*, climbing the Huber Boulder Problem pitch, a delicate V7 slab at 1,700 feet.

With nowhere to stop, Honnold linked the two 5.12b Enduro Corner pitches into the *Freerider Traverse* (5.12b), a 150-foot section usually broken up into three pitches with hanging belays. From Roundtable Ledge, at the end of the *Freerider Traverse*, Honnold climbed the last 600 feet of 5.11+ crack and offwidth in 20 minutes, topping out at 9:28 a.m. He'd been on the wall for 3 hours 56 minutes.

In the summer of 2006 in Squamish, British Columbia, I met a 21-year-old kid from Sacramento with big ears, huge puppy hands, and doe eyes. He wore sweatpants all the time and abstained from all vices save free soloing.

We climbed on the Chief, the slabs on the Apron, and on the sport routes at Cheakamus where he onsighted his first 5.12d, *Boiler Maker*. We spoke often of free soloing. I had free soloed hundreds of pitches across the United States, but in 2004, I fell 100 feet onsight free soloing *North Overhang* in Joshua Tree. My desire to climb cordless had been tempered by eight surgeries and a body full of metal. Still, I could relate to Honnold's desire for the freedom and purity. That summer, Honnold onsight–soloed *Pipeline*, a 170-foot 5.10+ offwidth at Squamish. "It's pretty much been all downhill after *Pipeline*," Honnold jokes. He soon transferred his granite skills to Yosemite. In September 2007, Honnold climbed *Astroman* (V 5.11c) and the *North Face of the Rostrum* (IV 5.11c) in a day unroped, attracting media attention and sponsorship.

In 2008, I drove into Zion and called Honnold, who had been mini traxioning on *Moonlight Buttress* (V 5.12d). We talked beta on *Moonlight*, then made plans to meet up. Then, I received a text from Mikey Schaefer: "Did you hear Honnold soloed *Moonlight*?" Honnold had neglected to mention it. It didn't surprise me that he'd soloed this 1,000-foot climb, a finger-crack staminafest. Though Honnold's most difficult ascents have been three 5.14c sport climbs and two V12s, he has established a huge base of endurance and fitness. He rarely tires on long routes and thus rarely gets scared on them. As George S. Patton Jr. wrote in *War as I Knew It*, "Fatigue makes cowards of us all." Over the next few years, Honnold continued to push his soloing.

Later in 2008, he free soloed the *Regular Northwest Face of Half Dome* (VI 5.12). In February 2010, he made the second ascent of *Ambrosia*, a 50-foot V11 highball in Bishop, California. In 2011, it was *Astroman* and the *Rostrum*, exiting the *Rostrum* via the *5.12 Alien*.

In 2012, Alex and I shared an apartment in Bishop. That winter, Alex convinced a crew to hike thirty-four pads out to the Luminance Boulder in the Buttermilks so he could establish the 50-foot *Too Big to Flail* (V9), after he'd worked out the moves on toprope. The boulder problem/short solo contained some of the hardest unroped climbing he had done—delicate patina crimping way off the deck.

By the time of his solo of the *Freerider*, he'd climbed an estimated 2,000 individual pitches ropeless, including multiple 50-pitch days and a day of 290 pitches in Squamish for his 29th birthday.

Not all of Honnold's solos have gone smoothly. Early on, in 2005, he fell twice soloing in Owen's River Gorge: once while downclimbing a 5.10 and another time climbing to the first bolt on *Pippy the Zenhead* (5.9). In 2008, on Half Dome, he stood 2,000 feet off the ground, stroking a carabiner, contemplating grabbing the metal to pull past an insecure slab move. He compromised, placing a single finger pad on the biner and making the move. On the *Rainbow Wall* (V 5.12b) in Red Rock Canyon in April 2010, Honnold climbed up and down into the dyno crux, 750 feet off the ground. He had climbed the route years before but barely remembered it. As he wrote in *Alone on the Wall*, referencing a recent breakup, ". . . in the mood I was in, I wanted to finish what I'd set out to do." Honnold crimped so hard on a dimple he got a blood blister, making the move. He climbed into 5.12 terrain above, which felt harder than he wanted to solo but that he now had to no choice but to climb.

In September 2011, Honnold called me from the *Direct North Buttress* (V 5.10b) of Middle Cathedral, looking for directions. In late 2011, Honnold created a short film with Corey Rich. *Why* showcases the Nikon D4, which Rich used to film Honnold soloing Equinox, a 5.12c finger crack in J-Tree. After lap three, Honnold was tiring. On his last effort, his foot skated slightly. He caught himself on a finger lock. In 2012, he backed off John Bachar's infamous J-Tree solo *Father Figure* (5.13a). In Zion in 2012, Honnold onsight-soloed *Shune's Buttress* (IV 5.11+). As he scrambled to the summit through snowy, loose terrain, Honnold broke a hold, fell into a tree, and landed on a pedestal, narrowly avoiding the plummet to the valley floor. Though Honnold climbs well, he's not flawless.

Over the years, Honnold began a symbiotic relationship with film media. Most of his solos have been re-created on film, as were *Moonlight Buttress*, Half Dome, and his 2014 free solo of *El Sendero Luminoso*, a 1,750-foot 5.12d in Potrero Chico, Mexico. To some extent, Honnold has used the film crews not only to advance his career but also to help with logistics—and they've been there to bail him out in a pinch. While filming for a 2014 Squarespace campaign with Jimmy Chin, Honnold soloed *Heaven* (5.12d) in Yosemite. On his second lap, on a hot day, his fist greased in the crack and he asked the film crew for a rope.

In fall 2016, Honnold arrived in Yosemite with hopes of soloing El Cap. Jimmy Chin and his wife, Chai, had been working with Honnold to produce a feature film. They'd documented him soloing *Excellent Adventure*, a 5.13 finish to the Rostrum, and *Les Riveres Pourpres*, a 1,600-foot 5.12c in the Taghia Gorge of Morocco. His first day in the Valley, a cold and dreary one, he fell on *Freeblast* with his girl-friend, Sanni McCandless, spraining his ankle badly. Later that fall, he tried to solo the *Freerider*. On a delicate 5.11 slab on *Freeblast*, he got scared, grabbed a bolt, and pulled through. The camera crew gave him a double-length sling and an ATC, which he used to rap from the fixed lines up to Mammoth Terraces.

The June 3 solo, obviously, was a smoother affair. A few cameramen watched from the meadow, while Chin and Cheyne Lempe waited near the top third where the climbing—what Honnold calls "fun exit climbing"—was more secure. There were also two remote-control cameras at the crux boulder problem on pitch 23. Whatever happened at the crux, the cameras would document it.

In August 2014, a friend and I attempted the *University Wall* (5.12a) at Squamish. On the hike down I ran into Honnold.

"What are you doing?" I asked.

"Just going for a hike," Honnold said.

"Like, you're gonna hike my project?" I asked looking at his rock shoes and chalk bag. Over the years, Honnold had talked about soloing *U-Wall*. We went over the difficult undercling section on pitch 2. Honnold said he kneebarred there and it felt secure.

At the base, I grabbed a pair of binoculars. Honnold moved smoothly through the first pitch, a wet 5.12, and launched into the undercling section. As I watched, his body started shaking. He looked ready to gyrate off. I put the binoculars down, breathed lightly, steadied myself, and then picked the binoculars back up. Honnold was climbing smoothly. He had been the whole time. It had been my hands shaking the binoculars. I had been projecting my own fear onto Honnold.

While Honnold's plans to solo big routes are often known, he tries to minimize any nervous energy around him—thus, his skittishness around the *U-Wall*. "He's always had the foresight to not tell me beforehand—actually ever, until Half Dome when it made news," Deidre Wolownick, his mother, says. She didn't climb at the time and didn't comprehend what he did until months later. "When it's in the magazines, you can't keep it from mom," she says.

The secrecy spares his mother the worry. Says Wolownick, "It would be harder for him if he knew that I knew. His mind has to be clear, and if he knew I was sitting home worrying about him, it would muddy the waters."

Before soloing the *Freerider*, Honnold and McCandless agreed that she would leave Yosemite for a few days. He'd been training hard, practicing front levers and trying to do the 7b Beastmaker hangboard workouts; he'd also given up sugar for the two months prior and taken a sabbatical from social media, to sit in his van and visualize soloing the route. He wanted to keep distractions at bay.

"It's called enabling," I told Will Stanhope this spring beneath *Midnight Light-ning*. Stanhope, like many climbers who have freed the *Freerider*, thought that solo-ing El Cap was a bad idea. In fact, the only person in the world who thought it was a good idea was Alex Honnold. Still, I'd agreed to support Honnold on *Freerider*, jugging behind him while he practiced the climb. In 2014, Honnold had supported me during one of my forty days prepping to climb *Freerider* in a day. With Hon-nold, I fell off the Boulder Problem, but so had he. Though I'd been disappointed to fall, I was also excited that Honnold had failed. It meant he would live a few years more. I jokingly wrote, "Don't solo my projects!" on his Facebook wall.

Our ascent this May went smoothly: round-trip in eleven hours. Honnold led every pitch, short fixing the rope for me. Most of the route he climbed with an enormous loop of slack, little gear, and 60-foot fall potential. He had climbed the *Freerider* at least a dozen times at that point, including his first trip in 2006, when he fell only once. In spring 2008, a loaf-hold on the crux twenty-third pitch broke, upping the difficulty. Honnold had invested significant time on the route, climbing it slightly differently than he would have roped to make it feel more secure. He did the same on a few other sections. In the meadow, I said good-bye to Honnold and we hugged. I was unsure if I would see him again. Back at work at *Climbing*, I told my editor we should leave space either for an article about his ascent or an obituary.

Over the years, large sections of El Capitan proper have been free soloed. During speed-solo ascents on the *Nose*, Dean Potter often skipped belaying himself on cracks, soloing up to 5.11. In 2012, Potter took the first steps toward a big El Cap solo when he established *Easy Rider* (5.11d), a 1,000-foot U-shaped route on the top of El Capitan.

"I downclimb . . . *Lurking Fear* then come across Thanksgiving Ledge and tra-verse farther via a magical passage I discovered out a bucketed roof and finally end up on the top quarter of the *Freerider* without EVER using a rope," Potter said in an *Outside Online* interview.

In 2012, Potter and Sean "Stanley" Leary climbed the *West Face* (V 5.11c) into *Easy Rider* at 5.11d. This variation had solo potential, and Potter began working the *West Face* to prepare. I mentioned as much to Honnold. A few days after Potter and Stanley finished their variation, Honnold on May 22, 2012, made the first free solo of the *West Face*.

Deterred by Alex's competitive nature, Potter moved on. In late May, Honnold simul-climbed *Freerider* with Tommy Caldwell in a record 5.5 hours. All told, Hon-nold had climbed the delicate Boulder Problem crux nearly thirty times this year, falling only once, two days before his send. He was as solid as he could be. On June 3, I came into cell range late in the day after climbing. I saw Honnold's message and knew he had sent. The world congratulated Honnold.

National Geographic and Jimmy Chin worked their exclusive angle, with a film due summer 2018. The North Face, his main sponsor took out a full-page ad in the sports section of the *New York Times* congratulating Honnold. "The really good thing about it is that I'm probably not gonna get fired any time soon," jokes Honnold.

Honnold's solo sets him up for bigger objectives. Perhaps he'll link more routes in Yosemite or solo the Fitz Roy Traverse in Patagonia. Perhaps he'll retire. "After El Cap, what's left? What more could you possibly do as a free soloist?" his mom muses. Honnold will likely solo more—but at what level is unknown. "I don't know if I'll do anything extreme. We'll see," Honnold says. "What if some 16-year-old kid does everything I've ever done in, like, a day? I'll be, like, 'Uh-oh. I better get back to work or I won't be able to eat.'"